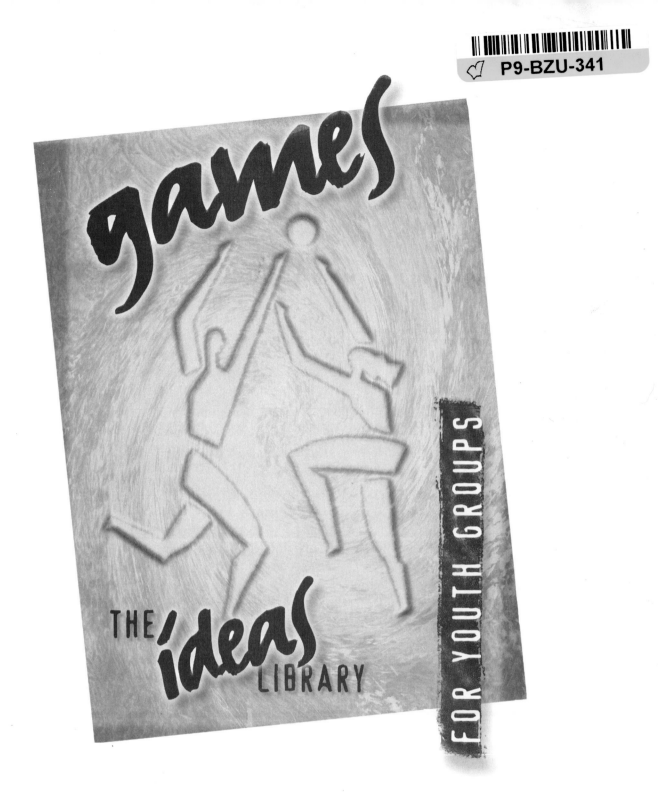

games

THE ideas LIBRARY

FOR YOUTH GROUPS

THE IDEAS LIBRARY

Administration, Publicity, & Fundraising
Camps, Retreats, Missions, & Service Ideas
Creative Meetings, Bible Lessons, & Worship Ideas
Crowd Breakers & Mixers
Crowd Breakers & Mixers 2
Discussion & Lesson Starters
Discussion & Lesson Starters 2
Drama, Skits, & Sketches
Drama, Skits, & Sketches 2
Games
Games 2
Holiday Ideas
Special Events

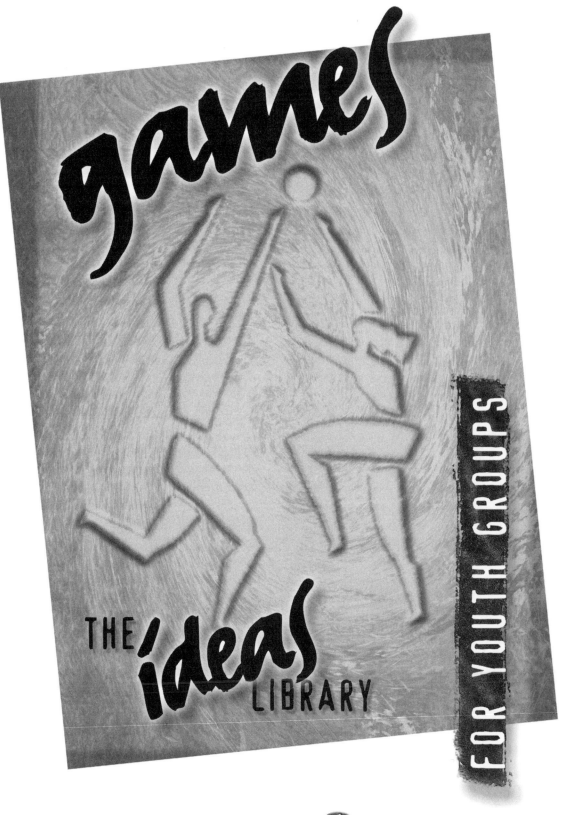

games

THE ideas LIBRARY

FOR YOUTH GROUPS

ZondervanPublishingHouse
Grand Rapids, Michigan
A Division of HarperCollinsPublishers

Games

Youth Specialties Books, 300 S. Pierce St., El Cajon, CA 92020, are published by Zondervan Publishing, 5300 Patterson Ave. S.E., Grand Rapids, MI 49530.

Ideas in this book have been voluntarily submitted by individuals and groups who claim to have used them in one form or another with their youth groups. Before you use an idea, evaluate it for its suitability to your own group, for any potential risks, for safety precautions that must be taken, and for advance preparation that may be required. Youth Specialties, and Zondervan Publishing are not responsible for, nor have any control over, the use or misuse of any of the ideas published in this book.

Project editor: Vicki Newby
Cover and interior design: Curt Sell
Art director: Mark Rayburn

Printed in the United States of America

09 10 11 12 / VG / 21 20 19 18

CONTENTS

LIVING ROOM GAMES

MIND READING GAMES

PING-PONG VARIATIONS

VOLLEYBALL GAMES

SO WHAT KILLER GAME HAVE YOU INVENTED LATELY?

Are your kids still talking about that game you invented for last month's party? Youth Specialties pays $40 (and in some cases, more) for unpublished, field-tested ideas that have worked for you.

You've probably been in youth work long enough to realize that sanitary, theoretical, tidy ideas aren't what in-the-trenches youth workers are looking for. They want—*you* want—imagination and take-'em-by-surprise novelty in parties and other events. Ideas that have been tested and tempered and improved in the very real, very adolescent world you work in.

So here's what to do:

- Sit down at your computer, get your killer game out of your head and onto your hard drive, then e-mail it to Ideas@YouthSpecialties.com. Or print it off and fax it to 619-440-0582 (Attn: Ideas).
- If you need to include diagrams, photos, art, or samples that help explain your game, stick it all in an envelope and mail it to our street address: Ideas, 300 S. Pierce St, El Cajon, CA 92020.
- Be sure to include your name, your addresses, phone numbers, and e-mail addresses.
- Let us have a few months to give your game idea a thumbs up or down*, and a little longer for your money.

*Hey, no offense intended if your idea isn't accepted. It's just that our fussy Ideas Library editor has these *really* meticulous standards. If the game isn't creative, original, and just plain fun in an utterly wild or delightful way, she'll reject it. Reluctantly (she has a tender heart), but she'll flush it. Sorry. But we figure you deserve only the best game ideas.

ALPHABETICAL LIST
OF EVERY GAME IN THIS BOOK

BALLOON GAMES

BALLOON GAMES

Twice the fun of a church board meeting with only half the hot air, balloon games are an inexpensive good time. Whether the object is to keep the balloons afloat or pop them like pimples on prom night, most of these games work with any size group. For even more balloon games, simply adapt some of the ball games in this book by substituting a balloon for the ball. (For water balloon games, see Games 2 in the Ideas Library.)

BAIL-O-WACK

This game is like volleyball, but it's played with a balloon and without a net. To set up use masking tape to make a straight line across the middle of the playing area. The length of the line in feet should be twice the total number of players on both teams (for example, for 10 players use a 20-foot line).

center for Team A ↓

TEAM A	X	X	X	(X)	X	X	X
TEAM B	0	0	0	(0)	0	0	0

center for Team B ↑

Divide into two teams, and have each team stand facing the other across the line (as if it were the net) in a single row on each side. Players should stand four feet apart from teammates, and two feet back from the line. Players cannot move from this position during play, though one foot may leave the floor to kick the balloon if the other stays in place.

The object is to volley a balloon back and forth across the line without allowing it to touch the floor on your team's side. The balloon can be batted with hands or kicked. As with the ball in volleyball, contact with the balloon may alternate between players on the same team, but the balloon cannot be touched by the same player twice in a row. Unlike volleyball, however, teams are not limited to three contacts in order to get the balloon back over the line to the other team.

The middle player in each team's line is the "center." Each round begins with one of the centers serving by tapping the balloon across the line to the other team. The team that won the point in the previous round gets to serve. A team scores a point when the balloon touches the floor on the opposite team's side of the line. There is no out-of-bounds play, so if the balloon is batted over the heads of players and out of their reach, the opposite team scores a point. A team also scores a point when a player on the opposite team makes contact with the balloon twice in a row or moves out of position.

You'll need extra balloons in case one bursts and a referee to make sure players stay in position. *Phil Blackwell*

BALLOON BALANCE RELAY

Form teams and give each team one baseball cap or painter's cap. The first player from each team dons the cap and balances an inflated balloon on the bill (bouncing on the bill is permitted). The players then walk to a point 10 feet away and back again while balancing the balloon on their hats. Then, using their hands, they pass the balloon and hat to the next players in line, who do the same thing.

A player whose balloon falls to the floor or is held up by any part of the body has to start over. (No fair blowing on the balloon to keep it in place.) The first team whose players all complete the circuit are declared the uncontested balloon balance relay champions of the world. *Michael Frisbie*

BALLOON BASKETBALL

Divide into two teams with an equal number of players. Arrange chairs as shown in the diagram, back to back in rows except for the two outer rows that face inward. One team faces in one direction, the second team faces the other direction.

After all the players are seated, toss a balloon into the center of the chairs. Players aren't allowed to stand as they try to bat the balloon with their

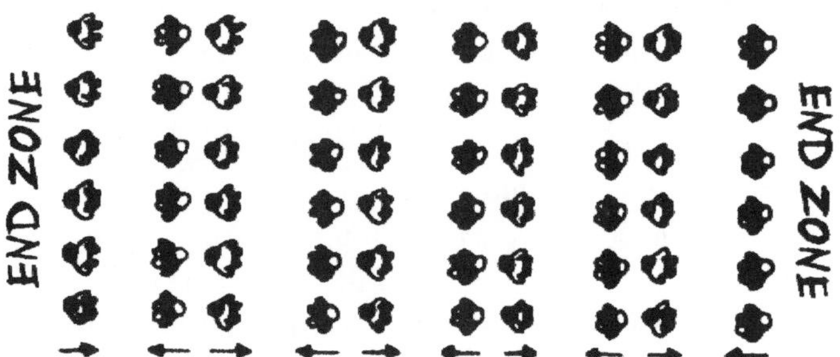

hands into the end zone that the teams face. As soon as the balloon drops into an end zone over the heads of the last row of people, the appropriate team scores two points. If the balloon goes out of bounds, just throw it back into the center. Play ends at 20 points or after 15 minutes, whichever comes first.

BALLOON BAT RELAY

Teams line up, single file, with kids as close together as possible. There should be a space between the legs to bat a balloon down the line, through the legs, with the hands. This is not easy if all the kids are standing close together. The person at the front of the line starts the balloon back and when it reaches the last person, he takes it to the front and continues until the team is once again in starting order. *David Parke*

BALLOON SMASH

Tie an inflated balloon around your waist and let it hang from behind. Try to break everyone else's balloon with a rolled up newspaper without allowing someone to bust your own balloon. You win if you are the last person wearing an inflated balloon. (Newspapers are the only weapons allowed.)

BALLOON STOMP

Blow up a balloon and tie it to your ankle with a piece of string. Try to stomp and pop everyone else's balloon while keeping yours intact. You win if you are the last person wearing an inflated balloon.

Or try **Balloon Stomp Flickers**—same game but played under a strobe light. (By the way, a strobe light is a great variation for air hockey, Ping-Pong, and pillow fights.)

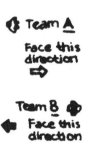

Or make it a team game with **Technicolor Stomp**, for which you'll need lots of colored balloons. Divide into teams and assign each team a color—red, blue, orange, yellow, etc. Then give each team an equal number of balloons of its color. For example, the red team is given, say, 20 red balloons. They begin by blowing up all the balloons and tying them off. When the actual game begins, the balloons from all the teams are released onto the floor, and the object is to stomp on and pop all the balloons that are not your team color while attempting to protect your own team's balloons. After the time limit is up (two or three minutes should do it), the popping of balloons stops and each team gathers up its remaining balloons. The team with the most balloons intact is the winner. *David Coppendge and Christine R. Rollins*

BALLOON BUST

Here is a creative way to pair up people for competition. Half of the group members write their names on small pieces of paper, which are then put inside balloons (one name per balloon).

Blow up the balloons and tie them off. The rest of the kids randomly grab a balloon, pop it, and pair up with the person whose name is found inside the balloon. The last two people to pair up lose.

BALLOON BUMP

Here's an indoor game for moderately sized groups (20 or more kids). Divide players into groups of four to six or so; place about as many chairs as there are groups randomly around the room; place lots of deflated balloons on each chair; then instruct each group to form a huddle of people, arms around shoulders, in the middle of the room.

On "Go!" each huddle shuffles to a chair. One person from each huddle grabs a balloon, blows it up, ties it off, and drops it into the middle of the huddle. Players in the huddle must keep the balloon from touching the floor by pressing against the balloon with their stomachs. As they do so, they must move toward another chair to repeat the process. At the second chair they visit, they must blow up two balloons; at the third chair, three balloons, etc.—all the while maintaining their huddle and keeping their balloons from falling to the floor.

If a balloon falls, the huddle must stop and put it back in the middle again (which takes time). A huddle cannot visit a chair where there is already another huddle working. Call time at three minutes, count how many balloons each huddle has in its middle, announce a winner—and play again! *Michael Capps*

BALLOON POP RELAY

Teams line up single file at a starting line. Place a chair about 30 feet away. Give each team member a deflated balloon. One at a time, kids run to the chair, blow up a balloon, tie it, pop it by sitting on it, and go to the end of the team line. First team to pop all of its balloons wins.

BALLOON BOMB

Remember the leftover party balloon that you'd bounce around in the air when you were a child, trying to keep it from hitting the ground? What was rainy day entertainment then still works with youth groups today.

Formalize the game a bit—form two teams that try to hit the balloon away from the opposition, require that teams alternate hits (only one hit per team), and forbid hitting the balloon directly at the floor. Scoring can run like this: Intentional grounding scores a point for the opposition, as does two consecutive hits by members of the same team. If the balloon touches the ground, the point goes to the opposition of the team that hit it last.

Variation: Instead of the two teams intermingling in the playing area, put them on opposite sides of a six-foot-wide dead zone, and permit—volleyball fashion—two hits per team (by different players) before returning the balloon across the dead zone. More than two hits per team or more than one hit per person scores a point for the opposition. If the balloon lands in the dead zone, the point is scored against the team that last hit it. A team serves until it loses a point.

• **Balloon Bomb Dress-up Relay.** For this variation of Balloon Bomb, each team needs a dress-up box with the same number and kinds of objects—old coat, gloves, hat, scarf, boots, etc. As teammates take their turns racing to the box and then dressing and undressing with the old clothes, they must keep a balloon in the air. If the balloon touches the ground, they must start their dressing over again. *Julie D. Anderson, Karen Friday, and Len and Sheryl DiCicco*

Balloon Burst

Divide your group into two teams and pick a captain for each. Arrange teams as shown in the diagram. Each team tries to hit the balloon in the direction of

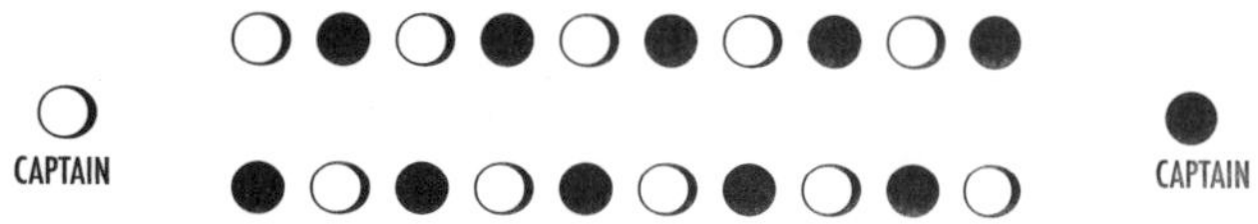

its captain, who then tries to burst the balloon with a pin. One point is scored for each popped balloon. Players must stay seated and use only one hand. *Kathie Taylor*

Balloon Pin Throw

Here's a crazy little game for as few as four people, or it can be used for larger groups in a relay style.

Each team has one of its members sit down in a chair, wearing a baseball cap with a stick pin taped to the bill, protruding just a little bit. If this is done as a relay, each person on the team has a balloon with a piece of string tied to it and stands a short distance from the person who is seated in the chair wearing the hat. Players then try to toss their balloons toward the hats, so that the pins will pop the balloons. They hold on to the piece of string so that they can retrieve the balloon if they miss the pin. As soon as a balloon pops, the next person on the team does it, and so on until everyone on the team has popped a balloon.

You might test this a few times before you play it so that you can determine the proper distance from the foul line to the chair. It should be a challenge to accomplish but not impossible. *Ira Pacheco*

Balloon Sucking Relay

Before the meeting cut off a small (about one-quarter of an inch) portion of the tip of cone-shaped drinking cups, and blow up several six-inch balloons. Divide your youth group into two equal teams arranged in parallel lines. Hand out one cup to each student. Place one balloon at the feet of the first person in each line. Place tape or some other marker about 30 feet away from the two lines.

At the sound of the whistle, the first person in each line must bend over, inhale through the small end of the cup to suck up the balloon, and stand up straight. Students may not tip their heads back. The players must then race to the goal line and back, passing the balloon to the next person in line. No hands are allowed during the transfer. If the balloon is dropped, the runner may only pick it up by inhaling through the paper cup. The team that finishes first wins. *Tony Avila*

Balloon Sweep

In this relay players maneuver a balloon around a goal and back using a broom, sweeping the balloon along the floor. It's much harder than you think. Run small groups of players in each relay.

Blind Balloon Hunt

Begin by placing a number of balloons in random locations on a large floor or field (if on a field, they may need to be anchored). A person is selected from each team to be a hunter. Two additional people from each team are selected to be the guides. Blindfold the hunters. At a signal the hunters proceed to locate as many balloons as possible (all teams going at the same time). The guides may not touch the hunter or the balloons. They only give verbal commands to lead the hunters to the balloons. Allow as much time as you feel necessary. The object is for the hunters to locate as many balloons as possible and bring them back to a starting point (unbroken). They must bring them back to the starting point to count. Keeping them informed of time is important in this event. *Doug Dennee*

Balloon Drop Relay

All you need are 40 or more inflated balloons (round ones) and two or more teams; each with a "dropper" (person who drops balloons) standing on a folding chair. Place the balloons in a box, line up the teams, and you're ready to go.

The idea is to get the balloon to the other end in the fastest time. Before you start, the dropper positions herself up on the chair with the balloon ready to drop to the floor. Two teammates sit on the floor in front of the dropper, back to back, leaving enough room for the balloon to slip down between their backs. The pair then carefully stands, keeping the balloon between their backs and shuffles their way to the other end.

Upon arrival the next balloon is dropped to the next pair and so on until the entire team reaches the other side. If the balloon should burst or fall to the floor before reaching the finish line, the pair must return and start over. The dropper may drop as many balloons as needed in order to get one positioned just where the pair wants it. The dropper is the only one allowed to touch balloons with her hands. This relay game is just as much fun to watch as it is to play! *Tom Bougher*

Bubblehead

For this simple game, have two people stand facing each other about four feet apart. Blow up a round balloon and have one player bump the balloon off his head to the other player. The second player bounces the balloon off her head back to the first player and so on, back and forth. See how many times they can bounce it without dropping it.

The balloon must be hit with the head only. The distance can be varied for greater or lesser difficulty. Each player can move only the left foot while reaching to hit the balloon. The right foot must remain planted. Each player may pivot on the ball of the right foot, but no jumping is allowed.

A variation of this game is to have teams line up, with players about four feet apart. Each team must bounce a balloon all the way down the team line, from one head to the other. Again, right feet must remain planted. If a balloon is dropped, the team must start over again. The first team to succeed is the winner. *Scott Rokely*

Carnival Concentration

For this variation of the old TV game show "Concentration," ask one of the kids with artistic flair to create a Concentration-style puzzle to put on a bulletin board. The puzzle could be a common expression, a line from a popular song, the title from a TV show or movie, or a verse of Scripture. Then tape inflated balloons over the entire puzzle using clear tape.

When it's time to play, break the group into two or three teams. Teams take turns throwing darts at

Balloon Drop Relay

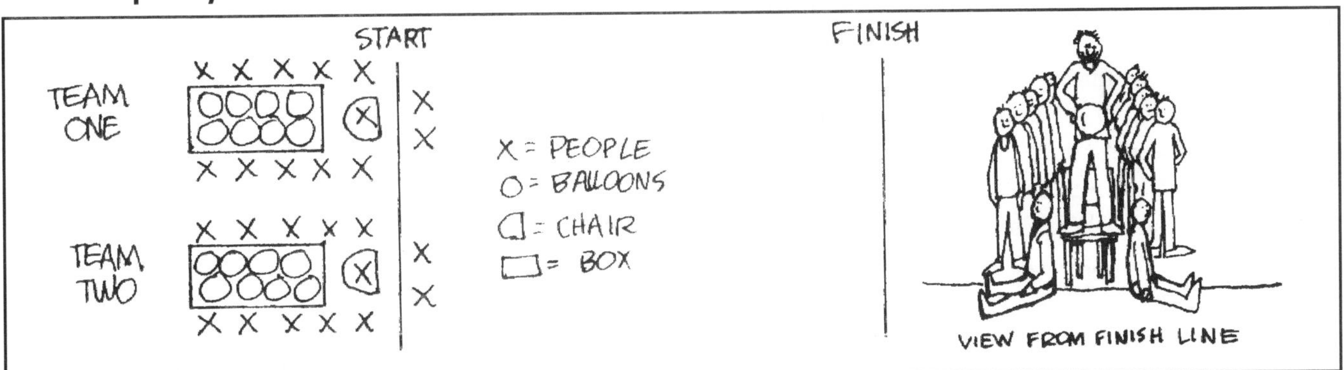

the balloons. When a player pops a balloon, that player's team gets 15 seconds to try to solve the puzzle. A team can only guess the puzzle when one of its members has popped a balloon. The winning team is the first to solve the puzzle successfully. *Jim Bell*

Let It Blow

Divide your group into teams and give each person a deflated balloon. Line the teams up for a relay, with a goal line about 15 feet away. On a signal, the first person on each team blows up his or her balloon and lets it go. The balloon will sail through the air. That person must then go to where it lands, stop, blow it up again, and let it go. The object is to get the balloon across the goal line and then run back and tag the next player on the team, who does the same thing until the relay is finished. This game is really wild, since it is almost impossible to predict where the balloons will land each time. It is especially fun and interesting when played outside, because the slightest breeze blows the balloon in a different direction. *Judy Groen*

Fan the Balloon

Each team gets an inflated balloon and a fan (a piece of cardboard). At the signal, one player from each team must fan the balloon, without touching it, around a goal and back. The balloon cannot touch the floor. Teammates hand off the cardboard during the relay until one team is declared the winner for finishing first.

Garbage Bag Ball

For this game, take a large plastic garbage bag and fill it full of balloons (blown up). Tie it with a twist-tie. You now have a "garbage bag ball." Here's an exciting game that makes good use of it:

1. Have all but 10 of the kids form a large circle on their knees. The remaining 10 kids then form a "pinwheel" formation in the center of the circle, lying on their backs, heads toward the center.
2. Everyone should have their shoes off for best results.
3. The garbage bag ball is then tossed into the circle. The object is for the kids on their backs to kick or hit the ball out of the circle, over the heads of the kids in the outer circle. The outer circle tries to keep it in play. If the ball is kicked over a player's head in the outer circle, then he or she must take the place of the person in the inner circle who kicked it. Play for as long as you wish. *David Washburn*

Head Hacky Sack

Give each team (seven to 10 people per team) a punch-ball-type balloon. The teams form circles and try to keep the punch ball in the air using only their heads. Play by the same rules as hacky sack, except that the head is the only part of the body with which players can legally hit the ball. If the punch ball falls to the floor, pick it up and start over. The team with the most consecutive hits is the winner. *Michael Frisbie*

Popping Pairs

This crazy relay is as much fun to watch as it is to participate in and works well with large groups. All you need is a large box of penny balloons and several clean inner tubes.

Divide your group into several equal teams of 20 or more. Line the teams up behind a start/finish line, having team members pair up. Place piles of balloons 50 feet or more from that line, one pile for each team. Make sure you have enough balloons in each pile (one for each team member).

Instruct the teams that the object is for each pair to run to its pile of balloons, each pick up a balloon and blow it up, and then pop them with their feet before returning to tag the next pair on their team. There is, however, a catch! Each pair must face back-to-back and place its inner tube around both players at waist height. With one runner running forward and the other backward, the partners run to their pile of balloons. Each one must bend down, pick up a balloon, blow it up, and break it with his foot while his partner is doing likewise. The inner tube must stay at waist height at all times. After both balloons are popped the pair is allowed to run back to its team to tag the next pair of runners. The person who ran forward must now run backward and vice versa. The first team to get all its members back across the start/finish line is declared the winning team. For added variety, use two inner tubes per pair instead of just one. *Mark W. Kaat*

Shaving Cream Piñatas

At your next slopfest (or whatever you call messy-game night), fill several large balloons with shaving cream and let some burly hunks take turns bashing the balloons. The game doesn't have to have a point—it's just fun. You could also fill the balloons with whipped cream or anything that comes in a pressurized can. All you need is patience to fill the balloons. *Michael Frisbie*

Swat War Mixer

First gather up what you'll need for this crowd breaker:

- One balloon for each person (all same color)
- Newspapers
- One small slip of paper for each person
- One six-inch length of string for each person
- Pens

Ask players to write something about themselves that nobody else knows—a quality, a memory, a trip, a skill—on a slip of paper. Then they should roll it up, push it into a balloon, and blow the balloon up. Mix all the balloons. Teens can then choose any of the balloons to tie to their back belt loops with the string. Give everyone a section of newspaper to roll up—and let the swatting begin! Kids should try to pop the balloons on others' backsides.

By the time the last balloon is popped, everyone should have retrieved a slip of paper. Gather the group into a circle, and take turns reading the information and guessing who the information is about—the reader should make a few guesses before others in the group have a chance. Writers can explain more about their idiosyncrasies and uniquenesses. *Russell Waddell*

Sticky-Buns Balloon Burst Relay

Ask the kids to line up in pairs behind a line on one side of the room. On the other side of the room spread inflated balloons across the floor. Give each team of two a roll of masking tape, and tell the kids that on "Go!" they are to apply the tape around the midsection of the team member whose birthday is closest to today. The pair must use the whole roll of tape and it must be put on sticky-side out.

When the tape is used up, the taped players must crab-walk to the balloons and bring back to their partners waiting at the starting line as many balloons as they can carry without using their hands. The waiting partner must then burst the balloons and save the ring part of the balloon (where you blow it up) to verify the number of balloons retrieved. Balloons popped by the sticky-bunned teammate don't count. The pair with the most rings wins.

This is a game to videotape. The kids are so dizzy from spinning around to get the tape on that they have a hard time doing the rest of the relay. *Keith Posehn*

Blow-Hard Bomber

You remember the old tug-of-war across the mud pit? Here's the same idea (do the dirty work unto the others, before they do it unto you)—except that the penalty for losing isn't a mud pit, however, but a balloon filled with talcum powder that explodes in your lap.

Collect the following materials:

- 2 plastic hoses, ¾-inch diameter by 6½-foot length
- 2 large balloons per round (heavy-duty punching type work well)
- talcum powder
- duct tape
- 2 chairs
- 2 pairs safety glasses
- 2 volunteers

Pour talcum powder into deflated balloons until they are half filled. Fit the plastic tube into the balloon, and seal it with duct tape so the air can't get out and the balloon won't fly off. Sit the two kids in chairs, back to back. Give each contestant the end of their tubes to blow in—and tape the balloon ends of their tubes to their opponents' thighs. (Be sure to tape the tubes, not the balloons themselves, to the players' thighs.) The winner is—well, the one who isn't white. *Matt Klein*

BASKETBALL GAMES

BASKETBALL GAMES

Some of these games are slight variations of good ol' hoopball as we know it. And then there are those less recognizable forms of the game that don't even require a court or a regulation basketball. A few are the hideous spawn of an unnatural mating of basketball and, say, baseball or dodgeball. But all of 'em are slam dunks.

ARENA NERFKETBALL

If you have a large room and can mount Nerf ball baskets and backboards at either end (or construct simple, portable frames to mount them on), your group can generate all the enthusiasm of a tournament play-off. Create two teams that must devise team names and cheers. Have groups of five rotate in and out every few minutes to give everyone a chance to play. Use refs to maintain order and keep the game moving. And since the baskets may be fragile, tape off the area four feet out from each basket and declare it out-of-bounds.

Other rules that keep the game active:

- Since Nerf balls can't be dribbled, players must pass after taking three steps.
- No touching opponents.
- No roughness.
- Play stops at ref's whistle, and ball goes to ref (violation of this rule results in a penalty).
- All penalties result in a free throw (free-throw shooters must rotate).
- Ref's decisions are final.

A fitting and frenetic finale? Invite everyone onto the floor for the game's last minute! *Jim Reed*

BALLOON BLOWER BASKETBALL

Have two teams line up, with each behind the free-throw line at one end of the basketball court. Each team designates a balloon blower. At a signal the first person in line shoots a basketball from the free throw line or dribbles as close as desired to the net and shoots. The second person in line must stay behind the free throw line until the ball is thrown back to him by the person who just shot. After a person shoots, he gets back in line. Each time someone makes a basket, the balloon blower makes one giant blow into the balloon. The team that pops its balloon first wins. If you want the game to go longer, you can give each team two or three balloons. *Jon Hantsbarger*

Basketball Pass

This is a simple relay game in which two teams line up single file in two lines. Each team must have an equal number of players. At the front of each line, a basketball (or several basketballs) is given to the first player. He passes it to the player behind him by passing it *over his head*. The next person passes it between her legs to the player behind her and so on. The ball(s) continue to the end of the line going over and under, and the team who finishes first wins.

Basket Brawl

Here's a coed basketball game that can be played with both junior and senior highers together. Divide your youth group into two teams. Try to distribute boys, girls, tall kids, short kids, junior highers, and senior highers equally among the teams to make the competition as fair as possible. Each team should also have an adult captain to help everyone get organized. It doesn't matter how many are on the team, and even the leaders can play.

Give each team identifying armbands. There should also be a scorekeeper, a timekeeper, a referee, and any other officials you desire.

The game is a continuously played, seven-period, 21-minute game. Each period is three minutes long and involves players from a particular category or mix of categories such as:

- Mixed players (boys, girls, junior highers, senior highers)—five players per team on the floor. Only girls can score.
- Junior highers only.
- Senior highers only.
- Girls only.
- Guys only.
- Mixed guys and girls. Only guys can shoot, and only girls can carry the ball. Girls must move the ball to the boys who shoot. Five players per team on the floor.
- Everybody! The entire team plays in the grand finale. If you have ball hogs who tend to dominate the game, you can insert an alternating rule: a guy shoots, then a girl, then a guy, and so on.

The clock never stops. A period is indicated by banging a pan lid with a wooden spoon at the end of three minutes. The team captains should have a period order sheet so that they can have their teams ready to change. If a team scores while the other team is getting organized, the point counts.

The referee needs a whistle, but he can only stop the game for an injury. The ref can call fouls if they are serious and continuous. Keep in mind that many younger kids may not know how to play basketball, so fouls may be unavoidable. But if flagrant fouls are being committed, just award free points to the other team rather than stopping to shoot free throws.

Each basket can be worth any number of points you choose, or a different number of points in different periods. The winner of the game can be the team with the most points or the team that wins the most periods.

You can adjust other rules as needed to deal with dribbling, boundaries, rotating players, and so on. The object of the game is to allow everyone to play and have a great time. Anything you can do to make that happen is good. *Mark Simone*

Basketball Derby

Play a game of basketball on roller skates. It is extremely funny to watch as well as play. There is no out-of-bounds or dribbling, but the other regular rules apply. Other games (such as softball, football, etc.) can be played on roller skates as well with excellent results. Make sure you have appropriate safety gear. *Joe Wright*

Basketball Squat

Divide your group into teams (approximately six to 10 per team). Have the teams choose a captain for each group. Have the teams line up in a straight line facing the captains (approximately five to 10 feet away from the captains). The captain throws the ball to the first person in the line who returns the throw and then squats down. The captain then throws the ball to the second person who does the same thing and on down the line to the last person. The captain then throws the ball a second time to the last person who throws it back and stands back up. This process is repeated till everyone has received another pass, working its way up to the first person in line. Anytime the ball is dropped, the team must start all over again. The first team to get everybody standing up again is the winner. *Eddie Benton*

BASKET-DODGEBALL

For this game you need a gym or a full basketball court with two hoops, four basketballs, and a playground ball.

Divide players into four teams. Each team lines up in a corner of the court in tallest-to-shortest order (see diagram below). Each player on the team is assigned a number—1 for the tallest, 2 for the next tallest, and so on. (To accommodate uneven teams, assign some players two numbers.)

Here's how to play. After you make sure all players are sitting, yell out a number—"Three!" The four 3s leap up, grab their basketballs, and dribble them to the basket at the opposite end of the gym. Only when a player makes a basket can he run back to his team without dribbling and set down the ball.

And here's where dodgeball enters. The first player back from replacing his basketball runs to center court, picks up the dodgeball, and begins the dodgeball game. Whoever he hits is out (the ball must hit the person without first bouncing)—unless the intended victim catches the ball, in which case the thrower is out. Woe to the player who's still struggling with making a basket when the other three start dodgeball!

When three players are eliminated from a dodgeball game, the survivor's team earns one point. Return balls and players to starting positions, then call another number. Play as many rounds as you like, or play until a team reaches a predetermined score. With kids dribbling in opposite directions and two of them shooting at the same basket, you'll get some wild collisions.

With few people or only one hoop, have just three teams that shoot in the same basket. Adapt the game for indoors with a Nerf ball. *Jeff Callen*

BASKETCASE

Here are the crazy twists to this basketball variation: the ball is carried overhead instead of dribbled down

Basket-Dodgeball

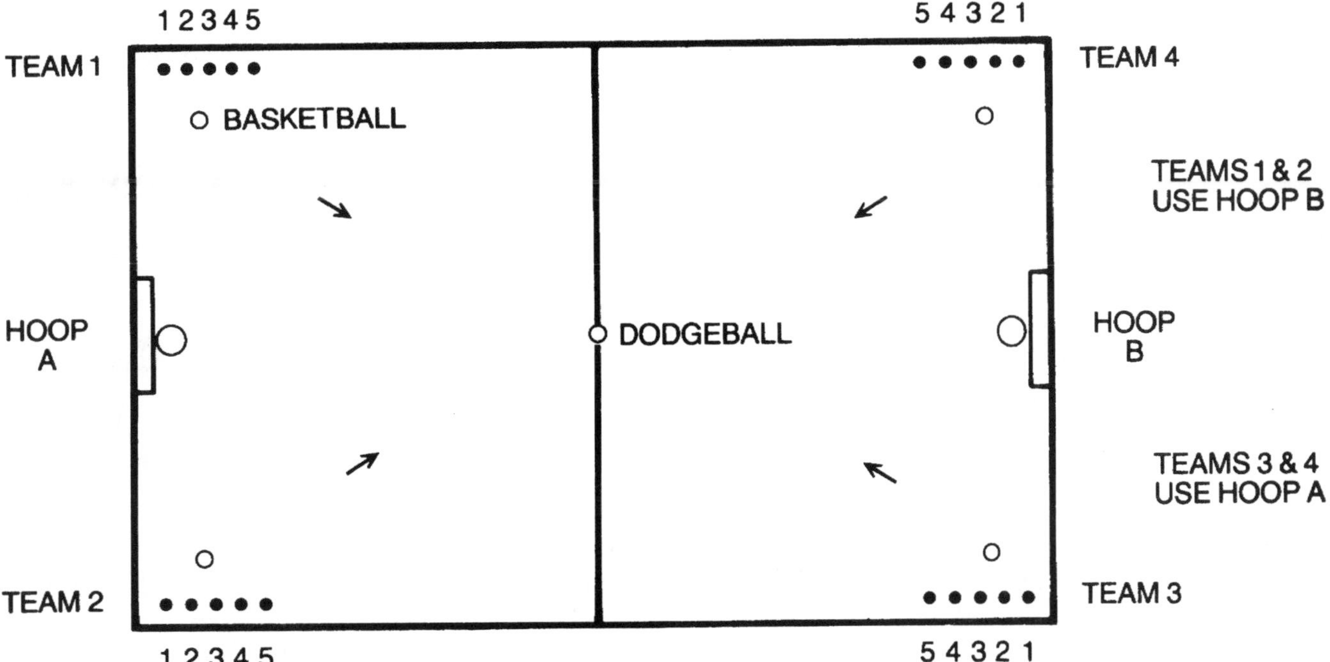

the court, and it is passed to a teammate by rolling it. Baskets are scored by throwing the ball up through the bottom of the hoop. Here are some details players need to know:

• Teammates of the player who passes the ball may use their hands to pick it up and carry it downcourt.
• Opponents of a passer, however, cannot use their hands to intercept a passed (rolled) ball—they must snare the ball between their feet, after which they can use their hands to carry and pass the ball.
• Foul shots are taken this way: the shooter rolls the ball to a teammate along the key, who may pick it up and make a basket a la "Basketcase."

Play to 21—the odd point must come from a foul shot. *Michael W. Capps*

BLIND BASKETBALL

You'll need a Nerf basketball hoop, a ball, and two blindfolds.

Divide the group into two teams, one offense, the other defense. Blindfold one member of each team; these two will do the actual playing. Following the verbal instructions of their teammates, the blindfolded offensive player tries to find the hoop and make a basket; the blindfolded defensive player, doing his best to hear his team's instructions, defends the basket.

Play periods of five minutes or so, then offensive and defensive teams switch and new players are blindfolded. Also during the switch, move the hoop so the blindfolded players don't know where it is.

Reference the game later when you want to illustrate how we are bombarded by messages and need to be selective in who we listen to. *Randy Isola*

CHAIRBALL

This exciting version of basketball can be played on any open field or in a large room. Instead of using a regular basketball, use something lighter, like a playground ball or a Nerf ball. You may have any number of people on the two teams. At each end of the playing area have someone standing on a chair holding a wastebasket or a similar container. A jump ball starts the game, just like regular basketball. The players then try to move the ball down the field so that someone on the team can shoot a basket. The person on the chair who is holding the basket may try to help by moving the basket if necessary to catch the ball when it is shot. All shots must be made beyond a 10-foot foul line. The ball may only be moved downfield by throwing it to a teammate or by kicking it. You may not run or walk with the ball. You may score baskets just like regular basketball, or you can come up with any point system that you choose. *Julie Von Vett*

CRAZY BASKETBALL

Divide your entire group into two teams with any number of players. The game is played on a regular basketball court, but without regular basketball rules. In this game, anything goes. The object is to score the most baskets any way you can. You can run, pass, dribble, or throw the basketball with no restrictions. All that matters is to make a basket. Kids can ride piggyback for height. This game works best with 50 to 200 participants.

FREE THROW UP

This is an exciting game if your young people have the guts (literally) to do it. Have one basketball and one basketball goal per team, and at least 12 ounces of root beer per player. The teams should have an equal number of players. The root beer can be either warm or cold, but should be put in pitchers, an equal amount given to each team. The teams line up and take turns shooting free throws, keeping strict order in taking turns. All players must shoot the same number of free throws, give or take one. The object of the game is to be the first team to empty its pitcher by drinking its contents. This is done by appointing someone to drink six-ounces poured into a paper cup whenever a free throw is made. Obviously, the same person does not do the drinking; this duty should be shared by as many players (using their own cups) as have a tolerance for the brown foamy fluid.

The game can also be played with darts, spitballs, snowballs, or anything else aimed at a target. The important features are (1) emptying the pitchers of root beer rather than hitting the target a certain number of times and (2) each player shoots at the target in the designated order. *Lew Worthington*

Donkey Basketball

Remember those wooden riding horses made out of broomsticks? You can still buy them, or you can make your own for a rousing game of Donkey Basketball. You play it just like regular basketball, except that you must "ride" your horse around the court while you play. It's not only fun to play—it's great to watch. *Donna McElrath*

Foul Shooting Marathon

If you have access to a basketball court, here's a good game that anybody can play and which allows everyone a chance to get in on the action. You can play with as many teams (at once) as you have baskets, or each team may go one at a time if you have only one basket.

The team lines up at the foul line and the first person in line gets the basketball. On a signal, he or she begins shooting regulation free throws (foul shots), while one teammate stands under the basket and returns the ball as quickly as possible. (The person under the basket can be the person who just finished shooting. That way each person does this job once. Begin with the last person in line.) The shooter continues to shoot until the whistle blows, then he or she becomes the person under the basket, and the next person starts shooting as quickly as possible.

The leader (who is blowing the whistle) may blow the whistle at even 30-second intervals (plus or minus) or may blow it at uneven intervals, giving some players more time than others. The latter is most applicable when all teams are throwing at the same time. That way a player doesn't really know how much time he has to shoot. A scorekeeper should be counting the total number of successful foul shots made, and the team which has the most after everyone has had a chance to throw, wins.

To make the game a bit longer, play four quarters, a quarter being the time it takes for everyone on the team to throw once.

Variations of this game include the following:

- Two teams can play best out of three rounds, rather than adding the total number of baskets made. In other words, a winner is declared after each round (quarter) and the first team to win two is the champ.
- You can have each shooter shoot a certain number of shots and then the next person takes over. No whistle is necessary here. Also, the round could be over as soon as one team finishes making all its throws, whether or not the other teams have finished. That way speed enters into the picture.
- You could also have a shooter shoot until he makes a shot and then move to the next person. If you do it this way, each round can have a set time limit, say 10 minutes, or the first team to get one free shot successfully out of each player is the winner of that round.

Norma Bailey

Parliff

This is a gym game for 16 or more kids, played with a basketball. One team spreads out across the court while the other goes up to "bat" next to one wall of the gym. The batter takes the ball and either punts or throws it in any direction (no boundaries). Immediately he or she then runs to the far wall, touches it, and runs back to touch the "home" wall. Meanwhile, the team in the "field" is chasing down the ball and passing it to a designated shooter under the goal next to their own home wall.

If the shooter can make the basket before the batter touches the home wall, the batter is out. If the batter makes it home first, his or her team wins a point for the "run." Allow three outs, and then the opposing team is up. Highest score after nine innings wins. *Chris Thompson*

Double Dribble

This game is played by regular basketball rules except that two balls are used at the same time and two teams of 10 are on the court. The game starts with jump balls at both ends of the court. Play with one ball does not stop because of the actions of the players with the other ball. One team could be shooting a free throw because of a foul, and the other group could come through on a lay-up.

The teams can be divided up as the players wish: two five-on-five games, super zone defense, eight-on-three, or other creative strategies. As the game develops, the teams will be able to see how to set up their own offenses and defenses.

A variation is to have the goals set at eight feet to minimize pure basketball skill and to allow for more slam dunk shots.

This is a great mixer where a lot of youths (and their parents) can get playing time. *Clark Barton*

NERFKETBALL

Here is a fun version of basketball using a Nerf ball and chairs. Choose two teams of equal numbers and seat them alternately on sturdy chairs (see below): two rows of players facing each other. For best results, players should be spaced at least double arm's distance apart both sideways and across. Place a "basket" (small bucket, gallon plastic bottle with top cut off, etc.) on the floor at each end of the double row, approximately six feet from the players at the ends of the rows.

The two basic ground rules of the game are: (1) Chairs cannot be moved or tipped; (2) Each player must remain seated while the ball is in play.

Using a coin flip, one team is chosen to take first possession of the ball. Play begins as the player farthest from his team's goal is given the ball by the referee. The team tries to work the ball toward their goal by passing it while opponents try to block passes and steal the ball. Any player may take a shot at the goal at any time, but the advantages of passing the ball to the player nearest the goal are obvious. If the ball is intercepted by the other team, play continues in the opposite direction.

When an attempted field goal misses, the ball is automatically given to the other team and play then goes the other way. When a field goal is scored, all players rotate one seat to the right. This will give each player the opportunity to be his team's prime shooter during the game. After rotation, the ball goes to the other team and goes the other way.

Any ball loose within the playing area is a free ball. Any ball going outside the playing area is given to the player nearest the last player to touch the ball.

Penalties may be assessed and free throws awarded for players leaving their seats or for unnecessary roughness. Limit the game by using a kitchen timer for quarters or halves, or by setting a scoring limit. *Ed Stewart*

FRISBASKETBALL

Next time your group wants to play basketball, try this game. Instead of a basketball, use a Frisbee and as many players as you wish on a regular basketball court. Of course, you can't dribble a Frisbee, so you must advance it by passing. The refs should call penalties such as fouls, traveling, and out of bounds just as they normally would in a basketball game. Points should be awarded as follows: one point for hitting the backboard, two for hitting the square on

Nerfketball

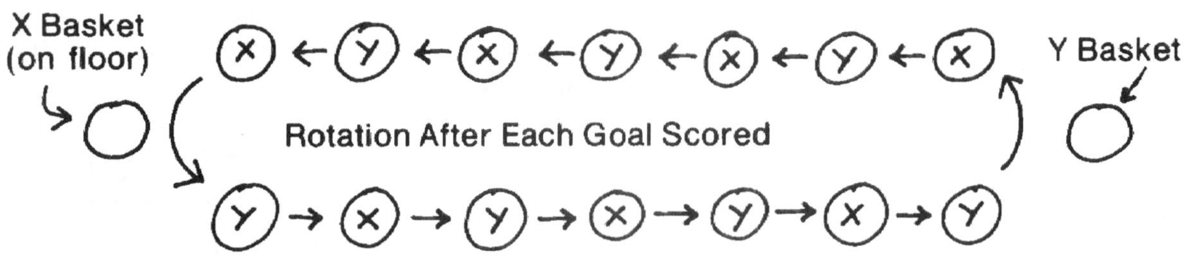

X Basket (on floor)

X ← Y ← X ← Y ← X ← Y ← X

Y Basket

Rotation After Each Goal Scored

Y → X → Y → X → Y → X → Y

the backboard, and three for making a goal (including foul shots). Double the scores for any shot made from behind half-court. Make sure you are in shape before you try out this one! *Kim Hall*

PEOPLE BALL

Here's a basketball game that includes everyone, not just the competitive hoopsters. After you divide your group into two teams, five from each team should take their place on the court and play regulation basketball—except that they cannot dribble the ball. In fact, they cannot move when they have the ball.

Here's how the ball is moved down the floor: all the rest of the team not on the court spreads out along both sidelines, alternating teams. The 10 players on the court must throw the ball to a sidelines teammate, who then throws it to a court player on his team. There are plenty of chances for interception, of course, both on the sidelines and the court.

Players should wear identifying colors or jerseys for quick recognition. There are no fouls on sideliners, and the ball is always put into play by a sideliner. *Michael W. Capps*

REFRIGERATOR BALL

Here's a good game that might come in handy at your next retreat when it starts raining outside. You need an indoor playing area and a standard refrigerator (or something similar). You also need a light ball and a cardboard box.

The box is weighted and placed on top of the refrigerator. The refrigerator is moved into the center of the room. A circle is drawn on the floor around the refrigerator so that kids can't get closer than four feet or so. Then you just play regular basketball. The team that has the ball may pass it around and then take shots at the basket, trying to get the ball to stay in the box. The excitement is increased by missed shots going over the box to the opposing team, shots being tipped, etc. Make up your own rules as you go along. A referee can call fouls and try to keep things from getting out of hand. *John Pierce*

RING-NET BALL

Here's a basketball-type game for gym night. As in baseball, the defense scatters around the basketball court. From the sideline at midcourt, an offensive batter throws a basketball into the field. He then runs out to the circle at midcourt—the base—and runs around it as many times as possible before the defense can grab the ball and sink a basket. Score one point for each completed circle around the base. Everyone on the team throws before the inning switches. *Phil Blackwell*

ROLLER BASKETBALL

Using an outdoor basketball court, two teams on roller skates attempt to score points by hitting the opponent's backboard with a beach ball. (Teams can have between five and 10 players each.) Players may either carry the ball or tap it as in volleyball. If a player is tagged by an opponent while carrying the ball, the ball goes over to the other team. The ball is put in play by a player passing it in from out of bounds.

Roughness penalty gives the opposing team a free-throw from the basketball free-throw line. *Chuck Williams*

SHORT ARM BASKETBALL

This game is played relay style and is fun to watch or play. Line up in any number of teams. The first player in each line runs out to a line about eight feet away with the ball, which is a ball of wadded-up newspaper wrapped in masking tape that is about six inches in diameter (or you could use a Nerf ball). He tosses the ball to the second player (standing now at the front of the line) who must catch it with his elbows while his hands are on his chin.

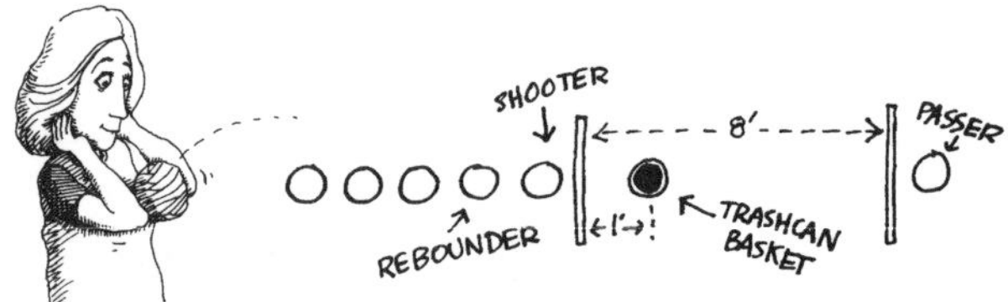

After catching the ball, that person (the shooter) then bounces the ball off the backboard (his knees) and into a bucket (or trash can) that is on the floor, one foot in front of him. The ball must bounce off his knees in order for the basket to count. If he misses, the rebounder (the next person in line) picks up the ball and tosses it back to the first person and the whole process repeats until a legal basket is made. You might want to set a limit on unsuccessful tries (like three), but usually that is not necessary.

Once a basket is made, the shooter grabs the ball, runs out to the passer's position, and the rebounder becomes the shooter, while the passer runs to the end of the line, etc. Everybody on the team plays all three positions once. The first team to get back to the original position is the winner. *Richard Moore*

Three-Way Giant Basketball

Instead of two teams for basketball, why not three? All three teams have seven players on the court at a time. Each team can have up to two "giants" (à la chicken-fight style) but a girl must be one of the two people comprising the giant. Teams can score at either basket. A player cannot dribble more than two times. Three fouls and a player is out of the game. Be sure to substitute freely so that everyone can play. *Bill Calvin*

Trash Can Basketball

This is an indoor version of basketball that can be played when the real thing is not available. Set up large trash cans at each end of the room (kids love to shoot things into trash cans). There should be a ring drawn around the trash cans about six feet out from the cans, which is a no-man's land. Use a soft, children's ball about eight inches in diameter, or anything else that will work. Rules are all the same as normal basketball except for a few:

- There is no dribbling. All movement of the ball is by passing. This helps to make the game not only more practical, but a lot fairer in a coed situation.
- No running with the ball. You can only pass it to a teammate.
- If you touch a player with the ball, that's a foul. The fouled player gets a free shot.
- No one is allowed in the no-man's land circle. That prevents goal tending and dunking, making the game a bit more fair for everyone.

Jim Walton

Strengthball Relays

The only equipment needed for these relays is one ball that bounces for each team and one basketball goal, or a target, for the game. Both (all) teams shoot at the same goal. The starting point should be the same distance from the goal for all teams. The playing area should be set up as diagrammed, with the path of each team indicated by the arrow.

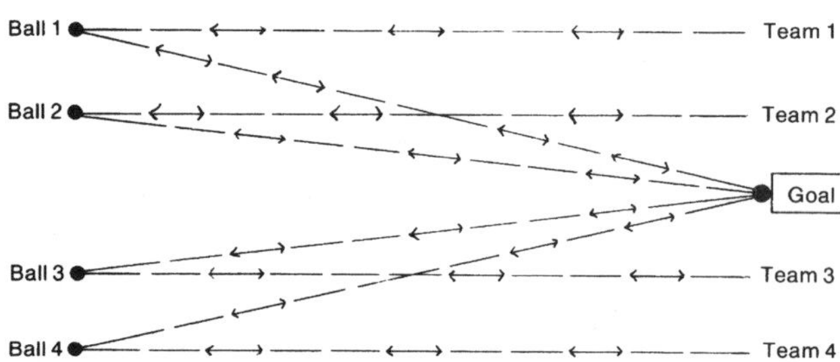

The teams should sit on the floor, with each player standing only to do his part. When each player is finished he should sit down in line. No interference with the balls is allowed by those in line. The team that is seated and finished first wins. The following rules apply to the types of Strengthball Relays that can be played:

- **Piggyback Strengthball.** Team members pair off. One partner takes a piggyback position on the other partner's shoulders. On a signal the first pair in line piggyback to the other end of the room, where the team's balls are sitting on the floor. The bottom partner picks up the ball for his/her team and passes it up to the partner riding piggyback. The pair proceeds to the goal with the upper partner dribbling the ball. Upon arriving at the goal, the upper partner attempts to score a goal (or hit the designated target) while still riding piggyback. The pair remains at the goal until one score is achieved. Then the pair returns the ball to the other end of the floor (where it was originally picked up) with the upper partner again dribbling the ball. Once the ball is placed, not thrown or dropped, in its original spot, the pair returns to their team. A tag is made to the next pair in line and they repeat this process. The team to finish first faints from exhaustion.

• **Wheelbarrow Strengthball.** Team members pair off. The familiar wheelbarrow positions are assumed by the first pair in each line (back people hold up the feet of the front people, who then walk on their hands). On the signal the first pair proceeds to the team's ball, in wheelbarrow fashion. The ball is corralled by the front person and guided with head and shoulders (no hands) to the goal (target). When the pair arrives under the goal, the back person lets go of the front person's legs. The back person must score one goal. After scoring, the pair returns the ball to its original spot, wheelbarrow style, then returns to their line. A tag is made to the next pair and the process is repeated until one team is finished.

• **Chair Strengthball.** (Additional equipment needed—one chair per team, placed close to the goal.) Team members run individually in this relay. The first person in each line runs, on a signal, to the team's ball, dribbles it to the team's chair in front of the goal (target), sits in the chair and shoots until a goal is scored (with seat on the chair and feet on the floor). The person then dribbles the ball back to its original spot, runs back to the line, tags the next person, and the process is repeated until one team finishes.

• **Soccer Strengthball.** Team members go individually in this relay. The first person in each line runs, on a signal, to the team's ball. That person dribbles the ball soccer style (with the feet) to the goal (target). Once near the goal, the player shoots until one goal is scored (shoot with the hands). The ball is then placed on the floor and dribbled, soccer style, to its original spot. The player then runs back to her line, tags the next person, and the process continues until one team finishes. *Ed Merrill*

TRIPLE THREAT BASKETBALL

Here's a new way to play basketball. It requires one basket and three teams. You can have three teams of any size, however a maximum of five players and a minimum of two would be best. The rules of the game are pretty much the same as regular basketball, but with these changes:

• Baskets are worth one point. The game is played until one team has 10 points and is leading the other two teams by at least two points each.

• After each basket is scored, the team in last place is awarded the ball out of bounds, even if it is the team that just scored. In the event that two teams (or all three teams) are tied for last, the team that has had the low point total the longest is awarded the ball. Or, you may want to come up with some other system that seems fair.

• In the event that play is stopped for some reason other than a basket, such as the ball going out of bounds, traveling, double dribble, etc., the team in last place is again awarded the ball. If the last place team was guilty of the violation, the ball is given to the team that is next to last.

• In the event of a foul, the team that was fouled takes the ball out of bounds. No foul shots.

This game can be played with two baskets on a regular basketball court, and having the teams rotate baskets after each goal is scored. Part of the fun then is trying to remember which basket is yours. Another variation is to play with four teams and four baskets on each side of a square, if you have baskets that can be moved. You could, of course, play the game with a Nerf ball and cardboard boxes or trash cans for baskets. Use your own creativity and have fun! *Merle Moser, Jr.*

TURTLE BASKETBALL

This idea adds a twist to the game of basketball. Instead of running up and down the court, everyone walks. Everyone, however, can walk as fast as they can. If the offense is caught running, the ball goes over to the other team. If the defense is caught, the offensive team member wins the ball and shoots two free throws. Each person caught running is assessed a foul. Also, everyone must keep their feet on the floor when rebounding. If someone is caught jumping, the ball goes to the other team. No foul is given here. This is really hilarious to watch. Except for the above, regular basketball rules are used for scoring. *Doug Simpson*

Two-on-Two Basketball

Here's a twist to the standard two-on-two game that's especially adaptable to tournament play. Each two-person team designates one of its members as the stationary shooter (Player S), who must remain at one end of the free-throw line, Player S cannot move her feet, and only she can do the shooting for her team. The remaining person on each team is the moving player (Player M), who grabs, rebounds, blocks shots, intercepts passes—everything but shoot.

Variations are endless. In coed games designate the girls as shooters, the guys as moving players. Or place your shooters anywhere on the court in order to vary the difficulty of the shots. Or add players and designate more shooters or more moving players. *Andrew Winters*

Indoor Games for Large Groups

These games are geared toward groups of thirty or more and are designed to be played in a gymnasium, fellowship hall, or similar room. But no matter how large your group is or what the confines of your meeting area are, you'll find crowd breakers, mixers, and contests that will work for you.

AMOEBA

Divide into teams and simply tie a rope around teammates at their waists. To do this, the teammates huddle together and hold their hands up in the air while you tie the rope around them. After they are tied, they race to a goal and back. Unless they work together as a team, they will get nowhere.

• **Amoeba Lift.** This game is a simple variation of the game Amoeba. This can be done as competition between teams or as a cooperative game with the entire group trying to break its own record. Each group should not be much larger than about 15, however. If you have more kids than that, divide into more groups, all of equal size.

Each group becomes an amoeba. Each amoeba is to develop a strategy whereby it must lift the entire group and stand on as few legs as possible. The amoeba must stand in place for a minimum of 10 seconds. Any legs that touch down during that time are counted. Have several leaders available to count legs during the lift and to pick up the pieces when the walls come tumblin' down. Obviously, the amoeba that is able to lift itself up on the fewest legs is the winner.

• **The Amoeba That Ate Manhattan.** All you need for this game is a clearly defined area (ball field, room, etc.) and lots of kids—though smaller groups will enjoy it, too. Two people are designated to be the young amoeba, who immediately join hands and try to capture others by encircling them. Those so captured join the growing chain and continue the quest, running roughly single file until they surround a victim and close the circle.

As each amoeba grows it may capture groups of people at a time, or even another, smaller amoeba.

The game ends when the entire group is part of a single amoeba, and the winner is the last one caught. *Dan Scholten and Jim Larsen*

A Day at School

The object of this game is to see who can go through a day of "school" the fastest by completing the assignment in every "class" (see page 37). Choose 11 locations around the church facility (Sunday school classrooms are best) and station a staff "teacher" in each one with the appropriate assignment from the list below. Then have the "students" meet with you in another room—their "homeroom"—where they are given a copy of the "report card" (see page 37).

Students must go to every class, answer the question or complete the assignment to the teacher's satisfaction, and have the teacher grade and initial the report card. The first and last classes students "attend" must be the same as their first and last classes at school (if it's summer, they can use the previous year's schedule). Other classes may be attended in any order they wish. To make it a little more complicated, don't tell the students where each class meets; let them find out on their own. The first student to return to "homeroom" with all assignments completed (regardless of grade) and all classes initialed is the winner. *Todd Capen*

Barnyard

Divide your group into six equal teams. Give each person a folded piece of paper with the name of an animal written on it. When you turn off the lights, players are to make the sound of their animal and search in the dark for other people making the same animal sound. Assign one of these six animal names to each player or make up your own:

Pig Horse Cow

Duck Dog Chicken

When teammates find each other, they lock arms and find more of their teammates. When the lights are turned on, everyone sits down. The team that locates the most teammates wins. (For more fun—or frustration—give one person the word donkey, so that he or she can't find *any* teammates.)

Car Stuff

For this wild game, you need a car that can risk damage or dirt. Kids line up on one side of the car (with front and back doors open) and, on a signal, run through the car—in one side and out the other. After going through the car, the players return to the end of the line and run through again until the time limit is up. The object is to see how many kids can run through the car in the time limit (one minute, two minutes, etc.). Two members of each team function as a Timer and a Counter. Each team gets a try. To play this game *without* a car, use a large cardboard box or a bench that the kids must crawl under.

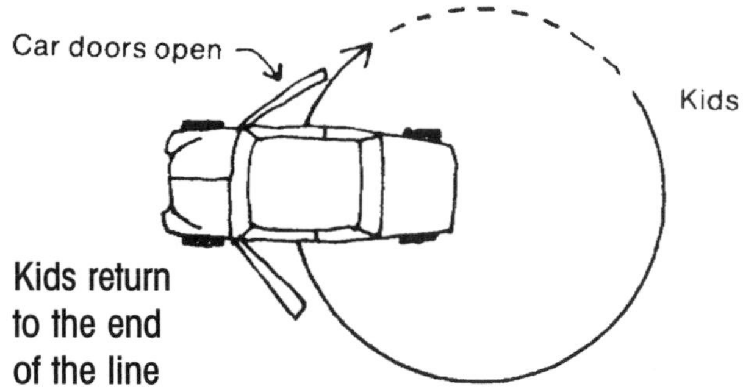

Chariot Races

This game works best on a slick floor, as in a gym. Set up a circular track. Have two strong people from each team (horses) pull each teammate (chariot driver), one at a time, around the circle on a thick blanket (chariot). The chariot driver should be sure to hold on tightly to the blanket. The first team to complete three laps or to give every teammate a ride is the winner. Any teammate who falls off the blanket must return to the starting line with his horses and try again.

Clumps

This game can be played with as many as 1,000 people. Everyone gently crowds toward a center point with their arms at their sides until the leader blows a whistle or horn. The leader calls out a number, 12 for instance. Everyone must break up into groups of 12, lock arms, and sit down. Leaders then eliminate

REPORT CARD

CLASS	GRADE (PASS/FAIL)	TEACHER'S INITIALS
Math	_______	_______
English	_______	_______
Literature	_______	_______
Science	_______	_______
P.E.	_______	_______
Lunch	_______	_______
Band/Choir	_______	_______
Drama	_______	_______
Vocational Ed	_______	_______
History	_______	_______
Foreign Language	_______	_______

SAMPLE CLASS ASSIGNMENTS

(To be given to the "teachers")

Math: Have them add the number of the apostles and the number of the Gospels.

English: Have them write "Jesus Loves Me" as a title for their next composition. (Check their spelling!)

Literature: Ask them what was the first book ever printed on a printing press. (Answer: the Bible)

Science: Ask them where they can read about the origin of the universe. (Genesis 1)

PE: Calisthenics—Have them do five push-ups and five deep-knee bends.

Lunch: Have them give you directions (a map) to their favorite off-campus eatery.

Band/Choir: Have them sing "The B-I-B-L-E."

Drama: Have them act out "And they were sore afraid!"

Vocational Ed: Tell them to "charade" any occupation of their choice until you can guess what it is.

History: Ask them "Who was buried in Joseph of Arimathea's tomb?" If they say Joseph of Arimathea, give them an "F".

Foreign Language: Ask them to translate the Greek word *agape*. (Godly love) all those who are not in groups of 12 within a brief time limit. This process is repeated, with different numbers each time, until all have been eliminated.

• **Anatomy Clumps.** Players begin by milling around the room as the leader stands in the middle. After a few seconds the leader blows a whistle and yells out two things: a part of the body and a number ("Elbow! Three!"). All players then rush to get into groups of whatever number was called and connect with each other whatever body part was called. After the call "Elbow! Three!," for example, players form groups of three and touch elbows with each other. The last group to do this correctly or a group of players not in a proper group is eliminated from the game.

Other examples: knee (4), nose (3), ankle (6), back (2), rear (5), neck (2), shoulder (6), head (4), lip (2).

• **Bread and Butter Clumps.** Divide the group into equal halves, giving one group the name "Bread" and the other group the name "Butter." Have kids mingle, saying only their group name—Bread or Butter. When the whistle is blown, the leader calls out a number, and the players must form a clump of that number—but only with members of their team. Anyone left out of a group, or in a group that accidently mixes the two teams, is eliminated. The last person left is the winner.

More variations can be made using different team names, such as "Peas and Carrots" or "Peanut Butter and Jelly." It's a lot of fun to play.

• **Freckle Clumps.** Use a felt-tipped pen to draw freckles on each player's face. Give 10 freckles to 10 players, two freckles to 10 more players, three freckles, and so on, depending on the size of your group. At the signal, players are to find everyone else who has the same number of freckles and to sit down on the floor. The last group to get together loses. Now that your teams are divided up, you can play team games or relays.

• **Pyramid Clumps.** Your kids mill around the floor. Then the leader blows the whistle or horn and yells out any number. After the number is called, the participants seek out the called number of kids, get down on their hands and knees, and build a pyramid. The pyramid group must have exactly the number of kids called or they are out of the game. Extra people are also out. The game continues until one individual or one small group remains.

• **Tin Pan Bang Bang.** The leader stands on a chair in the middle of the room with a stainless steel pot in his hand and a metal spoon. The crowd begins milling around the room. Everybody has to keep moving. The leader then bangs on the pot with the spoon a certain number of times and then stops. The players count the number of beats and then get in a circle holding hands with the same number of persons as the number of beats. Those who are not in a circle with the right number of people when a whistle blows are eliminated from the game. This is continued with a varied number of beats each time, until all are eliminated except for one person. *Michael W. Capps, Glenn T. Serino, Dallas Elder, and Norma Bailey*

DROP THE KEYS

Have the group sit in a circle facing inward. "It" is chairless and the object is to get a chair. "It" begins by running quickly around the circle (on the inside) and grabbing the hand of someone of the opposite sex. The person whose hand was grabbed grabs someone else's hand (again, of the opposite sex). This continues as they are running around the circle (boy, girl, boy, girl). As the line gets longer, "It" goes under arms and between people to thoroughly tie the line in knots. All the while, the last person chosen is still attempting to reach out and grab another person's hand sitting in the circle. When "It" chooses he drops the set of keys he has been carrying and everyone makes a mad dash for a chair. Whoever is left without a chair becomes the next "It." *Roger Lucas*

FOUR-LETTER WORD

Every member of the group has a large letter of the alphabet pinned on. At the signal, each person tries to find three others with which she can form a four-letter word within a one-minute time limit. Those failing to form a word are out, and the game continues until everyone is eliminated.

GORILLA-MAN-GUN

This game is a lot like the old paper-rock-scissors game kids play. Have everyone in your group pair off and stand in two lines, with each pair across from each other, back-to-back.

The leader, who merely directs the action, shouts "One, two, three!" And on "three" all players turn around to face their partners and—without hesitation—instantly assume one of three positions:
1. Gorilla—hands up in air, teeth snarling, and shouting, "GRROOWWWLLL."
2. Man—hands on hips, says "Hi, there!"
3. Gun—both hands draw imaginary guns from hips and shoot, shouting "Bang!"

After this is done, each pair decides which of them won:
• MAN beats GUN (the man has power over the gun).
• GUN beats GORILLA (the gorilla can be shot by the gun).
• GORILLA beats MAN (gorilla can kill the man).
• Tie? Then they try again. If they tie a second time, both lose.

After the first try, all the losers are out, all the winners pair up again, and it is repeated again. The idea is to eliminate the group down to one final pair who do it a last time, which will give you one final winner. It is best to demonstrate this game several times to the group before playing.

Happy Birthday Race

Divide the group into teams. Members of each team must line up according to date of birth, with the youngest person at one end of the line and the oldest person at the other end. Any team that is out of order after the time limit (or the last team to get in the correct order) loses.

King of the Goats

Divide the group into two teams. One team stands on the sidelines. Another team forms a circle around one opposing teammate who is blindfolded and called the goat. The people in the circle hold hands. The goat tries to tag people in the circle around him. The circle must move away from him as a group, without breaking the link. The kids standing on the sidelines shout directions to the goat to help him tag an opposing player. Just before you end the game with the last goat, blindfold him, begin the game, and have the circle silently disband. The kids on the sidelines should continue to shout instructions to keep him playing for a while. *Larry Lyon*

Kooky Kickball

The group is divided into two teams. Each team numbers off consecutively so that for every number on one team, there is a corresponding number on the opposite team. The teams line up facing each other, but in opposite order; i.e., the number "ones" of each team are at opposite ends of the line. A beach ball is used in the game with junior highers and a volleyball with senior highers. The ball is placed in the middle of the floor. When the player's number is called, the players from each team run and try to kick the ball through or over the opposing team line. They may use only their feet. The team members standing on the line may try to block the ball with their hands, but may not try to kick the ball. *William C. Moore*

Nylon Game

Divide the group into teams. Get all the old nylon stockings possible and put them in the middle of the room. Have players remove their shoes. One team sits in a circle around the pile. They are given one minute to put on all the nylons they can, one over the other, on one leg only. The team that gets the most nylons on wins. *Senior High Fellowship, First Congregational Church, Webster Groves, Mo.*

Bedlam

This game requires four teams of equal size. Each team takes one corner of the room or playing field. The play area can be either square or rectangular. At a signal each team attempts to move as quickly as possible to the corner diagonal from their corner. The first team to get all its members into its new corner wins that particular round.

Now for the fun. For the first round, announce simple *running* as the way for teams to travel to their corners. But after that you can use any number of possibilities: walking backward, wheelbarrow racing (one person is the wheelbarrow), piggybacking, rolling somersaults, hopping on one foot, skipping, crab-walking, etc. There will be mass bedlam in the center as all four teams crisscross.

• **Bedlam Elimination.** Designate "safe" areas in the room's four corners (with masking tape, perhaps), and give all members of all four teams a flag like those used in flag football, which must hang free from his or her waist (in back). The object of the game is to get to the safe area in the opposite corner of the room without losing your flag. As you pass through the middle, you can grab one or more of the other three teams' flags, as long as you still have your own flag in your possession.

Once the flag is gone, so is the player. He's out of the game.

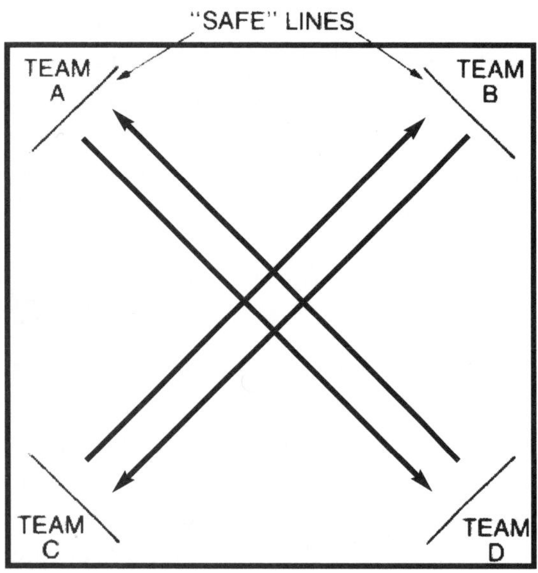

For best results, each team should have a different color flag. This will prevent players from replacing their own missing flag with a captured flag. Once all of the team's flags have been captured, the entire team is eliminated from the game. The game continues until only one team is left. Create your own variations of this game, with your own rules.

Don't forget to have the kids run across the playing area in a variety of different ways: on one foot, piggyback, on their hands and knees. In fact, such antics might be a good idea for slowing them down a bit to avoid injuries in the middle when everyone is moving in four different directions. *Tom Beaumont and Norma Bailey*

PULL UP

Everyone gets a chair and forms a circle, everyone sitting in a chair and facing the center of the circle, except for five boys and five girls who start the game. They are in the middle, standing. At a whistle the 10 youths in the center of the circle run to the people sitting in the chairs and "pull up" a person of the opposite sex, by taking the person's hands and pulling him up out of their chair.

For example, a boy would go up to a girl, pull her out of her chair, and then take her seat. The girl can offer no resistance. She then turns to the other side of the circle, pulls a guy out of his chair, takes his seat, and so on. This continues for one minute. The whistle blows, and players stop where they are. The boys and girls left standing are counted. The idea is sort of a random musical chairs, boys against the girls. For example, if there are two more girls standing than boys, the boys get two points, and the game continues. Every time a minute goes by, the whistle blows and those standing are counted. The team with the most points wins.

LINE PULL

Mark three long parallel lines within three feet of each other. Have teams face each other, lining up on two sides of the center line. Players try to grab and pull opposing players onto their side of the line without stepping over the line that lies three feet behind them. Anyone who is pulled across the center line is automatically a member of the opposing team. At the end of the time period, the team with the most players wins.

CATASTROPHE

This game can be used with a group of 15 or more people. Divide the group into three teams, and have each team sit in chairs in three lines, parallel to each other and with about three feet between the teams. All players should be facing the same direction, which is toward the front of their team's line. (Each player sits facing a teammate's back.)

Each team has the name of a town, such as Pottstown, Mudsville, and Dry Gulch (any name will do). Each player on each team is assigned an occupation—plumber, carpenter, policeman, preacher, teacher, doctor, etc. Each team should have the same occupations, and they should be seated in the same order on each team as well.

The leader then calls out an occupation and a town, such as, "We need a policeman at Pottstown." At that point, the policemen on each team must get up out of their chairs, run around their teams, and return to their chairs. The first person back in his or her chair wins a point for his or her team.

An additional twist to this game is that players must run around their teams in the right direction. This is determined by which town is called. For example, if the team lines are arranged so that Pottstown is on everyone's left, Mudsville is on the right, and Dry Gulch is in the middle, then if Mudsville is called, players must get out of their chairs on the right, and run around the team in a clockwise (right) direction. Pottstown would be left, and if Dry Gulch is called, either direction is okay. If you don't run in the correct direction, you lose.

If the leader calls out, "There's been a catastrophe in (town name)", then everyone on all three teams must get up and run around the team, again in the correct direction. The first team completely seated gets the point. Remember that everyone must get up from their chairs on the correct side, as well as going around in the right direction. *Scott Herrington*

Snow Fight

Place a line down the middle of two teams. Give each team a high stack of newspapers and one minute to wad up each piece of paper. At the signal, teams try to throw as many newspaper snowballs as possible on to the other team's side of the line within a given time limit. The team with the most paper snowballs on its side loses. Flat paper is not allowed to be thrown or counted. Include in the count the team's own snowballs that may not have been thrown yet. Anyone you catch throwing or kicking a snowball after the whistle is blown costs his team 20 points. Play lots of rounds!

Roundup

All the kids are divided into two teams with the same number of boys and girls on each team. The girls of each team are the cowboys and the boys the cows. The cows must stay on their hands and knees throughout the game. The object of the game is this: the girls of each team try to get the cows of the opposing team into an area designated as the corral. The girls can drag, carry, etc., a cow to that area. Of course, the cows can resist but must stay on hands and knees. After a designated time interval, the team with the most cows in its corral wins the game. *Jerry Summers*

Shoulder Shove

Each player puts his left arm behind his back and grabs one ankle with his right hand. The goal is to try to knock everyone else off balance while everyone is hopping around in this position. Anyone who falls down is out of the game. The last player to remain standing is the winner. No elbowing, please.

Clothes Pinning

Here's a wild game that is simple, yet fun to play with any size group. Give everyone in the group six clothespins. On a signal each player tries to pin the clothespins on other players' clothing. Each of the six pins must be hung on six different players. Players must keep moving to avoid having clothespins hung them, while trying to hang their pins on someone else. When a player hangs all six clothespins, he remains in the game, but tries to avoid having more pins hung on him. At the end of a time limit, the person with the least amount of clothespins hanging on him is the winner and the person with the most is the loser.

Another way to play this is to divide the group into pairs and give each person six clothespins.

Each person then tries to hang all their pins on the partner. The winners then pair off again, and so on until there is a champion clothespinner. *Prudence Elliot*

SQUATTERS SMASH

This game works well with large groups. Players squat on their heels, cross their arms, and hop or walk around in that position while trying to knock the other players over. A player is out of the game if he is knocked over. The last person to remain in the game is the winner.

FOUR TEAM DODGEBALL

This is a fast-moving game that is best played in a gym or similar room. Divide the group into four teams of equal size. If you have a basketball court marked on the floor, this can be used as the playing area. Otherwise you will need to mark off your own boundaries with tape or some other method. The floor is divided into four square quadrants.

Each team is assigned one of the four areas and team members cannot leave their assigned areas during the game. A volleyball, beach ball, or playground ball should be used (not as hard or as large as a basketball). The rules are basically the same as regular dodgeball, except that a player may throw the ball at anyone in any of the other three quadrants. If a player is hit below the belt with the ball, he or she is out of the game. If the ball misses and goes out of bounds, the referee tosses the ball into the team that was thrown at (where it went out of bounds). If a player is thrown at and catches the ball before it hits the floor, without dropping it, the player that threw it is out.

The winning team is the team that lasts the longest (the team that still has at least one player after the other teams have been eliminated), or the team with the most players left at the end of a specified time limit.

• **Boundary Ball.** Kids love dodgeball, but as they become young adults, a game of dodgeball can become deadly. Thus, Boundary Ball.

Divide into two teams. If your group combines junior and senior highers, make the competition fair by including kids of both age groups on both teams.

For a playing field, choose an area with a square boundary. A gym, parking lot, or roped-off field all work well. Establish a center dividing line and have teams take their sides.

The game is played by rolling or bouncing the play ball back across the boundary behind the opposing team. The ball must be rolled or bounced. (This eliminates potential bodily injury inflicted by strong-armed throwers.) The game can be played up to 25 points (or whatever). A referee is helpful, and point judges can be a great help as well in determining whether a point is valid. Points are not valid unless the ball is rolled or bounced over the line.

• **Scatterball.** This game is a fast-moving variation of dodgeball. There are no teams. To begin the game stand everyone in the center of a kid-proof room or gymnasium and throw a four-square ball off one of the walls. At this point everyone scatters.

The ball is up for grabs for the rest of the game. Anyone may handle and throw the ball after a bounce off the floor, ceiling, or wall but may not take more than two steps before throwing it at one of the many human targets (who are free to run as they please). A target is out if hit by a direct throw of the ball without catching it. A thrower is out if the ball is caught in the air or if anyone is hit in the head.

Boundary Ball

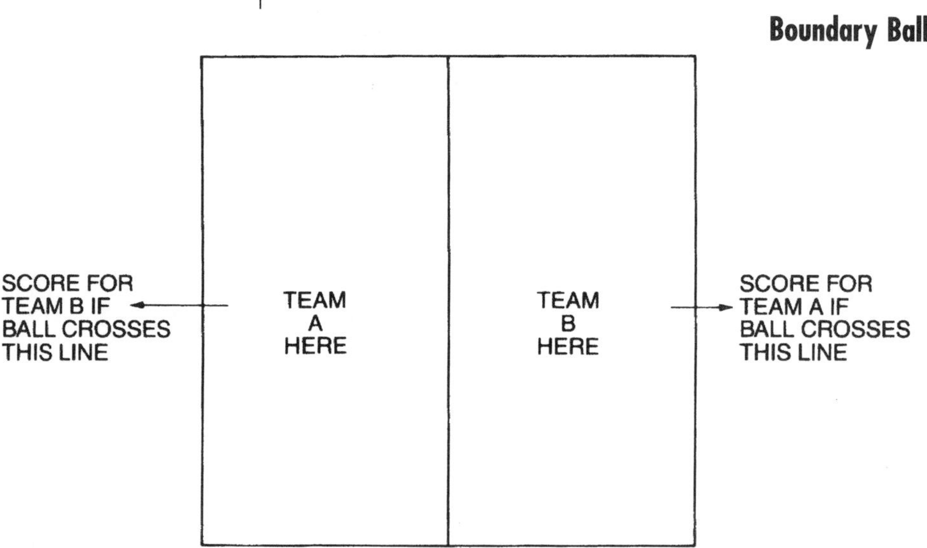

The Scatterball twist is that players who are out sit on the floor right where they are tagged; they must stay seated and may not move across the floor. They can still get throwers out by catching a ball in the air or by hitting a runner with the ball, and they may pass the ball to other sitting participants. Their presence increases the risk to running players, especially as the game progresses when more and more of them dot the floor. A thrower may collaborate with seated players by rolling or bouncing the ball to one of them.

The last person left standing is the winner and starts the next game. *David Buck, Samuel Hoyt, and John Gilbert*

Circle Bowling

Place as many bowling pins (or 12-inch long 2x4s) as there are pairs in a circle. Then have the pairs hold hands and form a circle around the pins. At a signal each person in a pair attempts to pull their partner into a pin and knock it down. Whoever hits a pin is eliminated, new pairs are formed, the appropriate number of pins reset, and a new round begins until a winner emerges. *Fred Winslow*

Marshmallow Bagging

Put your team in a circle at just slightly further apart than arm's length. Determine a beginning point in the circle and place two bags there. In one bag dump a number of marshmallows. The other remains empty. At the whistle the person nearest the bag begins pulling out the marshmallows (one at a time) and tossing them to the next person in the circle—one at a time. The person at the end of the circle next to the empty bag then drops the marshmallows into the bag. The team has one minute to see how many marshmallows they can get around the circle and into the bag.

For an interesting twist to this game, have a member of the opposite team seated by the empty bag, and as the marshmallows are fed into the bag, he eats them as fast as he can. He can only pull them out one at a time with one hand. A fast eater can get the final count in the bag to a minimum.

Another marshmallow game takes the place of bobbing for apples. Instead of apples in water, use marshmallows in chocolate sauce. *Doug Dennee*

Page Scramble

Give each team a children's storybook with titles such as Waldo the Jumping Dragon or Big Albert Moves into Town. The dumber the better. You must also make sure each book has the same number of pages. Before passing them out, however, carefully remove the pages from each book cover, and mix them up so that each team has a book with the correct number of pages but not the correct pages. On a signal, the teams distribute the pages among team members and they begin trading page for page with other teams. The whole place becomes a giant trading floor. The first team with a completed book, with pages in the correct order, wins. *Lee Bracey*

Poopdeck

Here's a great game for 10 to 100 participants. Play in a fairly large room or outside. Clearly mark off three sections on the floor with tape, chalk, etc. One section is the poopdeck, one the main deck, and the last the quarter deck. Begin with everyone standing in the poopdeck area. Call out the name of a deck (even the one that they are standing in) and the kids then run to the deck or section that you have called out. The last person into the section which you have called is out. If the kids are in poopdeck, for example, and you call out poopdeck, any kid who crosses the line, jumps the gun or in any other way (except being pushed) goes out of poopdeck, is out. The game continues rapidly until one person is the winner.

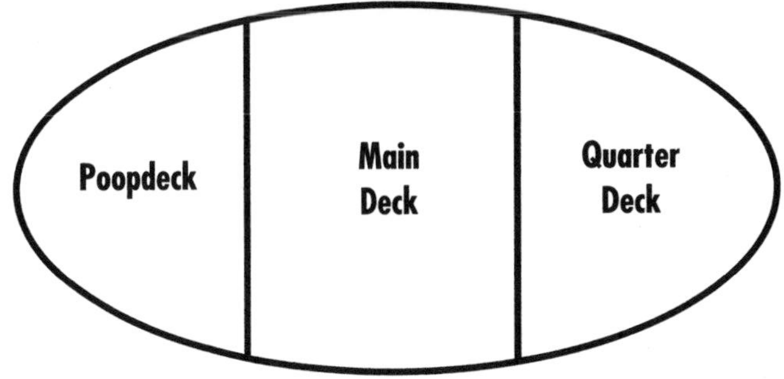

Hints on directing this game:

- Give them a few trial runs to warm up and for new kids to get the hang of the game.
- Call the decks loudly and distinctly.

• To get them really frustrated, point to the opposite deck from which you call.

Here are additional "decks" you can add to the original Poopdeck game to complicate things further:

Second Deck	**Bridge Deck**
Third Deck	**Flight Deck**
Fourth Deck	**Hanger Deck**
Promenade Deck	**Upper Deck**
Boat Deck	**Forecastle Deck**
Sun Deck	**Cabin Deck**

If you like, add special activities to each area, such as having kids flap their arms while in the Flight Deck. In addition, the following commands, if interspersed with the deck commands, can generate a great deal of playful confusion:

• **Hit the deck!**—Participants must drop to a prone position.

• **Clear the deck!**—Participants must step completely outside the marked area and may not step back in, no matter what other command may be issued, until they hear "On deck!"

• **On deck!**—Participants are free to step back inside the marked area.

Rick Bundschuh and Steve Perisho

SLIP OF WAR

Here's a fun version of tug-of-war. It works great if you have a room (like a gym or fellowship hall) that has a slick floor. Wax it up real good, and have all players take off their shoes. They should leave their socks on. Then have a tug-of-war. The results are hilarious, as there is very little traction, and everyone slides around, falls down, and generally has a lot of fun. *Greg Thompson*

SPACE BALL COUNTDOWN

Here is a fast, exciting, and rough game that requires teamwork ... and kids love it. Form two equal teams with one team forming an evenly spaced rectangle or circle and the other team inside the circle as dispersed as possible. On a signal the team outside tries to hit with the ball (a playground ball) every member inside as quickly as possible. Head hits and bounce hits are illegal.

When everyone has been hit, the clock stops, the time recorded and the teams change places. The team with the shortest time in the outside circle wins. You can score the best two out of three rounds or combine total times. Be sure to have players remove glasses and aim shoulder level and below. Do not use hard, soccer-type balls. *Norma Bailey*

SQUAT

This game can really be fun, but if everything is not done quite right, it can be a spectacular flop. First get everyone in a circle shoulder-to-shoulder. Then have them turn right, facing the back of the person in front of them. On the count of three, sit down.

If everything is done right, everyone will simultaneously sit down on the lap of the person behind him. If the timing isn't quite right...

To make the game even more precarious, have everyone cross their right leg over their left before sitting down. Make sure everyone's hands are out to the side. *Marshall Shelley*

THROUGH THE LEGS SHUFFLE

Here's the old through-the-legs game with a new twist. Have the teams line up single file spreading their legs apart enough so that someone can crawl through them. Players must have their hands on the hips of the person in front of them. The lines must be behind the starting line. On the signal, the last person crawls through the legs of the team and stands up at the front of the line. As soon as he stands up, the person who is now at the rear of the line crawls through, etc. The line moves forward and the first team to cross the goal line wins. Only one person per team can be crawling at a time. *Ken McCoy*

Underdog

Choose one player to be "It." "It" tags the free players, who must "freeze" when tagged. Frozen players must obtain freedom by spreading their legs apart, allowing a free player to pass between their open legs. "It" must freeze all the free players and the game is over. Spice the game up by making two or three players "It." *Steve Illum*

Big Bopper

This exciting game is similar to frozen tag. Instead of the one who is "It" tagging people, "It" (called the "bopper") bops people with a "bataca bat," rolled-up newspaper or a similar object. When someone is bopped they must not only stay frozen, but they must begin making appropriate sounds (such as "ohhh" or "aghhh") that sound like they have been bopped. They must remain frozen and moaning until someone who is free tags them. You can have a safe area for resting. Big Bopper is best played in the dark. *Mark Masterson*

Chain Tag

Here's a fast moving game of tag that can be played indoors or out. One person begins as "It," but as soon as she tags someone, that person must take her hand and they continue tagging people as a unit. Once there are eight in the tagging group, it breaks apart and becomes two groups of four. This continues with each group of four trying to catch the remaining people. Every time they catch four more, they break off and form a new group of four. The result is several groups of four chasing the free single players who have not been caught yet. The game is played until everyone is caught. Running in group is a lot of fun and the effect is something like Crack the Whip. *Joyce Bartlett*

The Jail Game

Divide your group into the Posse and Felons. This game is played in and surrounding a large room, preferably one with at least two exits. A jail is constructed in the room by making a square with chairs, tables, or benches. The Posse tries to capture all the Felons by tagging them and sending them to jail. The Felons, while avoiding being tagged, attempt to free their fellow Felons in jail. To free them, they must simply touch the jail. No more than three jailers (members of the Posse) can be in the jail room at any time—if there are more than three, all Felons in the jail go free.

Have the teams switch when all Felons have been caught or after a certain time period has elapsed. To make it easier, Felons who have just been freed should have a 10-second count before they can be recaptured. *Andy Brown*

Toilet Tag

This version of tag brings a new flush to that time-worn game. Mark off the playing area suitable for your size group. Designate one or more players to be "It". Those who are "It" run around attempting to tag other players, who are then "dead" and must kneel down on one knee with one arm out and to the side. Dead players can reenter the game only when a free player sits on their knee and pulls down their hands—"flushes the toilet." The game ends when all the players except "It" are kneeling. *Randy Hausler*

Air Raid

Next time you are playing games, announce at the beginning that the group is always in danger of an air attack from enemies of unknown origin. If the leader shouts out "Air Raid," everyone would be well advised to fall flat on the floor. The last person to do so will be penalized by a substantial number of points from their team score.

The element of surprise works best with this. Every so often during the regular games, the leader should just yell out "Air Raid." There are always a few youths who forget and are left standing, thus costing their team some valuable points. It's a great little "extra added attraction" to a recreation time. *Joe Falkner*

Banana Whistle

Divide your group into three or more teams. Position three people from each team about 20 feet apart as shown in the diagram below.

A fourth person from each team goes to the starting line and is blindfolded. At a signal, the people positioned on the playing field begin to yell at the blindfolded person trying to get him to come toward them until they can touch him without moving from their positions. This must be done in order

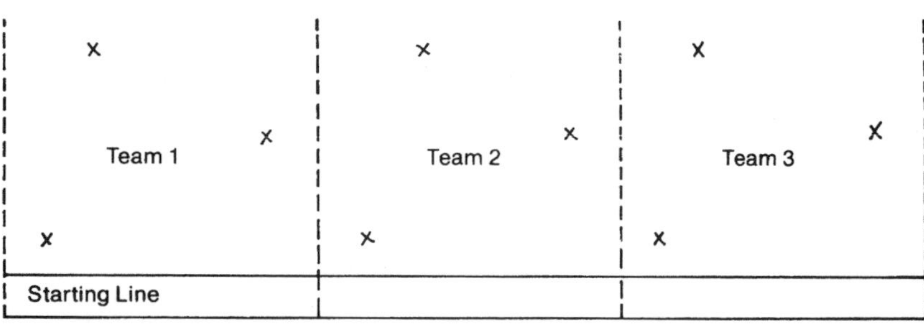

(player 1 first, then 2 and 3). After reaching all three players on his team, the runner removes the blindfold and runs back to the starting line where a fifth person is waiting to feed him a banana. As soon as possible after eating the banana, he must whistle an assigned tune as loud as he can for at least 15 seconds.

This is good for a lot of laughs and team competition. If there are more people on each team, you can have more than three on the playing field, or they always come in handy for cheering the person on. *Brenda Clowers*

BERSERK

Here is a unique game that requires little skill, includes any amount of people, and is 100 percent active. The object is for a group of any size to keep an equal amount of assigned tennis balls moving about a gymnasium floor until six penalties have been indicated.

The vocabulary for this game is unique and essential to the success of the game. It goes like this:

Rabid Nugget: a moving tennis ball
Hectic: a stationary tennis ball
Berserk: a referee's scream, designating a penalty
Frenzy: an elapsed time period measuring six Berserks
Logic: a tennis ball that becomes lodged unintentionally on or behind something
Illogic: a tennis ball that is craftily stuck on or behind something
Paranoia: a player's feeling that the refs are picking on her/him

If 30 players are on the gym floor, 30 Rabid Nuggets are thrown, rolled, or bounced simultaneously onto the floor by one of the refs. There are three refs; one at each end of the court and one off to the side at mid-court. It is the duty of the two refs on the floor to try and spot Hectics and to generate a hysterical scream (a Berserk) so that all will recognize a penalty. The group has five seconds to start a Hectic moving again or another full throated Berserk is issued. The Berserking ref must point condemningly at the Hectic until it is again provided impetus.

Every 15 seconds after a start, the side line ref puts an additional Rabid Nugget into play until the final Berserk has been recorded.

The team is allowed six Berserks, at which juncture the ref on the sidelines, who is responsible for timing this melee, jumps up and down waiving his arms yelling, "STOP, STOP, STOP."

The object is to keep the Rabid Nuggets moving as long as possible before six Berserks have been recorded. This time span is called a Frenzy. After a Frenzy, ask the group to develop a strategy in order to keep the Rabid Nuggets moving for a longer span of time, i.e., increasing the Frenzy.

Other rules:

- A Rabid Nugget must be kicked (only kicked) randomly or to another player. It may not be held underfoot and simply moved back and forth.
- If a Rabid Nugget becomes a Logic or Illogic, the ref must get the Nugget back into motion. An Illogic receives an immediate Berserk.
- Official tennis balls are not essential for active and satisfying play. You could have a heck of a good game if everyone brought their own piece of Silly Putty.

Karl Rohnke

BLIND SARDINES

Here's a fun game that encourages community building within the group, and there are no winners or losers. All you need is a large room and blindfolds for everyone.

One person is appointed (or volunteers) to be the "sardine," and does not wear a blindfold. Everyone else dons a blindfold and tries to locate the sardine. When a person wearing a blindfold touches or runs into another person, she asks that person if she is the sardine. The sardine must say yes if touched. Once a person touches the sardine, he must hold onto the sardine for the remainder of the game, so that a chain of people is gradually formed. If a person touches anyone in the chain, it is as if she touched the sardine, and she adds herself to the chain. The sardine must not attempt to avoid being touched by anybody and is free to walk about the room. The game concludes when all are a part of the chain. *Thomas M. Church*

MAD HATTER

Here's a free-for-all that gets really wild. Everybody should have a cap or hat of some kind. If you want the game to last longer, use ski caps. Then give everybody a club—a sock stuffed full of cloth or something soft. On your signal players try to knock off everybody else's cap while keeping their own on.

Players cannot use their hands to protect themselves or their caps, and they may not knock off anyone's cap with anything except the sock club. Players who lose their caps are out of the game. See who can last the longest.

For a variation each player wears a paper bag hat that rests on the ears. Each player also receives a rolled-up newspaper. The object is to knock off everyone else's paper bag hat without losing your own. No one can hold onto the hat. *Ed Laremore*

HUMAN HUNT

Divide into teams and have each team choose a leader. All team members must stay within a designated area. A judge stands in a position that is an equal distance from all the teams. For example, if there are four teams, then the teams can position themselves in the four corners of the room and the judge can stand in the middle.

The judge calls out a characteristic similar to the ones below and the leader on each team tries to locate someone on her team who fits the characteristic. As soon as someone is found, the leader grabs that person by the hand, and they both run like crazy to the judge. The first team leader to slap the hand of the judge (pulling along the proper person) wins points for his or her team.

Here are some sample characteristics. Find someone who—

- Has blue eyes and brown hair
- Received all A's in the last marking period
- Ate at McDonald's today
- Jogs daily
- Is engaged to be married
- Likes broccoli
- Sent a card to a friend today
- Memorized a Bible verse this week
- Visited a foreign country this year
- Is wearing Nikes
- Is chewing green gum
- Came in a blue minivan
- Received a traffic violation this month
- Received a love letter today
- Recently wrote a thank-you note for a gift

Don Shenk

SHOCK

Two teams line up single file and hold hands. On one end of the team there is a spoon on the floor (or on a table) and at the other end there is a person from each team with a coin.

Shock

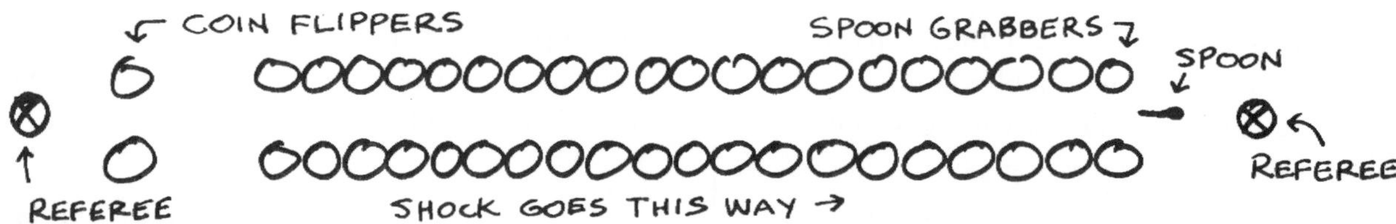

The two people with the coins begin flipping them (like a coin toss) and showing the coin to the first person on their team. If the coin lands with tails up, nothing happens. If the coin lands heads up, the first person quickly squeezes the hand of the second person, who squeezes the hand of the third person, and so on down the line. As soon as the last person in line has his hand squeezed, he tries to grab the spoon. After grabbing the spoon, the spoon is replaced and that person then runs to the front of the line and becomes the coin flipper. Everybody else moves down one. This continues until every player has been the coin flipper and the spoon grabber. The first team to get its original coin flipper and spoon grabber back into their original positions is the winner.

No one may squeeze the next person's hand until his own hand has been squeezed first. This is like an electric shock that works its way down the line. A referee should be stationed at both ends of the team lines to make sure everything is done legally. A false shock results in a new coin flip. You might want to have players practice their squeezes before starting, so that everyone knows to squeeze good and hard. Otherwise they might confuse a little twitch for a legal squeeze. *Adrienne Anderson and John Bohling*

HUMAN PIT

This game is based on the old card game of Pit except that you use people instead of cards. It works especially well at camp or with large youth groups.

First of all, decide on the commodity to be traded (such as animals, sports teams, schools, colors, and so on). Then determine the number of teams you wish to have. For each team, there must be nine cards of one suit. For example, if you have three teams, and you are using animals, there must be nine dogs, nine cats, and nine pigs, or whatever animals you decide to use. You will want at least two people on each team (the teams are the people who are not cards). The more teams you have, the more chaotic and fun the game is. For each suit chosen, make nine slips of paper which will identify the suit. For example, if your suits are colors, and one of the colors is red, make nine red slips of paper. Bring enough pins to pin these pieces of paper onto the people who will be cards.

Now you must choose people to be cards. If you have seven teams, you will need to choose 63 cards (nine times seven). Have everyone stand in a large circle and count off the number of cards needed. Instruct the "cards" to go to the middle of the circle where several assistants help with pinning the pieces of paper identifying their suit on the inside of their sweaters, cuffs, or whatever, so that their suit is not outwardly visible. While the cards are being prepared in the middle, number off the remaining teams. Space each team evenly around the outside of the circle. Instruct each team to choose one master trader to be responsible for trading cards for their team in the middle of the circle (the Pit).

Deal the cards to the teams by having nine cards randomly go to each team. From this point on, cards must move on their hands and knees. Be sure each team has nine cards and has a little time to identify the suit of the cards.

Now you are ready to start the trading. Announce that all trading is to be done in the Pit and only by the master trader on each team. To trade, a team must choose one to four cards of the same suit. The master trader then leads the cards to be traded (on their hands and knees) to the middle where he calls out "Trade one! One! One!" or "Two! Two! Two!" or "Three! Three! Three!" or "Four! Four! Four!" depending on the number of cards being traded. If the trader of one team wishes to trade cards with another team, he must call out

"One! One! One!" etc., and trade an equal number of cards with that team. When cards have been exchanged, each master trader must bring his new cards (on their hands and knees) back to his team before looking to see what suit the cards are that he has received. Then the team decides what cards they wish to trade next, and so on. Trading continues until one team gets nine cards of the same suit and wins the game.

After explaining all this, let them begin. It's a fast moving game and is hilarious to watch. There is usually absolute mayhem in the middle of the Pit. Following the game you may want to discuss how the cards felt when teams wanted to keep them or wanted to get rid of them. Play as many rounds as you have time for. This idea could also be used for other card games, by simply substituting people for playing cards. *Chris Keidel*

Mad Mad Mattress

For this game divide your group into several teams. Each team needs a mattress. If the mattresses are small, then give each team two mattresses that are placed side by side; or tailor the events to fit the size of the mattress. The team stands around the outside of the mattress. The leader then gives an instruction, and each team must perform that task on the mattress. The first team to correctly complete the task receives points for that round. Each task must be completed entirely on the mattress. Some sample tasks:

- Build a six (or 10) person pyramid.
- Get 12 people sitting in a circle with their feet together in the middle.
- Get four people to stand on their heads in each of the four corners of the mattress.
- Get the whole team on the mattress. (Works well if you have large groups.)
- Get four girls up on four guys' shoulders.
- Get 15 people laying flat on their stomachs, side-by-side.

You can make up more tasks of your own. It's a good idea to have a referee at each mattress to determine when the task has been completed successfully. *Judy Groen*

Kubic Kids

This game is simple, yet lots of fun. Draw a square on the floor (as large or small as you choose), and see how many kids each team can get inside the square. Anything is legal, as long as no part of the body is touching the floor outside the square. Set a time limit and have team competition. *Jim Bowes*

Random Scores

Next time your group is having competition between teams in several events, and you want to neutralize things so that no team is able to dominate the other teams, here's a way to hand out points that keeps the competition much closer.

Before the competition begins, determine the point value for each event. Make sure you have enough points so that every team will receive points following every event. For example, if you have five teams, you need at least five point entries—like 10, 8, 6, 4, and 2. After you've decided on that, make up a board for each, scrambling the points so that they are in no particular order:

6	10	2	4	8

Then cover the points with construction paper squares, with a letter on each one, like so:

A	B	C	D	E

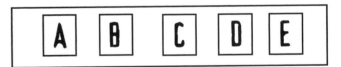

Now, following every event, the points are awarded this way: The team that comes in first gets first choice of the letters on the board. It's purely chance, but they do get to choose first. The second place team chooses second, and so on. Sometimes the last place team actually gets the most points because it doesn't know how many points lie behind each letter. Still, the first place team likes the privilege of being able to choose first, even though the whole thing is determined by luck. Not only does this keep the competition close, but watching teams choose letters adds extra suspense. *Billy Richter*

SQUIRREL

This game can be played indoors or outdoors. The group forms several small circles of four people each. Each circle represents a hollow tree; players hold hands. One person from each circle steps into the middle of the circle to become the squirrel who makes a home in the hollow tree. Two other players who are not part of a circle become a squirrel without a tree and a hound. The hound chases the homeless squirrel in and out among the trees. For safety the squirrel may crawl into any tree, but the squirrel already in the tree must leave the tree and flee from the hound. If the hound tags the fleeing squirrel, the squirrel becomes the hound and the hound the squirrel, and the game continues. *Glenn Davis*

STRIKE FORCE

So your kids make airplanes out of your Sunday school papers? Put their expertise to good use! You need a gym or a large room, marked into a court.

Divide the group into two teams, each having a home front (safe) zone, with a battle zone in the middle. Each person makes a paper airplane and a paper wad grenade. The object of the game is similar to dodgeball, using planes and grenades to hit opponents. If a player is hit with a plane, he hands over his plane and is out of the game. If a player is hit with a grenade, he forfeits his plane and can only throw grenades. He must also remain in the battle zone at all times and any planes that he picks up must be *handed* to a teammate.

Here are some more rules:

1. Airplanes and grenades must be thrown. Simply touching your opponent with your airplane or grenade is considered a self-destruct and you are out of the game, forfeiting your planes and grenades to your opponent.
2. Players may not cross over into the opponents' home front except during "air raids," which the referee will grant at certain times. However, players may stand at the line and throw planes and grenades into the opponents' home front.
3. A hit on the head or face of an opponent while he is standing (not ducking) is a self-destruct and the thrower is out of the game.
4. Grounder grenades and airplanes that slide or roll count the same as airborne ones if they touch you. Airplanes and grenades cannot be picked up until they stop moving. (They can't be stopped with your foot, either.) Grenades and airplanes that bounce off the wall are dead and don't count as hits.
5. Hand-to-hand combat is not permitted and is sudden death to the player who starts it.

Use these signals:

- One long whistle is a 15-second retreat to the home front by both teams.
- Two short whistles is an air raid.
- One short whistle ia an attack—all players must go to the battle zone.

Allen Johnson

FLOOR HOCKEY LIVES!

The game your grandparents played as kids is still around—and your teenagers will love it.

Order a set from any game distributor's catalog, learn the rules (usually included with the set), then adapt them to your own situation.

Schedule tournaments one afternoon or evening a month—and get ready for big turnouts. *Neil MacQueen*

INDOOR MURDERBALL

Here's an indoor game for two teams. You need at least five on a team, but you can play with a lot more, depending on the size of the room you have.

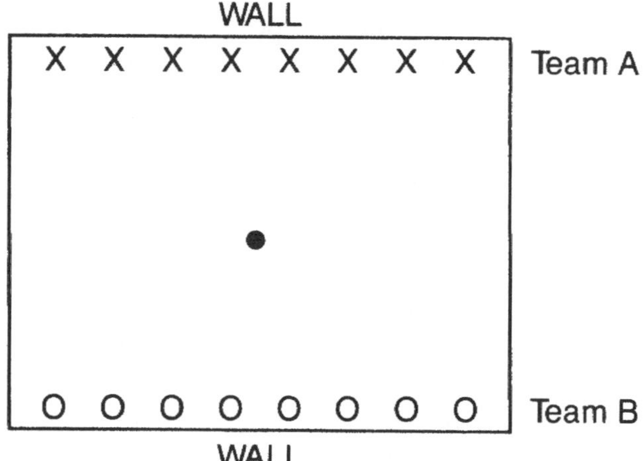

You need a room that is nearly indestructible, with space to run.

Two teams of equal size line up on opposite walls, about three feet from the wall. Team members then number off.

A ball is placed in the middle of the room. (Any large ball will work.) The leader calls out a number, and the two players with that number (one from each team) run out to the middle and try to hit the opposite team's wall with the ball. The team standing in front of the wall tries to prevent that from happening.

Players attempt to get the ball to the goal any way they can—carrying it across, throwing, kicking, rolling, whatever. Anything is legal. *Ralph Gustafson*

LIGHT WARS

"Stop running in the halls!" runs the continual warning to junior highers. With whatever board or pastoral or custodial permission you need, give the junior highers the run of the building just once. Play Capture the Flag inside one evening after dark, marking out each team's territory (a two-story building makes it easy).

Instead of tagging the enemy to make captures, each player is equipped with a standard flashlight (you'll probably want to ban five-volt lights, spotlights, fluorescent lights, and Bud Lites) in order to beam an enemy player and call out his or her name—which causes the beamed player to sit out for five minutes.

If you play several rounds of Light Wars during the evening, some kids may want to sit out a game or two to enjoy one of the Star Wars videos you can be showing at the same time. *Dick Read*

OFF THE WALL

Here's a high-energy competition that blends dodgeball with Capture the Flag.

Create a playing court in your gym (or large room, provided the walls are very sturdy) by assigning each wall a color and taping 50 inflated balloons of that color to the wall. Create a territory for each color that extends out 20 feet from the wall, leaving a large "free zone" in the center of the gym (see diagram). In the center of each of the four territories, set a "safe" (a large box). At the edge of each territory, mark off an area to be the team's "jail."

Now divide your group into teams—one team for each territory. Each team designates certain players as Invaders, Defenders, and one Jailkeeper.

• **Invaders.** Invaders try to hit opposing teams' balloons off the wall with soccer balls or playground balls thrown only from the central free zone. An Invader cannot throw a ball unless he or she remains in the free zone. Invaders may also steal balloons from an enemy's wall by invading their territory. Stolen balloons are taken back to the Invader's own team's safe. Invaders may not, however, steal balloons from an opponent's "safe."

• **Defenders.** Defenders defend their wall by catching or deflecting balls. They may capture Invaders by tagging them within the Defender's territory. Captured Invaders are taken to the jail. Defenders may not return to the wall balloons that were hit off.

• **Jail rules.** A team may ransom its Invaders who are in jail by exchanging three balloons from its safe for its incarcerated Invader. The team holding the

Off the Wall

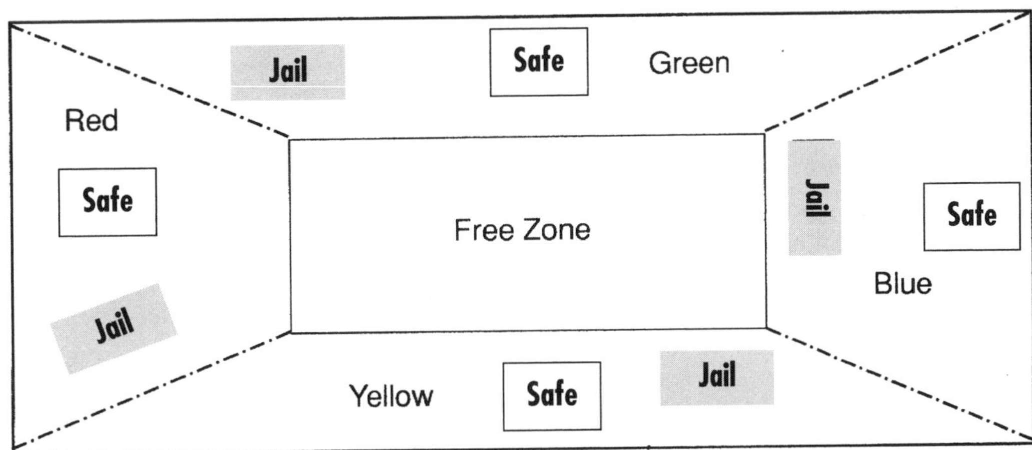

Invader in jail may then return these recovered balloons to its wall.

Assign a time limit for the game to be played out. At the end of the game, each team earns five points for every balloon remaining on its wall and 10 points for every captured balloon still in its safe.

James Bell

Masking-Tape Mazes

If you have a fairly large room with a clean floor, a few rolls of masking tape will set you up for these two games:

• **Tape Tag.** This tag game requires your kids to pretend that the wide tape strips that you lay down on the floor, maze fashion, represent invisible though impenetrable walls that cannot be crossed, jumped, or reached through. You'll probably want some refs to watch for corner-cutters and wall-climbers, who can be penalized by being made "It."

An autumn variation: play Tape Tag outside with raked-up lines of leaves instead of tape.

• **A-Maze-ing Grace.** Form a labyrinth with masking tape (see diagram). Divide your group into teams of exactly four. Rules are simple:

— Each team of four must stand shoulder-to-shoulder in a square, facing outward, north-south-east-west fashion, with tightly locked arms. Whatever direction a team member faces as he enters the maze, he must face that same direction until his team exits the maze. For example, if a player is facing north upon entering the maze, that player must always face north regardless of the turns and corners his team makes as they proceed through the maze. At any given time, then, one player is walking forward, another backward, one shuffling to his right, and another to his left.

— Teams are disqualified if they rotate from their original positions or disconnect arms.

— Teams are timed—fastest time wins.

— Teams earn penalty seconds if they cross the maze lines.

You don't want collisions in this game, so it's

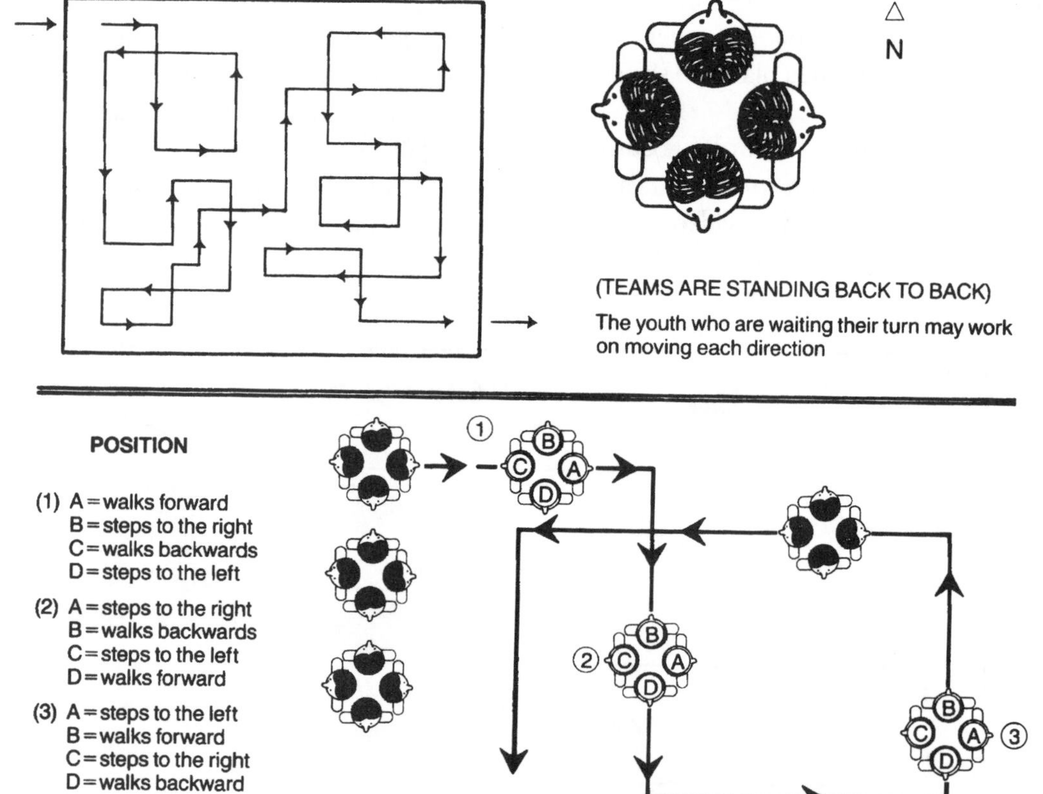

N
(TEAMS ARE STANDING BACK TO BACK)
The youth who are waiting their turn may work on moving each direction
POSITION
(1) A=walks forward
B=steps to the right
C=walks backwards
D=steps to the left
(2) A=steps to the right
B=walks backwards
C=steps to the left
D=walks forward
(3) A=steps to the left
B=walks forward
C=steps to the right
D=walks backward
1
2
3
A
B
C
D

usually best to start the next team only when the previous one has left the maze. This is a fun way to launch into discussions of unity, the body of Christ, etc., later on. *Michael W. Capps and Mark E. Byers*

Box Maze

A good substitute for a haunted house, this maze makes an exciting event around Halloween—but it works for any "A-Maze-ing Nite" on your calendar.

Solicit donations of refrigerator boxes from a box company, appliance and furniture stores, or your kids' neighborhoods. After you've collected at least 40 boxes, start plotting your maze. Remove all staples from the boxes to avoid injuring the kids or ruining their clothing. Insert the end of one box into another, and tape the seams well. A series of four-way intersections, T intersections, and dead ends will challenge your young people as they crawl through the maze on their hands and knees.

Before the kids come into the room containing the maze, turn out the lights so they can't picture how the maze goes. Station volunteers inside the maze with a flashlight in case any problems occur. Send kids through in groups of three or four, and assure them that there's someone inside the maze with a flashlight ready to assist them if they call out.

If you don't have the time to prepare the maze yourself, enlist some students to create the maze and staff it. Seniors, for example, delight in subjecting younger unfortunates to rigors of any kind. You can use the maze as a springboard for discussing God's guidance, decision making, fear, or walking in darkness. *Elliott Cooke*

Streets and Alleys

One person is "It" and chases another person through a maze of people.

Form the maze this way: everyone faces in one direction and holds hands, forming alleys. When a leader yells "Streets!" everyone in the maze faces the opposite direction and rejoins hands, which forms a different maze configuration. When the leader yells, "Alleys!" everyone turns 90 degrees again and rejoins hands.

Meanwhile, "It" tries to tag a runner in the maze. Neither "It" nor the runner can break through joined hands, although "It" can reach through joined hands to another aisle.

Nine-Legged Race

Just for fun or to demonstrate the value of working together, this variation of the three-legged race is best for large groups and lots of space.

Divide the kids into groups of eight or so (the numbers don't matter as long as the teams are even). Place five kids on one side of the playing field, and the team's remaining three kids opposite them across the field. From the five-kid side, two of them begin a traditional three-legged race. When they reach the other side, they add another team member, turn, and run back. At each end of their course, they tie up with another teammate until all eight kids are strung together at the ankles and running the last length. The first across the finish line wins. (The fun is watching them figure out how to turn around—but don't tell them this.)

For heightened hilarity, use thin plastic trash bag strips as ties, and add this rule—if a tie breaks, they have to stop and either re-tie it or replace it.

And even though you may not have specified the game as a foot race, the teammates cannot drop to their knees and pull themselves along with their hands. *Phillip Lopez*

The Great Giveaway

Buy some play $1000 bills or make youth-group dollars for this game. Hand out The Great Giveaway (page 54), one per person, and give each player as

many $1000 bills as there are players in the game. *Bradley Bergfalk*

$$$$$$$$$$$$$$$$$$$$$$$$$$$

THE GREAT GIVEAWAY

Instructions: You have been given $1000 for every person in the group. Your objective is to multiply your money as quickly as possible by approaching every member of the group and challenging each of them to one of the following activities. After you compete with those in your group, ask them to write their initials in the space at the left.

Some of these activities are based on elements entirely outside of your control; others demand a certain level of expertise (albeit not very much). Your time is limited, so play your hand wisely.

Oh, one other thing. You cannot approach the same person more than once for the same numbered challenge.

_______1. Find another person whose birthday is the in the same month as yours. The person whose birthday is closest to the first of the month earns $1000.

_______2. Play rock-paper-scissors (up to three times). Winner takes $1000 per time.

_______3. Bubble gum blow—the largest bubble wins $1000.

_______4. The person with the most pocket change between the two of you wins $1000.

_______5. The person who can recite John 3:16 from memory wins $2000. If there is a tie, the person who can recite an additional Bible verse from memory wins.

_______6. Say "ahhh" together until one person runs out of breath. Whoever can say "ahhh" the longest wins $1000.

_______7. The one who can curl his tongue takes $1000. In case of a tie, the one who can curl her tongue and flare her nostrils at the same time wins.

_______8. The one who can name the most Christian recording artists wins $2000.

_______9. Thumb wrestling—the winner takes $1000 (play up to three times).

_______10. The person with the longest fingernails wins $1000. In the case of a tie, the longest toenails.

_______11. The person who can stand on her head and hum the entire national anthem at the same time wins $3000.

_______12. The person who has the longest eyelashes without mascara wins $1000.

_______13. The person who can ask "Where's the bathroom?" in another language takes $1000.

_______14. Add up the number of letters in your first, middle, and last name. The competitor with the longest name wins $1000.

$$$$$$$$$$$$$$$$$$$$$$$$$$$

Musical Sponge

This game is like musical chairs, but with a few changes. Use the same number of chairs as there are players. As the players circle the chairs, they hold onto the shoulders of the person in front of them. They are all blindfolded.

Before the music stops, the leader places a wet sponge on one of the chairs. The unfortunate player who sits on the wet sponge when the music stops (or when the whistle blows) is out. *David Rasmussen*

Shuffle the Deck

Here's a simple, lively way to break a large group down into smaller ones—or to play just for fun. Distribute a deck of playing cards (or Rook cards) to the group, one per person. Then you call out different combinations, like these:

- "Get in a group that adds up to 58."
- "Find three people of the same suit."
- "Find five numbers in a row, of any suit."
- "Find your whole suit."
- "Find four of you—four 3s, four 8s, etc."

For larger groups use multiple decks of cards; for smaller groups eliminate cards. Then create your own combinations! *Scott Oas*

Sports Toto

This game has its origins in Europe. It's fun and adds the element of chance to some wild and crazy games.

To play, divide your group into four teams of equal size. It doesn't matter how many are on each team. Each team should have a team name and a team captain who will also act as scorekeeper.

To begin the game the leader asks each team to send one of its members out to the center of the room. After all four players (one from each team) are selected, the leader introduces each one. ("This is Jim Darby, representing Team 1!")

After the players are introduced, each team huddles together and "votes" on which player they think will win the yet unnamed event about to be announced. Each team must decide on a single person to receive its vote. A team does not have to vote for its own representative

After each team has voted, the leader draws an "event" or task out of a hat. It can be anything:

- Blow up a balloon and sit on it until it breaks.
- Peel a potato with a blunt table knife.
- Blow a table tennis ball from one end of the room to the other.
- Drink a can of warm soda pop and burp.

When the whistle is blown, the players begin competing, and the four teams cheer for the one they voted for. The winning player then earns a point for any team that voted for him or her.

You can add even more excitement by having teams guess who will win, place (come in second), and show (come in third). Bonus points can be awarded for guessing the correct order, 1-2-3.

Make sure that the events are things anyone can do. In fact, you should have a number of events which favor nonathletic kids, like trying to solve a rather complicated mathematical problem or guessing the number of beans in a jar. If you use a little creativity, your kids will ask to do it over and over again. *Eileen Thompson*

Tapeworms

Set up a table at each end of the playing area, form a semicircular safety zone in front of each table with pylons or chairs (see diagram), and stick a bunch of two-inch-long pieces of masking tape to the front edge of each table (two pieces per team member).

The game starts as both teams pile into their own safety zones, grab one piece of tape each, and then enter the battle zone in order to stick the tape on their opponents' bodies, below the shoulders. Players can't remove the tape once they're stuck. After sticking someone, players can return to their safety zone (for only 10 seconds) for one more piece of tape.

Tapeworms

After a specified period of time, the game ends, teams count how many hits they've received, and the team with the least hits wins. Colored tape gives the game a brighter aspect, perhaps to designate teams. *Daniel Atwood*

DOT TO DOT

Before this game, buy two packages (each package a different color) of one-half-inch self-sticking circle labels and number them one through half the number of kids in your group—that is, if there are 30 in your group, number one color of circles 1 through 15. Do the same for the other color circles. Bring along a few balls of kite string or embroidery yarn as well as some rolls of masking tape.

Divide the kids into two teams (or more, if your group is large), give each team a package of the numbered "dots," instruct all players to stick a dot on their foreheads—then have them mingle, perhaps playing another crowd breaker so that the members of the two or more teams are thoroughly mixed. At a signal all players should stand still, and a selected captain from each team is given the string and tape and told to string her team dot-to-dot fashion, in order according to the numbers stuck to her teammates' foreheads. Captains can tape the string wherever they want on their teammates, and the first team finished wins.

Can you guess the fitting reward? A children's dot-to-dot book! *Keith Curran*

SPELL MY FEET

The object of this hilarious game is for players to form words as quickly as they can. Two teams of five members each sit facing the audience. Using a large

black marker, the leaders inscribe letters on the soles of the feet of the players.

The first player on each team gets an A on one foot and an N on the other; the second receives an E and a T; the third G and R; the fourth O and M; the fifth S and P.

The leader then calls out a word, and the group that is able to line up their feet to spell that word in the shortest amount of time wins that particular round.

- Easy word, worth five points each: MASTER, ROAST, SMEAR, TOGS, SNORE
- More difficult phrases, worth 10 points each: TEN PROMS, GET SPAM, GREAT SON, MORE NAPS
- The last series, worth 20 points per word, requires teams to compose their own words: the team using the most letters to form a word or combination of words wins the round.

Jim Johnson

DIVE BOMBERS

Here's an indoor game that especially junior highers will scream for again and again. Two teams are chosen at random and seated on opposite sides of the room. Each team has a target, who sits with a Styrofoam cup balanced on his head somewhere near the back of the group. All players must stay seated in one spot throughout the game. The object of the game is to knock the cup off the head of the other team's target with wadded newspaper. The target cannot use his hands in any way, but other team members can bat down flying paper bombs as long as their seats don't leave the ground. A point is scored each time a team knocks off the other team's cup.

Kids can be very creative using a variety of large and small bombs, paper airplanes, machine gun blasts, cooperative barrages, protective seating, paper clubs to knock down bombs, etc. The game usually takes a stack of newspaper about four feet high. *Phil Butin*

EAT THAT FOOD!

Patterned after the game show "Name That Tune," this game requires contestants to guess the number of bites it will take them to eat the food.

Just for fun, set up your youth group room like a game-show studio—lights, video camera, scoreboard and scorekeeper, crowd motivator (who holds up signs for the audience: APPLAUSE, CHEER, BOO, THAT'S SICK!, MAKE ME BARF!, etc.), host with mike, offstage voice to enumerate what prizes winners receive, and sponsors who supply comic commercial breaks.

The host (probably you) should line up the contestants in chairs along the front, call for the particular food to be paraded across the room so all can see it, then work your way down the line, asking each player to bid how many bites they'll eat that food in. Have equal portions for each contestant. Bidders should remember these details:

- The fewer bites, the more points.
- A bite is the meeting of players' upper and lower teeth after having shoved the food into their mouths as far as they can; there is no limit, however, on chews.
- The low bidder eats first; if he succeeds, his team is awarded the points. If he fails, his team is penalized the same number of points.

Continue to query each player up and down the line until one desperate contestant bids so low that the others refuse to challenge him.

At that point turn to the audience and say, with your best Guy or Girl Smiley game-show host expression, "Tell Rick what to do!," to which the audience screams, "EAT THAT FOOD!"

After the low bidder's attempt, all contestants must eat their food. If they succeed in putting it away within the number of bites they bid, they are awarded points accordingly; if they fail, they are similarly penalized.

If anyone still has the stomach for it, end the game with a final eat-off—a mix of all the foods used during the several rounds of the game. Give contestants a serving spoon and two minutes to down as many bites as they can.

Keep some barf bags handy for this game. *Tim Baines*

DRESSING IN THE DARK

To play this game you need piles of activity-specific clothing and blindfolds. Each pile must contain the same type of clothing. On 3x5-inch index cards write instructions for which activity players are to dress for, followed by a list of specific clothing to put on. For example, the card reads, "You are going to play tennis. Put on: sweatshirt, socks, tennis shoes, T-shirt." Another card might read, "You are going skiing. Put on: ski jacket, gloves, socks, overalls."

Divide your group into teams of seven or eight, and give the index cards describing the first outfit to one player from each team. After the players have memorized the clothing they are to put on, blindfold them and guide them to their team's pile of clothing. The blindfolded players have three minutes to pull from the pile the correct articles of clothing and dress themselves correctly and neatly—buttons in the correct buttonholes, shirts on inside in, and pants on correctly. The only help the blindfolded players have is their sense of touch and shouted clues from their teammates. At the end of three minutes, if no one is completely dressed, the leader decides who is the best dressed. Otherwise, the team whose player finishes correctly dressing first gets the point. *Fay Wong*

MILLION-DOLLAR SPENDING SPREE

Do you know how much a thousand pounds of macadamia nuts cost? Your teenagers will know after they've played this game, which simulates what

many of them like to do best—shop at the mall. Their object is to be the first team to spend a cool million (on paper, that is) as they circulate through the mall shops. Give each team a calculator, a ledger sheet, and one pen. Here are the details to give the teams:

- The team members may not split up.
- No more than one item may be purchased from each store.

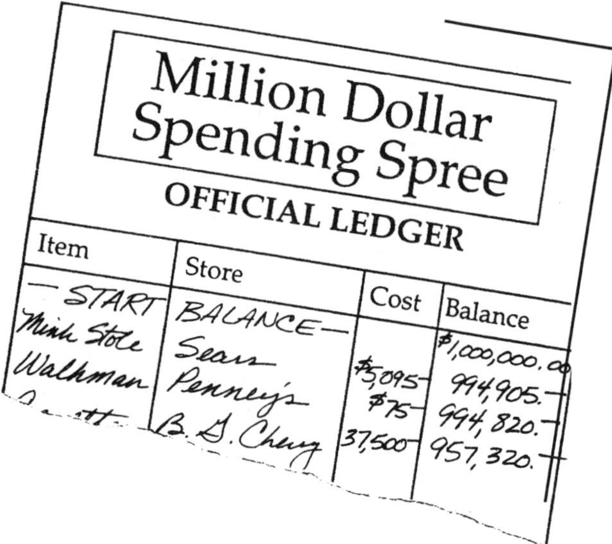

Million Dollar Spending Spree

OFFICIAL LEDGER

Item	Store	Cost	Balance
— START	BALANCE—		$1,000,000.00
Mink Stole	Sears	$5,095	994,905.
Walkman	Penney's	$75	994,820.
[illegible]	B. G. Chevy	37,500	957,320.

- No more then one kind of an item may be purchased.
- No one item over one hundred thousand may be purchased.
- On the ledger a team secretary must record the purchased item, the store from which it was brought, and the cost of the item (see sample sheet).
- If an item is sold by the measure (pounds, gallons, ounces, etc.), you are limited to a thousand units of that measure (1000 pounds of candy, 1000 ounces of perfume, etc.)
- Do not include taxes in your figuring.
- Do not record the original price for items that were on sale—record the sale price.
- You may purchase only what is marked for sale. For example, you may not offer to buy a cash register—or buy the whole store for a million.
- The first team to report back to start after spending their million wins.
- Teams have one and a half hours to spend their million and return to the starting site to verify their figures. If no team spends it all, the team that has spent the most at the end of the game wins.

The winning team will be treated to large Cokes after the game. *Jim Johnson*

SCRAMBLED LEGS

Divide your students into teams of six or seven; each group forms a circle, facing out. Then everyone's ankles are tied to their partners' on either side of them. The object of the game is then to shuffle around the room as a ring and collect strips of cloth or other material that were previously hung from the ceiling, walls, etc. Have a different color of strip for each team. The first team to collect all strips of its color and deposit them in a centrally located bucket wins. *Brian Sylvia*

POP-CAN BOWL

Divide your group into two teams; position them on opposite halves of a recreation room, gymnasium, or other playing area; and supply players with several playground balls. Between the two teams is a three-foot-wide "can zone," where dozens of empty pop cans stand.

Players must bowl the balls into the cans in order to knock them into the other team's playing area, though without crossing into the "can zone" themselves. The team with the least cans in its area after two minutes of playing wins. *John Krueger*

TURNS AND TRADES

Form two concentric circles of equal numbers of kids facing each other. Tell the kids to trade one thing they have on for one thing the person facing them has on—jewelry, shoes, socks, belts, hats, etc. The players must then put on the items they traded for.

Now ask the inner circle to move three people to their right so that each player has a new partner. Partners must make another trade; but they cannot trade anything they've received in a trade. Next ask the outer circle to move two people to their right and repeat the trading process. Call for one more turn and trade.

Kids will now have run out of jewelry, shoes, etc., and may be getting embarrassed about another impending trade. So have some fun with them: tell the outer circle to move two people to the right again. You'll hear moans, but when they move, tell them to trade something that has already been traded. Repeat this twice.

Now tell them they have two minutes to retrieve all of their items. Offer a prize to the first one to bring all of the items up to you, or you can time the group to see how quickly they can all retrieve their things and then sit down. *Terry Linhart*

DOMINO TEAMS

Make up 4x6 cards to look like dominos. Do as many sets as you plan to have teams, and each set in a different color. Also, put as many dots as you plan to have team members (i.e., for four teams of seven people make sets of cards in red, blue, green, and black with cards of one dot through seven dots in each color). Tape the cards on the backs of people as they come in and then explain, "At the whistle you are to discover what your domino number is and your color. You may ask yes or no questions of those around you. You may only ask one question per person. When you find out what your domino is, then go to your team area (areas should be designated prior to the start). The first team to get all their members in the right area and in order (one to seven) wins. *Doug Dennee*

CYCLOPS

For this game the group is divided up into teams of three to five and a volunteer is selected from each group. Each group is given a box of materials including tape, newspaper, aluminum foil, cellophane, or other similar items. On a signal the volunteer is covered completely, except for one eye, by the rest of the group (henceforth known as the pit crew) with the materials. Once the volunteer is completely covered, a referee checks the "cyclops" out, and if no clothing or skin is showing, the cyclops may begin the attack (without interference or assistance from the pit crew). No cyclops may attack without permission from a referee.

The object is to attack—by tagging— another cyclops who is not yet ready for attack. Once an unprepared cyclops is tagged, he is eliminated. The unprepared cyclops may flee the tag and the pit crew may keep working on the cyclops while he is fleeing. The attacking cyclops may remain in pursuit until a piece of covering falls off and some skin or clothing shows through. If this should occur the attacker must stop and allow the pit crew to make the necessary repairs. The event continues until there is only one cyclops left. *Mark Heiss*

HUMAN FOOSBALL

Many churches and recreation centers have a foosball table, which is a table version of soccer. Using an open field the foosball format may be constructed making for a wild and fast game of soccer.

Begin by dividing a playing field into 10 sections. (See diagram.) You may divide the field by using lime on the ground or an even better method is to use string or cord strung across the field about waist high as dividers. An easy way to do this is to run the string across the field and attach it at both ends to folding chairs.

Once the field is set up then it is time to arrange the players. Each team should use an equal number of players; normally 10 is about right but you may want to adjust that number depending on field size and the number of people who want to participate. Arrange the players in the sections as shown in the diagram. The players on the outer edges of the field are called spotters.

Once set up, the game itself is simple:

- The object of the game is to kick the ball into the other team's goal.
- The ball may be advanced using any part of the

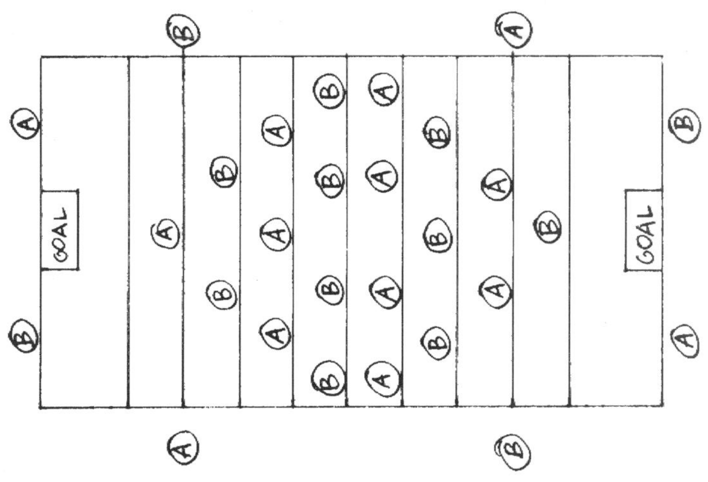

body except the hand and the arms. Unlike normal soccer, this rule also applies to the goalie, who is not stationed directly in front of the goal but in the first section away from the goal.

- Every player is required to stay within the limits of her section. One may advance the ball only while it is in her section. The players may move laterally as much as they like, but may not move upfield or downfield beyond the boundaries of their narrow section. (To enforce this rule any player who ranges out of her section is removed from the game for two minutes, along with everyone else who is in that section with her.)
- It is the job of the spotters (placed around the field alternately, in order to keep the game fair) to roll the ball back into play once it has been kicked out of bounds. Once again the number of spotters used will depend upon the number who are available to participate.
- Make sure the spotters throw the ball back in as soon as they retrieve it.
- It is best to develop a rotation system so that everyone can play the different positions.
- Any round ball will work; however, a slightly heavier ball such as a regulation soccer ball works best.
- For a more controlled game, everyone in a given line is required to join arms, like this:

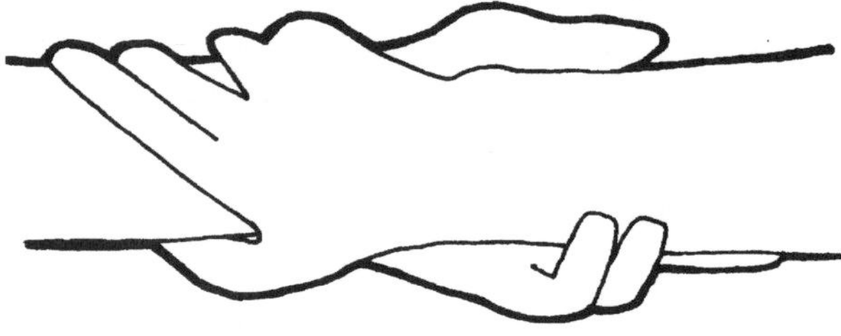

This forces each line to act (like an actual Foosball game) as a unit. It also makes it more difficult for players to break the rules (such as stepping outside the lines). *Billy Richter and Steve Perisho*

Mix 'Em Up

This variation on musical chairs works best with at least 15 players—the more the merrier. Set up a circle of chairs, one for each player except the leader. All the players sit down.

The leader calls out a random characteristic present in the group—"Everyone with purple socks!" All players who share that characteristic get up and scramble for new seats vacated by other players doing the same thing. The leader also darts for a seat. When the seats are filled, one player is left standing—who chooses the next characteristic, and so on.

If absolutely nothing comes to mind, "It" can always say, "Mix 'em up!" at which all players get up and find new seats. *Christopher Graham*

Newspaper Costumes

Divide the group up so that there are three people in a group. Each group is given 12 pieces of newspaper and eight straight pins. The contest is to see which group can make the most original costume—neatness counts. It is good to see how much creativity people have. Have a judge to choose the winning group. *Ora Barker*

First Day at School

Play this game close to the opening day of classes in September. It's a fun, frantic way for your kids to remember (or anticipate) the difficulty of finding their way around a new school building on the first day of school.

To begin, you need a very large room (at least a fellowship hall, preferably a gym) or, better yet, the entire church building. Throughout the room or building label different ROOMS with very small signs: MATH ROOM, SCIENCE ROOM, HOMEROOM, etc. or post sponsors ("teachers") throughout the room or building with name tags: Mr. Jones, Mrs. Schwartz, Ms. Gallagher, etc. In either case, the crucial thing is to make the sign or name tag absolutely tiny, so that kids will have to crowd up close in order to read it.

When your kids come, announce that they have to find a specific class or teacher (name one) and that the first couple of people to find the correct room will receive a prize, the last several will have to sit out. Continue this process until all but the last person or two are eliminated.

Things will get chaotic and frantic, of course, as kids streak around the room or building, trying to quickly read minuscule signs. So don't play this where your kids can maim themselves or demolish church property. *Dave Mahoney*

IMPROV GAMES

Take advantage of stand-up comedy's popularity with an evening of improv comedy competition. Select teams and an emcee, and get ready for an evening of laughter and memories. Here are some ideas to get things rolling.

• **Lists.** Select two people from each team. Ask the audience for a list of 10 emotions or states of mind (rage, euphoria, panic, etc.). Write them down. Then ask the audience for an infrequent household chore, such as taking down the Christmas tree.

One of the teams begins acting out the chore, using words and actions, and conveying the first emotion on the list. Every 30 seconds or so, the emcee calls out a different one of the 10 emotions. The actors change emotions immediately, carrying out the same chore. Switch teams and repeat the process. Use the ol' "applause meter" to determine the winner.

• **Talk or Die.** Select one person from each team and have those selected line up, facing the audience. The emcee begins a story, stopping halfway through a sentence and pointing to one of the players, who then continues the story. For example, the emcee says, "Two small children were standing in front of a candy store when, to their amazement—"

If a contestant hesitates or continues the story in a way that makes no sense, the audience and the emcee yell, "Die!" The last person standing is the winner.

• **Video Fairy Tales.** Ask the audience to list types of movies—musicals, romantic comedies, police dramas, horror, sci-fi, techno-thrillers, spaghetti westerns, etc.). Write them down, and each team picks one of the types. Then ask the audience for a popular fairy tale or nursery rhyme.

Give each team two minutes to plan how to enact the fairy tale or nursery rhyme in the cinematic genre they selected.

Appoint a "distinguished panel" of judges to score the acts on a scale of one to 10. Encourage the audience to voice approval or disapproval of the judges' decision. *Kevin Turner*

VIDEO SOUND EFFECTS

Before your party or event, videotape several objects that operate or run with distinctive sounds—a train, race car, photocopier, typewriter or keyboard, the youth-room door shutting, voices of individuals in your congregation, etc. Make sure the camcorder's microphone picks up the audio.

At the event, conceal the TV screen with a piece of cardboard and pass out pencils and slips of paper. Then play the tape, so that kids hear only the sounds of the operations you recorded. Pause between sounds so students can write down their guesses as to what produced that sound. When they're done, rewind the tape, remove the cardboard from the TV screen, and replay the tape, letting kids see and hear it this time. The student who identified the most sounds wins. *Len Cuthbert*

FOUR ON A COUCH

This is best played with at least 20 players. Write everyone's name on a slip of paper, one name per slip, and place the papers in a container.

Now sit everyone in a circle, with the couch (or four chairs) as part of the circle. Two boys and two girls (alternating) should sit on the couch. The teens sitting on the floor in a circle should leave one empty space.

The goal is to fill the four spaces on the couch with either all boys or all girls.

Once your teens are all situated, have each player draw a name from the container. Then start with the person sitting to the right of the open space: he calls the name of anyone in the group. Whoever holds the slip of paper with that name on it moves to the open spot and trades slips with the person who called the name. The play continues, with the person who now sits to the right of the vacant spot. (Pay attention, especially to the last name called.) Other players may not give hints to the player whose turn it is. *Christopher Graham*

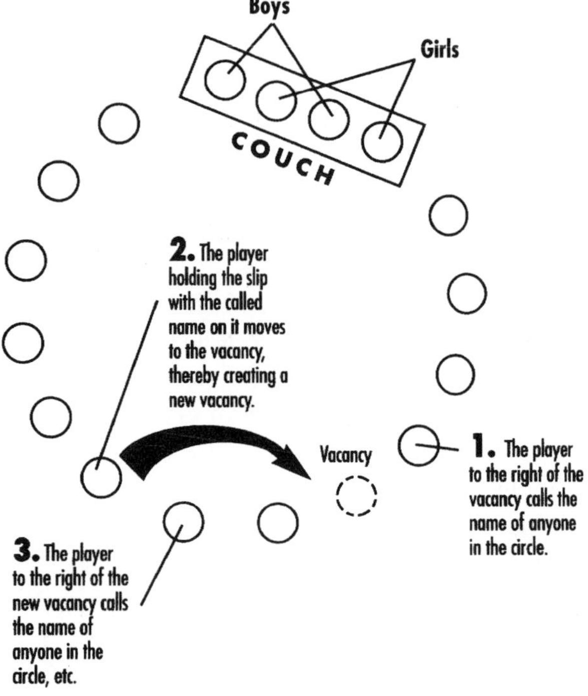

Boys
Girls
COUCH
2. The player holding the slip with the called name on it moves to the vacancy, thereby creating a new vacancy.
Vacancy
1. The player to the right of the vacancy calls the name of anyone in the circle.
3. The player to the right of the new vacancy calls the name of anyone in the circle, etc.

PRISON BALL

The more players, the better for this classic game that is played best indoors (where walls are the court's boundaries), but a playground version works okay, too. You'll need one, two, or three playground balls (depending on the size of your group). Divide your group into two equal teams—we'll call them Reds and Whites, for the sake of the diagram below.

The game begins with each team on its half of the court, and each team with at least one ball (unless the group is small—10 on side, say. In this case, use a single ball). Now for the rules:

- The object is to send all of your opponents to prison.
- You send opponents to prison by hitting them with the ball.
- Opponents who catch the ball, however, stay free and don't go to prison.
- Players in prison regain their freedom by hitting an opponent with the ball.
- Prisoners get a ball either by one slipping through their opponent's half of the court, or by their still-free teammates lobbing balls deliberately to their comrades in prison.
- You must stay on your side of the middle line.
- You may not step into the prison behind your half

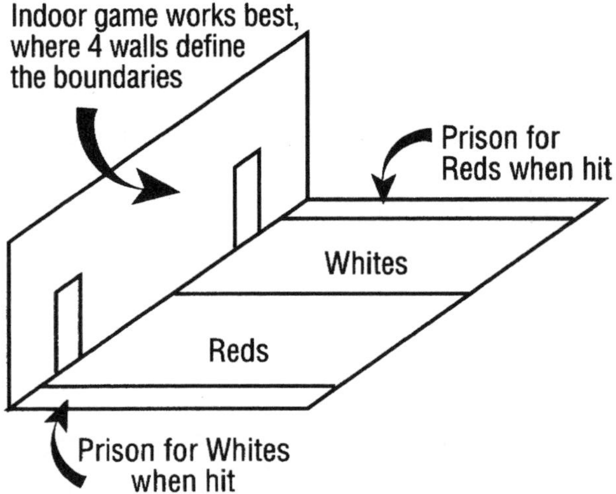

Indoor game works best, where 4 walls define the boundaries
Prison for Reds when hit
Whites
Reds
Prison for Whites when hit

of the court.

Teenagers can throw balls hard, so make rules appropriate to your group.

Possible variations: Balls must hit players below the waist (or thrower goes to prison)...use soft, mushy Nerf-type balls...boys hit boys, girls hit girls (just make sure there are equal numbers on each side)...etc. *Christopher Graham*

INDOOR GAMES FOR SMALL GROUPS

Flexibility is the key here. While these games will work best in groups of thirty or less, most of them can be adapted for use in larger groups. And while some require a large indoor space, such as a fellowship hall or gymnasium, others can be played in a living room.

BIG BAD WOLF

Give three-person teams enough newspaper and tape to build a newspaper shelter of some kind. It must be big enough to get all three inside. The wolf (youth leader) then attempts to blow the shelter down. A prize is awarded to the best job. Afterward have a giant paper fight. *Cynthia and John Baker*

BOTTLE BOWLING

Use plastic bottles (like milk bottles) for pins and a volleyball or similar ball for bowling. Works great for picnics and all-day game events. *Glen Richardson*

CONTEST OF THE WINDS

Draw a large square on the floor similar to the diagram below. The square is divided into four equal parts, designated as the North, East, South, and West. Divide the group into four teams of the same names. Scatter dried leaves or cotton balls evenly in each quarter of the square. At a given signal, the "winds begin to blow" and each team tries to blow (no hands allowed) the leaves out of their square into another. Set a time limit and the team with the least leaves (or cotton balls) in their square wins.

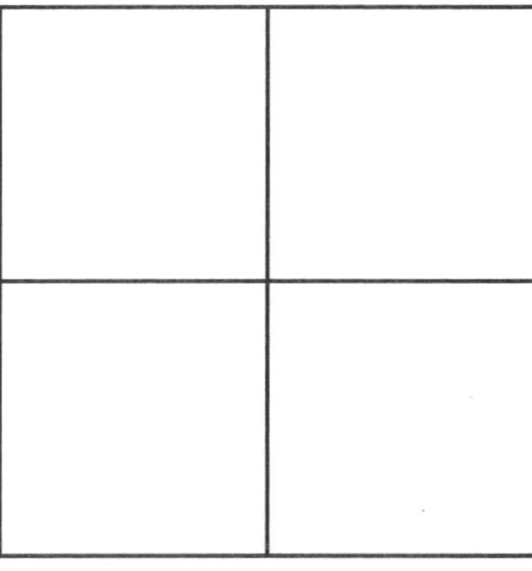

Don Womacks

CROSSWORD PEOPLE

Divide the group into teams of equal size (12 to 24 people per team). Write one letter on each 12-inch square card. Give each team a set of selected letters from the alphabet (one card per person). Teams get identical sets of letters. Choose frequently used vowels and consonants, plus two or three rarely used letters such as Q, X, or Z.

Here's a suggested letter list; for larger groups, add more vowels and consonants accordingly:

A—2	I—2	P—1
C—1	J—1	T—1
E—2	M—1	U—1
F—1	N—1	Y—1
G—1	O—1	

...and any *one* of these: Q, X, Z

At a signal each team tries to form a crossword puzzle within a given time limit, using as many teammates as possible, each holding one card. Each team should have a captain to direct the team. For example, a 18-person team, using the suggested letters AACEFGIIJMNOOPTUXY, above, could line up this way:

```
JUMPING
  I   O
TAX   O
     CAFE
      Y
```

Award points to teams that use more teammates, form the longest word, the most words, etc. Or assign a point value to each letter and add up points as if you were playing Scrabble.

Dr. Tangle

Have a group of any number of people hold hands. Have one person leave the room. Start in a circle, then without breaking hands, go under and over other people's arms. When the group is all knotted up, call the person back into the room to try to untangle the group without breaking hands. *Senior High Fellowship, First Congregational Church, Webster Groves, Mo.*

I Know That Voice

Everyone sits on chairs arranged in a circle, with one person standing in the middle. The person in the middle is blindfolded and given a rolled-up newspaper. She is spun around as everyone else changes seats. Everyone needs to be silent. The person blindfolded then finds a person's lap only by means of the end of the newspaper.

Once a lap is found, the newspaper is unfolded and placed on the lap. The blindfolded person sits on the newspaper and says any predetermined short phrase: "Duckie Wuckie" is the traditional one for this game, but it can be anything—"Go Wildcats ... Patriots rule ... our God reigns." In a disguised voice the person being sat upon says the appropriate response (also predetermined): "Quack quack" or "We're number one" or "Yes, they do" or simply "Amen!" The phrase and response can be repeated twice more, and the blindfolded person may venture a guess at the owner of the lap at any time. If the blindfolded person correctly identifies whose lap he or she is on within three guesses, the blindfold swaps to the person whose lap is being sat on; otherwise the blindfolded person finds another lap and tries again. *Steve Tigner*

Birdie on the Perch

Have kids pair up and form two concentric circles. Pairs should face each other.

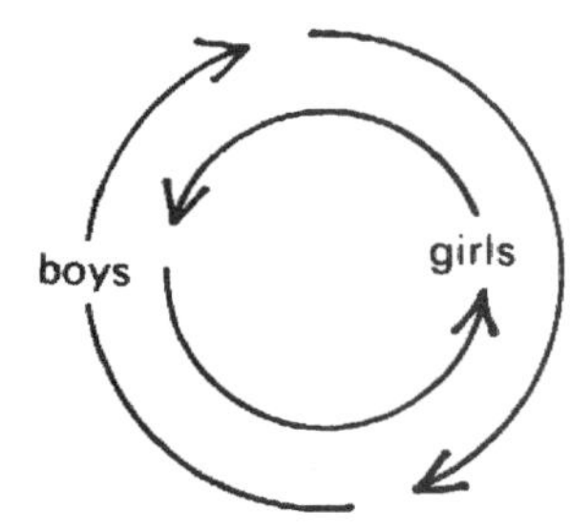

When the whistle blows, the outer circle moves clockwise while the inner circle moves counterclockwise. When the leader yells "Birdie on the perch!" players in the outer circle get down on all fours. Players from the inner circle then race to find their partner, straddle their backs, and sit. The game ends when only one pair remains.

Expandable Hopscotch

This is a grownup version of the old child's game of hopscotch. Secure small-size carpet remnants from any carpet store. These are then used as hopscotch squares. The game is played as usual, except that the squares are spaced further and further apart as the game progresses until the kids are jumping several feet between squares. It's a good competition and is great for laughs. *Dave Bransby*

Fickle Feather

Lay a sheet out flat on the floor. Have all the kids kneel around the sheet on all four sides of it, and then pick up the sheet by the edges. They pull it taut and hold it under their chins. A feather is placed on the sheet, and the kids try to blow the feather away from their side. Each side of the sheet is a team, and if the feather touches one of the team members, or gets blown over their heads, that team gets a point. The team with the fewest points is the winner.

FLEA MARKET

This is a good party game. You will need to prepare ahead of time a large number of one-inch square pieces of paper, all different colors. These are hidden all around the room. Some squares have numbers on them. On a starting signal all the group hunts for the squares, and as soon as they have been found, kids start trading with each other, trying to acquire the colors that they think are worth the most. (Only you know the color value.) The value of the colors and numbers is unknown to the players until the trading is over. You then announce the values and whoever has the most points, wins. (This is also good as an Easter Egg Hunt.)

Colors:	white = 1 point
	brown = 5 points
	green = minus 5 points
	blue = 2 points
	red = 10 points
Numbers:	7 = add 50
	11 = double score
	13 = subtract 50
	15 = add 1

FRUITBASKET UPSET

This game can be played with any number of people, usually inside. The entire group sits in a circle with one less chair than there are people. The extra person stands in the middle. Everyone is secretly assigned the name of a fruit.

The person in the middle begins by naming several fruits, then yelling "Go!"—and the people named with those fruits must change chairs.

At the same time, the person in the middle also tries to get one of the vacant chairs. The person who fails to get a chair is then the one in the middle and repeats the process.

For a raucous end to the game, play the final couple of rounds with this twist: the person in the middle calls out "Fruitbasket Upset!" at which time *everyone* must exchange chairs. Use sturdy chairs, for this game is really wild!

• **Birthday Shuffle.** In this variation the circle has as many chairs as there are people. The leader calls out any three months of the year, and everyone in the circle whose birthday is in those months must get up and find a new chair. While they're scrambling to find a new seat, the extra person tries to sit in a vacant chair. This will leave a new person in the middle.

If most of the kids in the group are roughly the same age, the leader can call out a year, and all those who were born that year must switch chairs. If the leader calls out some other pre-designated word or phrase (like "Happy Birthday!"), then everyone must get up and change chairs. *Randy Cooney, Scotty Shows, and Art Voltz*

GIANT JIGSAW PUZZLE

Obtain a used outdoor billboard sign from a sign company (they come rolled up and easy to carry), and cut it into a giant jigsaw puzzle. Use it as a game to see which team can put it together in the least amount of time.

HUNTERS AND HOUNDS

Kids pair up. One partner is the hunter and one is the hound. The hunter holds a paper bag and stays behind the starting line (the hunting lodge) while her hound searches for hidden peanuts. When the hound finds a peanut, he howls. Only then can the hunter run to retrieve the peanut and place it in the bag. When two or more hounds find the same peanut, each howls and the hunter who gets there first gets the nut. *Jerry Summers*

INDOOR OLYMPICS

• **Discus Throw.** Contestants compete like discus throwers. They take two hops and a step, then throw a paper plate as far as they can.

• **Hammer Throw.** Inflate and tie off large paper bags with a 30-inch string. Contestants swing the sack around their heads several times before throwing for distance.

• **Javelin Throw.** Contestants take three running steps and throw a toothpick as far as possible.

KILL THE UMPIRE

Two people are placed in the center of the room and are blindfolded. One is the umpire and one is the batter. The umpire gets a whistle, the batter gets a rolled-up newspaper. Every five seconds, the umpire must blow the whistle so that the batter can try to locate her and hit her with the newspaper (within two minutes). At some point, secretly remove one of the player's blindfolds. *Jerry Summers*

SHOE SCRAMBLE

All players remove their shoes and mix them up in a big pile. Divide the group in half. One half of the players rush to the pile, locate a matching pair of shoes, and find the owner of the shoes. The owner becomes that person's partner and must find his partner's shoes based on his partner's description. The first pair to put on their shoes wins.

KING OF THE CIRCLE

Mark off a large circle (10 feet or so in diameter) and put about a dozen people into it. At a signal, all the players try to throw everybody else out of the circle without stepping outside or getting pushed out of the circle themselves. The last person within the circle wins.

MURDER

This is a great indoor game for casual get-togethers. Place a number of slips of paper in a hat. There should be the same number of slips of paper as there are players. One of these slips of paper has the word *detective* written on it, and another has the word *murderer* on it. The rest of them are blank. Everyone draws a slip of paper from the hat. Whoever draws the word detective announces himself, and it is his job to try to locate the murderer, who remains silent. From this point, there are two ways the game may be played:

1. The detective leaves the room, and the room is darkened. All the players mill about the room and the murderer silently slips behind someone and very quietly whispers "You're dead" in his ear. The victim counts to three, screams, and falls to the floor. The lights are turned on and the detective reenters the room. He then may question the players for a minute or so before attempting to name the murderer. If he is correct, the murderer becomes the detective, and a new murderer is selected. During the questioning, only the murderer may lie. All others must tell the truth about whatever they saw, heard, felt, or otherwise sensed.

2. The detective remains in the room, and the murderer attempts to "murder" as many victims as possible (in the manner described above) before he is caught by the detective. The murderer gets points for every person he can kill before being discovered, and the detective gets points deducted for every incorrect guess or accusation. Everyone should get a chance to play both roles. This is best with at least 20 kids.

• **The Farmer's Dotter.** This indoor game is similar to Murder. A detective must reveal the identity of the mysterious "dotter" who is placing self-adhesive dot labels on other members of the group. Use a random, secret method for choosing the "dotter" and provide him or her with enough dot labels to stick on everyone in the room. The detective tries to do three things:

1. Let people know when they've been dotted (if they aren't aware of it).
2. Keep a record of all who've been dotted (in case labels drop off during the course of the evening).
3. Identify the dotter.

This kind of game can continue behind the scenes while other games are being played. If the dotter is identified, a new dotter and a new detective can be secretly chosen, and the game continues. The object is for the dotter to dot as many people as he can before the detective discovers his identity. *Michael W. Capps*

NUT HUNT

Hide peanuts all over the room, ahead of time. Divide into teams and assign each team an animal name (donkey, cow, etc.). Each team also has a leader. The idea is to find all the peanuts. The team members hunt for them and as soon as a peanut is located, the person must get down on all fours and make his animal sound (hee-haw, etc.), until the team leader comes and collects the peanut. Then, the team member can go find more peanuts. The team with the most peanuts at the end of the time wins. *Sue Broadhurst*

Musical Water Glasses

Give each team eight water glasses, three spoons, and a pitcher of water. Five minutes are given for the teams to put appropriate amounts of water in each of the glasses, forming a musical scale, and then practice a song using the spoons to tap the glasses. Points can be awarded for the best pitch, best song, best harmony, etc. It is best to put the teams in different corners of the room so they can hear what they are doing. *Ed Bender*

Pass It On

The entire group forms a circle. Everyone is given an object which can be large or small, and any shape (such as a bowling ball, a trash can, a shoe, etc.). On a signal, players pass their object to the person on the right, keeping the objects moving at all times. When a person drops any object, he must leave the game, but his object remains in. As the game progresses, more people leave the game, making it harder and harder to avoid dropping an object since the objects soon outnumber the people. The winner is the last person to "drop" out.

Shoe Shucking Race

Divide your group into teams of six players each. Teammates must lie on their backs in a circle and put their feet up so that all feet meet in the center of the circle. Place one container of water (dishpan) on all the feet. One at a time, each player is to try to remove her shoes without spilling the water. The team must figure out a way to prevent spilling while one teammate is removing shoes. The team removing the most shoes after three minutes wins.

Singing Charades

Divide your group into smaller groups. Each group sends one person to the center of the room where he and the others are given the name of a song (the leader whispers). Each rushes back to his own team with paper and pencil and draws out a picture that he thinks best describes the song. (No words can be written or said by the artist.) The team tries to guess what the song is and when they get it immediately sing it out. The first team to sing the correct song wins. Each team sends another entry. The game may be repeated for each team member or until the leader wishes to stop. This is a great game for informal Christmas parties, when you use carols for songs.

Strung Out

Have any number of teams stand in straight lines. Each team gets a cold spoon with a 20-foot piece of string tied to it. The spoon should come just out of the freezer. The object is to see how many people you can lace together by taking the spoon and passing it through your clothing (neck down to ankle). The first contestant holds end of string in his mouth. This is not timed. Anything goes from bending, lying down, crouching, etc. Anything to get more string out.

Swat

The group sits in a circle and in the center is a wastebasket turned bottom up. One person is "It" and stands inside the circle with a loosely rolled-up newspaper. "It" walks around the inside of the circle and swats one person's knee. He must then put the newspaper back on top of the wastebasket and return to the swatted person's seat before that person is able to grab the newspaper and hit him back.

If the newspaper falls off the wastebasket, it must be put back by "It." *Glen Richardson*

Swivel Hips

Have the group sit in a circle with their chairs close together. A chosen person then stands up and the person on her right moves and sits in her chair, the person on his right moves and sits in his chair, and as this continues the person who stands tries to get a seat. If the person is able to get a seat, the person whose seat was taken stands up and the circle continues to move.

Once the group has begun to master the movement, you can ask them to switch directions and to make it even more fun, you can have a whistle and when you blow the whistle they must change directions. If you have a large group, you can have two or three people trying to find seats. *David Worth*

Back-to-Back

Divide your group into pairs and have them sit on the floor back-to-back linking arms. Then tell them to stand up. With a little timing, it shouldn't be too hard. Then combine two pairs into a foursome. Have the foursome sit on the floor back-to-back with arms linked. Tell them to stand up. It is a little harder with four. Keep adding more people to the group until the giant blob can't stand up any more. *Marshall Shelley*

Beach Ball Pickup

Divide your group into two teams. Teams then number off and line up opposite each other about 20 feet apart. Between the two teams, six beach balls (light ones) are placed on the floor. Two numbers are called and the two players on each team with those numbers begin play. Each pair must pick up three balls without using their hands or arms. If they drop a ball, they must start over. All three balls must be held between the two players and must be off the ground. The first pair to succeed is the winner. Repeat by calling two new numbers, and so on. *Dave Gilliam*

Yarn Guess

This is one of those things you do just for fun. On one side of the room, put some numbers on the wall (on cards or just write on the wall). Attach to the number the end of a long piece of yarn. Then hang the yarn up the wall, across the ceiling, and down the opposite wall to a letter on the wall. Let the yarn make a few turns, go through things, etc., to make it interesting. With about 25 different lengths of yarn going across the room connecting numbers and letters, it really looks wild. The object is to have the kids try to figure out which number connects up with which letter. Whoever guesses the most right wins a prize. *Von Trutschler*

Bloody Marshmallow

Have the kids pair off. Partners stand about 10 feet apart facing each other. Each gets five marshmallows and a paper cup full of catsup. One at a time, each person dips a marshmallow in the catsup and tries to toss it in his partner's mouth. The partner tries to catch it in his mouth. The couple that catches the most out of all 10 marshmallows wins. *Steven Kjorvestad*

Marshmallow Pitch

Kids pair off, and each pair gets a sack of miniature marshmallows. Each pair should also have a neutral "counter." One person is the pitcher, the other the catcher. On "Go!" the pitcher tosses a marshmallow into the catcher's mouth, and the catcher must eat the marshmallow. The pitcher and catcher should be about 10 feet apart. The counter counts how many successful catches are made, and the pair with the most at the end of a time limit, or the first to reach 20 successful catches, is the winner. *Don French*

Porcu-Mallow

This game gets more difficult but funnier as you go along. Divide your group into two or more teams. Give each player a toothpick (round ones work best) and a marshmallow. The first player puts the marshmallow on his toothpick and then holds the toothpick with his teeth. All other players hold toothpicks in their mouths. You're now ready to start the game.

Pass the marshmallow from player to player by sticking your toothpick into the marshmallow and leaving it as you pass it along. You are not allowed to use your hands. As the marshmallow is passed, it accumulates one more toothpick from each player.

It's a riot to see players trying to avoid being stuck by the other toothpicks already in the marshmallow. The first team to finish is the winner. And the end product is a marshmallow that looks like a porcupine. *Glenn Davis*

Marshmallow Surprise

At first this game seems mild and old fashioned—but then the blindfolds come out and it becomes hilarious.

Before the meeting, tie marshmallows to 18-inch strings and suspend the strings from a line across the room. When the youths arrive, ask for volunteers to attempt to eat the marshmallows off of the strings. Also ask for volunteers to coach each participant. The coaches must tie blindfolds on the marshmallow-eaters and back them up about three or four feet from the line. After the blindfolds are in place, explain the rules slowly enough so that another accomplice has enough time to dip each marshmallow in chocolate syrup. At a signal each coach verbally directs his marshmallow-eater to her marshmallow and tells her how close she's getting, etc. The coach must make sure that the marshmallow-eaters don't use their hands.

Amazingly enough, very few realize that they're making a mess all over their face, and the spectators get a good laugh.

Another funny variation of the game is to remove the marshmallows altogether. It's a riot to watch kids hunting with their mouths for something that's not there. Of course the coaches should be clued in. *Brenda Clowers*

Marshmallow Mouth-to-Mouth

Thread a marshmallow to the middle of a long, thin string of licorice. Put a player on each end of the licorice, then tell them this is an eating race (no hands allowed); first one to eat his or her way to the marshmallow—including the marshmallow—wins.

If this contact is too close for your comfort, center a pair of marshmallows four inches apart on the licorice. The first teen to reach and eat the closest marshmallow wins. *Rob Church*

Bubble Blow Blitz

Give each team a bottle of bubble soap and a bubble pipe. Have the team captain stand 10 to 20 feet away from the goal line making bubbles while his teammates blow them across the goal line. The team that blows the most bubbles across the goal line wins. If you play this indoors, draw the goal line only 10 feet away from the person blowing the bubbles. Dead air doesn't allow the bubbles to be blown more than a few feet. When playing outdoors the goal line can be 15 to 20 feet away from the captain. This game is worthless on windy days. *Bill Calvin*

CHURCH TRIVIA

Divide the group into teams (or kids may compete individually) and give each a list of unusual things in the church to identify. Here's a sample list:

• The name of the company that manufactured the church's fire extinguisher.
• The number of steps in the baptistery.
• The number of fuses in the fuse box.
• The location of the first-aid kit.
• The last word in a specific book in the church library.
• The number of yellow lines painted on the parking lot.

Your list should include 20 or so items such as these. At the signal everyone tries to locate the various information required as quickly as possible. With teams, the questions can be assigned to the different team members. The first team to finish, or the one with the most questions correctly answered, wins. *Don Snider*

CHOP FOOEY

Provide chopsticks for each team and then race to see who can eat the fastest using only the chopsticks. The food can be anything from Jell-O to corn. *Shirley Peterson*

CINDERELLA

Arrange chairs in a circle. All the Cinderellas (females) in the group select a chair. The Prince Charmings (males) each pick a Cinderella and kneel down in front of her. He removes her shoes and holds them in his hand. The leader calls for the shoes and they are thrown to the middle of the circle. Then the Cinderellas blindfold their Prince Charmings. After each prince is blindfolded, the leader rearranges and mixes the shoes in the middle.

On a signal all the Prince Charmings crawl to the circle and attempt to find their Cinderella's shoes. The Cinderellas can help only verbally, shouting out instructions to their men. After finding the shoes, the princes crawl back to their girls (again guided only by verbal instructions). They place the shoes (right one on right foot, etc.) on the girls and then remove their blindfolds. The game continues until the last contestant succeeds. *Carol Wennerholm*

CATCH THE WIND

Divide your group into three-person teams. Have one person lie on the floor with a straw in his mouth. At his head, place a chair. A second person sits in the chair facing the person on the floor and has a party blower in his mouth. The chair back should be toward the person on the floor and the seated person should rest his chin on the chair back.

A third person sits next to the person on the floor and places tissues one at a time on the end of the straw. The person on the floor then blows the tissue up in the air and the person in the chair tries to catch it with the party blower. The winning team is the first to catch a given number of tissues. The distance from the blower on the floor to the catcher may vary depending on the vertical distance that people can blow. *Dave Gilliam*

COTTONTAIL TAG

This game needs to be held in a place where there can be easy cleanup. Have all the kids in the group bring a can of shaving cream to the meeting. When the kids show up, you give a bull's-eye belt to each kid. This consists of a square foot of cardboard with a circle drawn on it and a string strung through it big enough to go around a kid's waist. Each kid ties it on his waist with the cardboard around back in the general area that a tail would go. You split the kids into two teams and explain that the object of the game is to try and squirt a glob of shaving cream into the bull's-eye worn by members of the opposing team, while protecting yours at the same time. You may not touch your own cardboard or sit down on it. The shaving cream must stick to the cardboard and be inside the circle. The team that has successfully put the most cottontails on the other team within the time limit is the winner. *Andrea Sutton*

Feet on the Rocks

Divide your group into two teams. Have each team sit in chairs back-to-back with an approximate five-foot space between the chairs. The captain of each team sits in a separate chair at the end of the team row of chairs.

At a signal an ice cube is placed under one of the feet of each captain. The captains slide the ice to player 1 on their team. Player 1 must pass it from one foot to the other and then to the next player on the team. This continues until the ice cube is passed by the entire team back to the captain again. The captain is now allowed to stand up and devise a way to carry the ice cube with his or her feet only to the opposite end of the room and put it in a cup (no hands).

If the captain drops the ice cube, he or she can start from where it was dropped, but if the ice cube melts or slips out of reach while the team is passing it, they must start over again. *Barry Kolanowski*

No Trespassing

Tie a plastic-covered clothesline rope, approximately 20 feet long, to two folding chairs, so that the rope is about eight inches off the floor. The rope should be in the center of the room. Also, be sure to mark your rope with a masking tape flag approximately one foot from each chair. This is for the safety of whoever is "It."

Choose one person to be "It" and divide the rest into two groups. Each group takes one end of the field (or room) facing the other group. Blindfold "It" and also give him some knee pads to protect his knees if the floor is hard or rough. "It" then takes his position, kneeling with one hand on the rope. He is free to move on his knees as long as he is touching the rope. On a signal each team hops on one foot across the rope to get to the other side. Team members must cross the rope without tripping or being tagged by "It." Before jumping over the rope, each person must announce his jump by clapping his hands together five times. Any trespassers (jumpers) caught become an obstacle for the next round. They lie face down parallel to the rope, leaving room on each side for the jumpers. The first person caught becomes the next "It." *Tom Bougher*

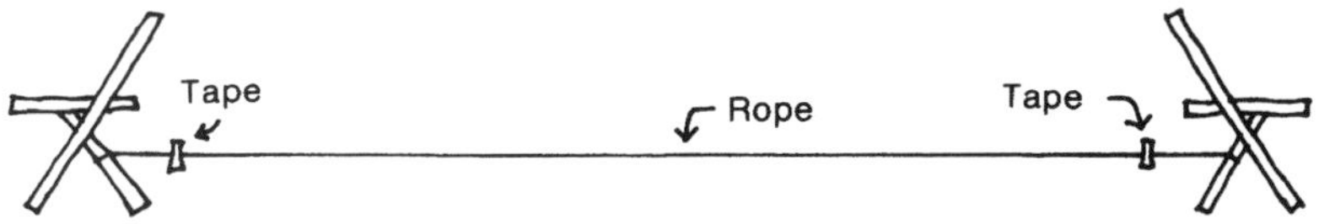

Tape

Rope

Tape

Flyswatter

This is a good little game taken from Pin the Tail on the Donkey. Blindfold a kid, give him a flyswatter (the type with holes in it), and spin him around a few times. Place a glob of shaving cream on the wall and have the kid try to swat it. On impact the "swatter" usually gets hit with flying shaving cream. Wipe it up and position a new glob in a different spot for the next contestant. The winner is whoever can swat the glob in the fastest time. *Andrea Sutton*

Grape Toss

Teams appoint one kid who is the "tosser." He gets a bag of grapes. The rest of the team gets in a circle around him. The tosser is in the middle. He must toss grapes to everyone on his team, one at a time, and each team member must catch the grape in his or her mouth. The first team to go around their circle (the whole team) wins. *Richard Reynolds*

Math Scramble

Divide into teams. Each person is given a number on a piece of paper which is to be worn. (Numbers should begin at 0 and go up to 10 or the number of kids on the team.) The leader stands an equal distance away from each team and yells out a "math problem" such as "2 times 8 minus 4 divided by 3" and the team must send the person with the correct answer (the person wearing the number "4" in this case) to the leader. No talking is allowed on the team. The correct person must simply get up and run. The first correct answer to the leader wins 100 points. The first team to reach 1,000 (or whatever) wins. *J.C. Heneisen*

Hook-Up

An active game, Hook-up works best with 10 or more people. Divide into pairs, and have the partners link elbows and form a circle of pairs with at least four feet separating each pair from another. Then choose one person to be the "chaser" and another to be the "chasee." The chaser attempts to tag the chasee while running inside, outside, and weaving through the circle of pairs. The chasee, anytime he wants to, can "pull into the pits" by grabbing the free elbow of one of the pairs. Doing so makes the chasee safe and takes him out of the chase and makes the person on the other side of the one whose elbow he grabbed the chasee. If the chasee is tagged, he becomes the chaser and the chaser becomes the chasee. *Marshall Shelley*

Paper Shoot

Divide into teams of four to eight kids each. Set a garbage can up in the middle of the room (about three feet high), and prepare ahead of time several paper batons and a lot of wadded up paper balls. Use masking tape to create a circle around the can about

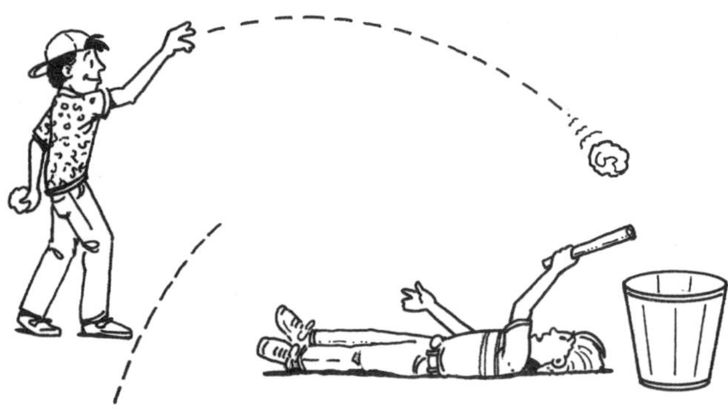

10 feet away. One team lies down on their backs around the trash can with their heads toward the can. Each of these players has a paper baton. The opposing team stands around the trash can behind the line and tries to throw wadded up paper balls into the can, while the defending team tries to knock the balls away with their paper batons. The opposing team gets two minutes to try to shoot as much paper into the can as possible. After each team has had its chance to be in both positions, the team that got the most paper balls into the can is declared the winner. To make the game a bit more difficult for the throwers, have them sit in chairs while they toss the paper. *Jeff Dietrich*

Number Numbness

As soon as the group arrives, tell them that you have hidden around your church or meeting area 20 sheets of paper, each with a number on it—the numbers ranging from 1 to 20. All the numbers have been taped in plain sight—if you are lying under a pew, that is, or sitting in the last row of the balcony.

Divide students into two or three teams (or let them search as a single cooperative group) and send them out with a 10-minute time limit (time should vary depending on how many numbers, kids, and the size of the hiding area). Numbers can be taped on rolls of TP, on the ceiling, in a drawer—the stranger the place, the better. The winner is the team with the most points (the 1 is worth 1 point, the 20 is worth 20), so they won't know till they all get back together who won. *Ed Baker*

Pillow Balance Beam Blast

Take an old railroad tie or make your own narrow, raised playing area. The two players stand at either end of the beam. Each is given a pillow. At the signal "Go!" they try to knock their opponent off the beam. The first one to touch the floor loses. However, the winner must remain standing after the other person falls. *Ron Wells*

Rattlesnake

For this game of stealth and skill, you will need two blindfolds, a small plastic bottle (a prescription bottle or empty film container works fine) with a rock in it, and a defined area for play. This can be done on large mats (of the wrestling variety) or on a carpeted floor. The referee blindfolds two people. One is designated the rattlesnake and given the bottle, and the other is the hunter. The hunter is spun in circles several times so he loses his sense of direction. We are now ready to begin play. It is essential that everyone remains absolutely quiet (everyone not playing is seated around the edges of the playing area). The referee says, "Rattlesnake." The rattlesnake must shake his rattler and then try to escape capture by the hunter. The game continues with the referee periodically saying rattlesnake until the hunter captures the rattlesnake. *Ron Wells*

SHUFFLE YOUR BUNS

Arrange chairs in a circle so that everyone has a chair. There should be two extra chairs in the circle. Each person sits in a chair except for two people in the middle who try to sit in the two vacant chairs. The persons sitting in the chairs keep moving around from chair to chair to prevent the two in the middle from sitting down. If one or both of the two in the middle manage to sit in a chair, the person on their right replaces them in the middle of the circle and then tries to sit in an empty chair.

• **Double Shuffle Toss.** In this variation, as players shuffle from chair to chair, they also pass or throw a rolled towel to anyone in the circle. If one of the two "Its" in the middle intercepts the towel, she trades places with the one who threw it. They also trade places if a middle person tags the player holding the towel.

For larger groups, add more people in the middle, more towels, and more empty chairs. *Scott Eynon and Mary McKemy*

STACK 'EM UP

Have everyone sit in chairs in a circle. Prepare a list of qualifying characteristics such as those found in the "Sit down if you..." elimination game. Here are a few examples:

- If you forgot to use a deodorant today . . .
- If you got a traffic ticket this year . . .
- If you have a hole in your sock . . .
- If you are afraid of the dark . . .

Then read them one at a time, adding " ...move three chairs to the right" or "...move one chair to the left," etc. All those who qualify—that is, all who forgot to use deodorant, or who got a traffic ticket this year—move as instructed and sit in that chair, regardless of whether or not it's occupied by one or more persons. Sure enough, as the game progresses, kids begin stacking up on chairs. *Mary McKemy*

STICK IT

Here's a game of skill that can be played by as few as two people. You need the following items: two light ropes (cords or string) about 10 feet long, several dowels (round sticks) about 12 inches long, a box big enough for the dowels to go in, a chair, and a lectern (speaker stand) or something similar.

Tack the two cords to the lectern two inches apart and stretch the ropes back to the chair, 10 feet away. One person stands on the chair and holds the ropes. The box is placed approximately two-thirds of the way from the chair under the ropes. A second player places the dowels (one at a time) on the two ropes at the holder's hands, and the holder tries to roll the dowel down the ropes and then dump it into the box. If he fails, he must try again. Players can be timed (best time to get them all in) or two can be going at once for a good race. For team relays, each person gets a dowel, and they must all get their dowels in the box.

After you're done with the dowels, give them to the children's department to be used as rhythm sticks or for rolling out clay. *Dave Gilliam*

SKUNK

This is a game of strength and agility. You need a defined padded area, either a carpeted floor or a large mat. In the center of the playing area, a skunk skin is placed (be creative with your substitutes!). The two players stand on either side of the skunk skin and lock arms over the skin. At a signal, each tries to force the other to touch the skunk skin with some part of their body. The first one to touch the skin loses. Have the other people sit around the playing area to keep the sprawling players on the mat. *Ron Wells*

SOUND-OFF

Divide into two teams (or as many teams as you can equip with the following items) and give each team access to a TV/VCR, a cartoon on videocassette, an audiocassette deck, and a blank audiocassette tape.

Now let each team record its own homemade soundtrack (recorded on the audiocassette deck) to the cartoon. Any sound effects, music, or dialogue can be used. Allow 20 minutes for this, then have the teams show their videos with sound. The results are a lot of fun. *Chuck Prestwood*

TURTLE RACE

Cut a number of turtle shapes out of thin plywood similar to the diagram below. Make sure that all the shapes are identical. Drill a hole in the neck. Thread a heavy string through the hole and tie one end to a fixed object.

When the string is pulled upward, the turtle lifts up and scoots forward. The legs must always stay touching the floor. The higher the turtle is lifted, the further it will scoot. But look out! You're liable to flip him over and lose ground while your opponents are in hot pursuit. For relays, have someone at each end of the string (one holding and one pulling). When the turtle reaches a certain finish line, flip him over and the other teammate takes him back. This game is great with all age groups. *Tracy Guthrie*

TARGET PRACTICE

Place a table against a wall. On the table place many "targets" made from paper folded in half. These targets should be various sizes from two inches to about six inches. Put point values on each one (10, 25, 50, 100) depending on how big the target is. Each team gets an "arsenal" of rubber bands and tries to shoot as many targets over in one minute as possible. All players must stand behind a line 15 feet (or so) away from the table. Points are scored each time a target is knocked over. The team with the most points wins. *J.C. Heneisen*

TOILET PAPER RACE

Students race to see who can unroll a roll of toilet paper by pushing it along the ground with their noses. The first person to unroll the entire roll or cross the finish line wins. For a switch, have other contestants do it in reverse, that is, roll it back up in the fastest time. *Andy Hansen*

TRUST TAG

This is the usual game of tag, except that the players play in partners or groups of two. One partner must wear a blindfold while his teammate must guide him by keeping his hands on his blindfolded partner's waist and shouting out directions. The object is for the blindfolded player to tag another blindfolded player. To make it even more difficult, the un-blindfolded player must give his partner directions without talking, just pushing or pulling him around. *Dick Babington*

TRIANGLE TAG

Have kids gather into groups of four. Three of them should form a triangle by holding hands or wrists. The fourth person stands in the middle of the triangle.

Choose one group to be "It." A successful tag occurs only when the person in the middle of a triangle tags another middler. The trick, of course, is for the triangle to track with their middler, to anticipate his or her direction and strategy—or at least to hear the middler's verbal instructions. The other groups, of course, try to avoid being tagged while staying inside the boundaries.

Every few games rotate members within their group, so everyone gets a turn inside the triangle. (Besides being fun Triangle Tag can effectively introduce sessions about submission, humility, and cooperation.) *Alan Rathbun*

Lightning Snake Tag

Play in a pitch-black room with periodic, strobe-like flashes of light.

Empty a large room of all obstacles and cover all possible sources of light with cardboard, rugs, heavy tape, or whatever else is required to completely darken the room. Make it really dark. Get a camera with a flash and fresh batteries (no film is needed).

Place one student—the seeker—in a brightly lit room while the remaining players scatter in the dark room. Bring the seeker into the dark room to tag whomever she can locate. Once tagged, players join hands with the seeker to make an ever-growing snake.

Every 30 seconds or so, flash the camera to help the seeker. The last person to be caught wins. *Matt Klein*

Slap Slap

Height, weight, and sex are not factors to win this game. Simply have two players face each other and raise their hands above their shoulders and then match hands. A distance of 18 to 36 inches may separate the players, but as the players match hands, they should be able to push each other's hands and arms back and forth comfortably (always above the shoulders). At a signal the players attempt to slap or push the other's hands so as to force the other off balance. The first person to lose his balance or move either foot gives way to another challenger, with the winner staying in. *Ron Erber*

Static Snow

For a hysterical fun activity, have your youth group get together in a small room. In advance, buy several large bags of white Styrofoam beads and funnel them into a vacuum cleaner. Then hook the hose on so the vacuum cleaner blows. (Be sure to run a test blow before adding the Styrofoam beads or you will blow dust over everyone.) Turn on the machine and spray the beads all over the room. The feather weight beads become charged with static electricity and stick to everything and everyone. They are difficult to clean up, but the effect is worth it. For a little more excitement, you might turn all the lights out so that the kids have no idea what is being sprayed on them. *Chip Sutton*

Bottle Ball

Here's a group game that can be played indoors or out. The ideal number of players for this game is five on each side, but it can be adapted for more. Make distinguishable boundaries similar to a soccer field, approximately 60 feet by 30 feet, with a center line. Place large plastic bottles about 18 inches apart along both ends of the playing area. Then put the teams on the field: three guards along the back to guard the bottles and two throwers along their side of the center line:

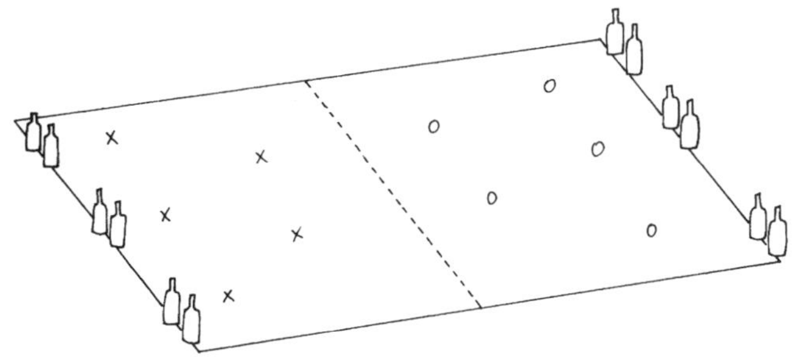

The throwers try to shoot a medium-size Nerf basketball (or another soft-type ball) through the opposite side at the opponents bottles. Players foul when they step over the center line. The scoring goes like this: five points for each bottle knocked down, 10 points for each shot that goes between the bottles, and one point for each shot rolling over the back boundary line.

You could also divide your group into four, six, or eight different teams and have a tournament. *J. Russell Matzke*

Swinger

This is a great game for all ages and is a lot of fun to watch as well as play. Take a small (15 inches) drain plunger handle and put a plunger on each end. Then attach 12 to 15 inches of string to a small jack ball with a straight pin. Tie the loose end of the string to the middle of the handle so the ball and string hang from the center.

Have pairs stand face-to-face with the rubber plungers resting on their foreheads and their hands behind their backs. With only body movement, the pair has to start the ball swinging and try to flip it over the handle. Time each pair with the winning pair having the shortest time. You might want to set a maximum time in case some just can't get it. *Vernon R. Red, Jr.*

Trade-In Poster Puzzle

Take as many posters as you have teams and cut them up into various jigsaw puzzle pieces. Mix all the pieces up together and put them in a bag. The competition begins by giving each person one piece of poster puzzle. At the signal each team tries to be the first to construct one poster.

Eventually each team will see that they have pieces of posters that they're *not* trying to piece together, and so will need to trade pieces to complete the puzzle. The teams can then trade pieces, one for one. If there are leftover poster pieces, pass them out randomly to teams a few minutes into the game. *Harvey Wilkie*

Crumbling Pyramids

Divide your youths into teams of six. On a signal each team must form a pyramid and complete a given task. The first team to complete the task receives points. After each task the teams must dismantle and wait for the signal to begin a new task. A list of tasks follows. If you make up your own, scale your points according to the number in the pyramid involved in the action.

- **Form a pyramid and say "The Pledge of Allegiance" in unison. (60 points)**
- **The bottom person in the middle must take off his shoes. (20 points)**
- **The two people on the second level must turn completely around. (40 points)**
- **The person on the second level on the left must turn around. (20 points)**
- **The bottom person in the middle must turn around. (20 points)**
- **The whole team turns around in a circle (only the bottom three have to move). (60 points)**

Andy Strachan

Dice Grab

To play this game, you will need to buy some oversized dice at a game or stationery store. Or, if you want to make your own, cut two small blocks of wood into 1¼-inch cubes. Sand and paint them if you wish, then mark them with dots similar to a pair of dice.

Mark a two-foot diameter circle with chalk on the floor, on a rug, or on the top of a card table. One person starts the game by rolling the dice toward the center and simultaneously calling out any single number between two and 12. If the dots total the number called, all may grab for them. Each die is worth one point on the grab and the scramble may continue out of the circle or off the table.

The game becomes more exciting as the time between throws is cut down. The roller continues until the number he calls is thrown, then he passes the dice to an adjacent player. A game is usually won when someone earns 11 points. *Bud Moon*

Down the Drain

For this game you'll need to get quite a few of those plastic tubes found in most golf club bags that protect the clubs. You can probably borrow these from someone, as the game won't damage them.

Divide the group into two equal teams. Each team gets half the tubes, or one for each player. The teams line up and the players hold the tubes end to end, using their hands to secure the joints.

At the beginning of each line, the team leaders or sponsors simultaneously place a marble in the end of the first tube. The object is for each team to move the marble down all the tubes and out the other end. The team that is the first to do this is the winner. If the marble slips through one of the joints and falls onto the floor, the team is disqualified. Once the kids get the hang of it, they should be able to do it rather smoothly. There is some strategy involved, however, and the kids will really enjoy the challenge.

To make the game go a little longer, go for best two out of three, or give each team 10 marbles to send down the drain. Only one marble is allowed in the drain at a time. Somebody should be assigned to catch the marbles when they come out. *E. Parke Brown*

ELECTRIC FENCE

For this game you need two poles and a piece of rope or string. The rope is tied between the two poles, about two feet off the floor to begin.

Divide into teams. The object of the game is for the entire team to get over the electric fence (the rope) without getting electrocuted (touching the rope). Each team takes a turn, with team members going one at a time.

After each successful try, the rope is raised a little higher, as in regular high jump competition. Eventually, teams will be eliminated as they find the rope too high to get over.

What makes this game interesting is that even though one player goes over the rope at a time, the other team members can help any way they want. Once a person is over the fence, however, she must stay over the fence and not come back around to help anyone. So the last person each time must somehow get over the fence without help on one side. This game requires lots of teamwork.

Teams can be eliminated entirely if one person touches the fence, or you can eliminate individual members only as the rope gets higher and higher. Make sure your teams are evenly divided according to height, age, and sex. *Jim Bowes*

HAND OVER HAND

Divide your group into two or more teams of five or more participants. Each team forms a circle and everyone holds his right hand in the middle of the circle. Have kids stack their hands basketball-huddle style. Then have them place their left hands in the circle in the same manner so that left hands are stacked on top of the right hand stack. At the signal, the person whose hand is on the bottom should take that hand and place it on top of the stack. The next person should do the same, and so on until the person who began the process is again on the bottom. The first team to complete this process is winner of round #1. For the next round try three laps. Then try five. After everyone is getting the hang of it, try going backward. *Ben Sharpton*

HUMAN TIC-TAC-TOE

As suggested by its title, this game is played just as it is on paper, except that people are used. It is very active and great for smaller groups. To play, set up nine chairs in three rows of three. Team One stands on one side of the chairs and Team Two on the other. Players on each team then number off 1, 2, 3, 4, and so on.

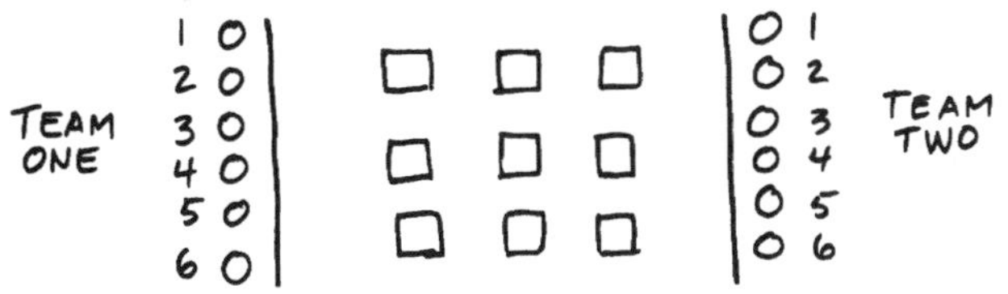

TEAM ONE 1 2 3 4 5 6 — TEAM TWO 1 2 3 4 5 6

When the leader calls out a number (four, for example), the two fours on each team scramble to sit down on any two chairs as quickly as they can. When they are seated, another number is called, and the same thing happens, until three teammates from either team have successfully scored a tic-tac-toe by sitting in a row of three, either up, down, or diagonally. If no tic-tac-toe is made, then the players return to their teams and the game is played again.

A variation of this would be to play with 10 people per game (5 on a team). They all take a seat in one of the nine chairs, leaving one person without a seat. When the whistle is blown, everyone must get up and move to a different chair, while the extra person tries to sit down somewhere. After the mad scramble for seats, the game is scored like tic-tac-toe. Any row of three people from the same team gets points. In each round, there will always be one person left without a seat.

An even crazier way to play this game would be to play as described above, but use guys on their hands and knees as chairs and the girls from each team sit on the guys' backs. When the whistle is blown, they try to sit on the guys' backs and try to hang on even when another girl tries to pull or push her off. It's really wild. Whether you use chairs, guys, lines on the floor (like real tic-tac-toe), or whatever, it's a lot of fun to play. *Glenn Davis*

Knock Your Socks Off

This is a survival of the fittest game. It's probably best if males and females in your group play separate rounds.

Draw a big circle on the floor. All the players get in the circle with no shoes, only socks. The object is to take off other player's socks and keep yours on. Once your socks are gone, you are out of the game. If any part of your body goes outside the circle, you are also out. The last person to remain in the circle with her socks on is the winner. *Glenn Davis*

Inversion

This game requires a great deal of teamwork. It can be played as a competitive game (teams compete against each other) or as a cooperative game (everyone is on the same team).

Draw two parallel lines on the floor, about 18 inches apart. The team lines up inside those two lines. They number off 1, 2, 3, 4, and so on from one end of the line to the other.

On a signal, they must reverse their order without stepping outside those two parallel lines. If there are 20 people on the team, then player number 1 must change places with player number 20, and so on. Only the person in the middle stays in the same place.

Let the teams practice this once and come up with a strategy for doing it quickly and accurately. Then compete against the clock (try to set a world record), or see which team can do it in the quickest time. It's a lot of fun to watch. Referees can penalize a team (in seconds lost) any time a person steps outside one of the two lines. *James Bowes*

Mini Grand Prix

If someone in your group has one or two of those radio-controlled toy cars, see if you can borrow them for this game. Set up a Grand Prix course around the room (be creative) and have the kids take turns to see who can maneuver the car around the track in the fastest time. Have a stopwatch handy and deduct seconds for knocking over objects, leaving the course, etc. Some kids will really get into this. *Jim Walton*

Terrible Twos

Here is a fast competitive game that can be organized in just a few minutes using ordinary household items. Locate about 30 or 40 pairs of things (like two shoes, two hammers, two books, two CDs, two bars of soap, two toothbrushes, etc.). Add several items as well that have no mate. Put all this stuff into a big box or into a big pile. Mix it all up. Then divide your group into two teams. Each team should be an equal distance from the pile or box. If this game is played indoors, it would be good to locate the pile of stuff in a separate room.

On "Go!" each team sends a player to the pile or box of stuff. That player returns to his team with one item from the stockpile. Each successive team member does the same thing in turn, taking care not to return with the mate of an item. The kids race through their lineup as many times as possible within a set time limit, bringing back as many items as they can.

If someone accidentally returns to the team with a mate, the next runner must return it to the pile and cannot take a new item back to the team on that turn. If the item is not spotted right away as a duplicate item and thrown into the team's stockpile, it will count against the team when points are added up at the end of the game. When the whistle blows (just before the stockpile is depleted) points for each team are awarded as follows:

- Each item is worth 10 points.
- Each item with no mate is worth 50 more points.
- Each pair of objects stockpiled by the same team is worth minus 50 points per item (100 total minus points per pair).

For experienced players, have each team's stockpile be a large box that items are dropped into (out of sight). This means that the kids must memorize each item as it goes in, and it increases the likelihood of ending up the game with more duplicate items in the box. Another way to add difficulty to the game is to make the pairs of items not identical to each other, but still creating a pair. For example, you might have a toothbrush and toothpaste, a hammer and a nail, a cup and saucer, etc. *Rob Moritz*

MUSICAL COSTUMES

Here is a funny game that allows everyone to look a little silly. Before you start, have a laundry bag or pillowcase filled with various articles of clothing—funny hats, baggy pants, gloves, belts, or anything that can be worn. (The leader can use her own discretion as to how embarrassing the items are.) Keep the bag tied shut so the clothing will not spill out.

Have your group start passing the bag around as music is played. If you don't use music, use a whistle, egg timer, or the like to stop the action. When the music stops, the person holding the bag must reach in and take out an article without looking at it. Then he must put it on and wear it for the remainder of the game. Try to have enough so that each person gets three or four funny articles of clothing. This can lend itself to seasonal clothing (Santa's bag, Easter parade, etc.). It may also be a fun way to create an instant costume for a Halloween party. After the game you can have a fashion show or take pictures to hang up on the group bulletin board. *Paul L. Fuqua*

PAPER BADMINTON

This variation of badminton can be played indoors. The racquet is made of a sheet of ordinary 8½x11 paper. Old church bulletins work fine. Fold the sheet in half and staple along two edges. Naturally, the thicker the paper, the stronger the racquet. Each player's hand goes inside the paper, sort of like a glove.

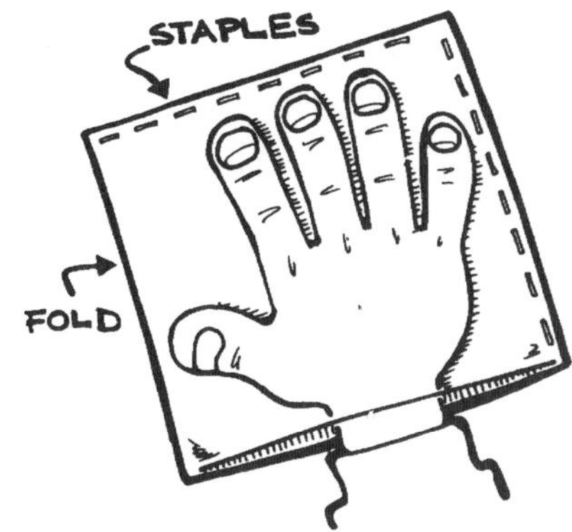

The net is a real one, and the birdie is a regular shuttlecock (or you can use a wad of paper). Play by whatever rules you wish: badminton, volleyball, or all-out war. *Keith Curran*

SHOE THE DONKEY

This game can be played indoors or outdoors. The only equipment needed is two chairs, eight shoes, and two blindfolds. Two chairs are set up in the middle of the area. These are the donkeys. Then two kids are blindfolded and seated on the donkeys. At least four kids donate their shoes and scatter them around the chairs. The object of the game is for the two players to locate and place a shoe on each leg of their donkey. The first one to shoe his or her donkey successfully is the winner.

To add excitement to the game, the players may be allowed to steal the shoes already placed on each other's donkey. This game guarantees squeals of laughter! *Cheri Brent*

CROUTON TOSS

Play this only if you designate a cleanup committee first! Kids sit in two rows, facing each other. Partners are opposite each other. Everyone has a Baggie of croutons—about a handful—and on "Go!" they throw their croutons into their partners' mouths, while at the same time catching—in their mouths—the croutons their partners throw. First pair whose Baggies are empty—and who have more croutons in them than on the floor—wins free salad at the next restaurant outing. *Randy Trotter*

Group Juggle

This circle game is something like hot potato, with a dash of Concentration. Throw a ball to one person in a standing circle of kids. That person throws it to another, and so on until everyone has received and thrown the ball once—but exactly once. No one should get the ball a second time, which means each player needs to remember where the ball's been. If your group's frustration threshold is high, increase the speed of the game and add more balls. *Tom Jackson*

Toilet Bowl

Sequel to the cereal bowl and the Super Bowl, Toilet Bowl requires minimal set-up. Construct one or two toilet seat-and-lid combinations from heavy cardboard (better yet, use real toilet seats), prop them open so that the open lids serve as backboards, distribute a Scotch-taped roll of toilet paper (the football) to each team, and make up some simple rules. The object of the game is to toss the toilet-paper football into the toilet.

Or make it a basketball free-throw game in tournament fashion, letting teams chart their advance to the Final Four and beyond. *E. Parke Brown*

Banana Duel

Team up your kids in pairs, have partners clasp their left hands, then tie those hands together. Give each player a banana with these instructions: they are to peel the banana any way they can (usually with teeth and right hands) before cramming it into their partner's mouth.

If your playing area can take the inevitable mess, enliven the game by blindfolding some or all the players. *Garr Williams, Jr.*

Epidermal Plunge

Choose male contestants who are more than just skin and bones. Each of them must suction a clean toilet plunger to his stomach; the guy who does the most jumping jacks before the plunger falls off wins. Award medals made of various-sized sink stoppers strung on colored ribbons. Contestants are sure to be flushed after this strenuous game. *Jim Johnson*

Back to School Shuffle

Form teams of eight students. Provide each team with a locker filled with items representing different classes in school: globe or map (history); calculator (math); gym clothes or tennis racket (P.E.); hammer (woodshop); paperback novel (English); protective goggles, beaker, or copy of the periodic table (chemistry); spatula or oven mitt (home economics); rubber nightcrawler (biology); sheet music (choir); brown bag or baloney sandwich in a Baggie (lunch); etc. Add other class subjects as desired.

Use the schedule provided on page 83 to make a transparency (for an overhead projector), or you can write your own schedules on a flip chart. Reveal the schedules one at a time: as you uncover each schedule, team members must rush to their locker, retrieve the correct items, return to the starting point, and line up in the correct order. The first team to do so wins the round.

Team members lining up out of order are sent to detention and sit out a round. Offer each person on the winning team a small or silly prize—an apple, eraser, folder, etc. *Dennis Leggett*

Tardy Trap

Here's a great game that is well worth the effort required to set it up. It's played like a board game in that players move from one space to the next, competing to be the first to arrive at the final destination.

You can lay out the game on the floor (as page 84 illustrates) using half-inch masking tape. Two rolls of tape should be enough. Use colored tape to indicate the red (vertical stripes on the diagram) and yellow (spotted squares on the diagram) penalty

Back to School Shufffle

Period
1 History
2 math
3 P.E.
4 woodshop
lunch
5 English
6 choir
7 Spanish

Period
1 band
2 history
3 biology
4 chemistry
lunch
5 home ec.
6 English
7 P.E.

Period
1 P.E.
2 English
3 home ec.
4 chemistry
lunch
5 math
6 history
7 band

Period
1 home ec.
2 English
3 P.E.
4 choir
lunch
5 Spanish
6 math
7 history

Period
1 woodshop
2 English
3 choir
4 Spanish
lunch
5 P.E.
6 biology
7 history

Period
1 band
2 history
3 biology
4 P.E.
lunch
5 English
6 chemistry
7 woodshop

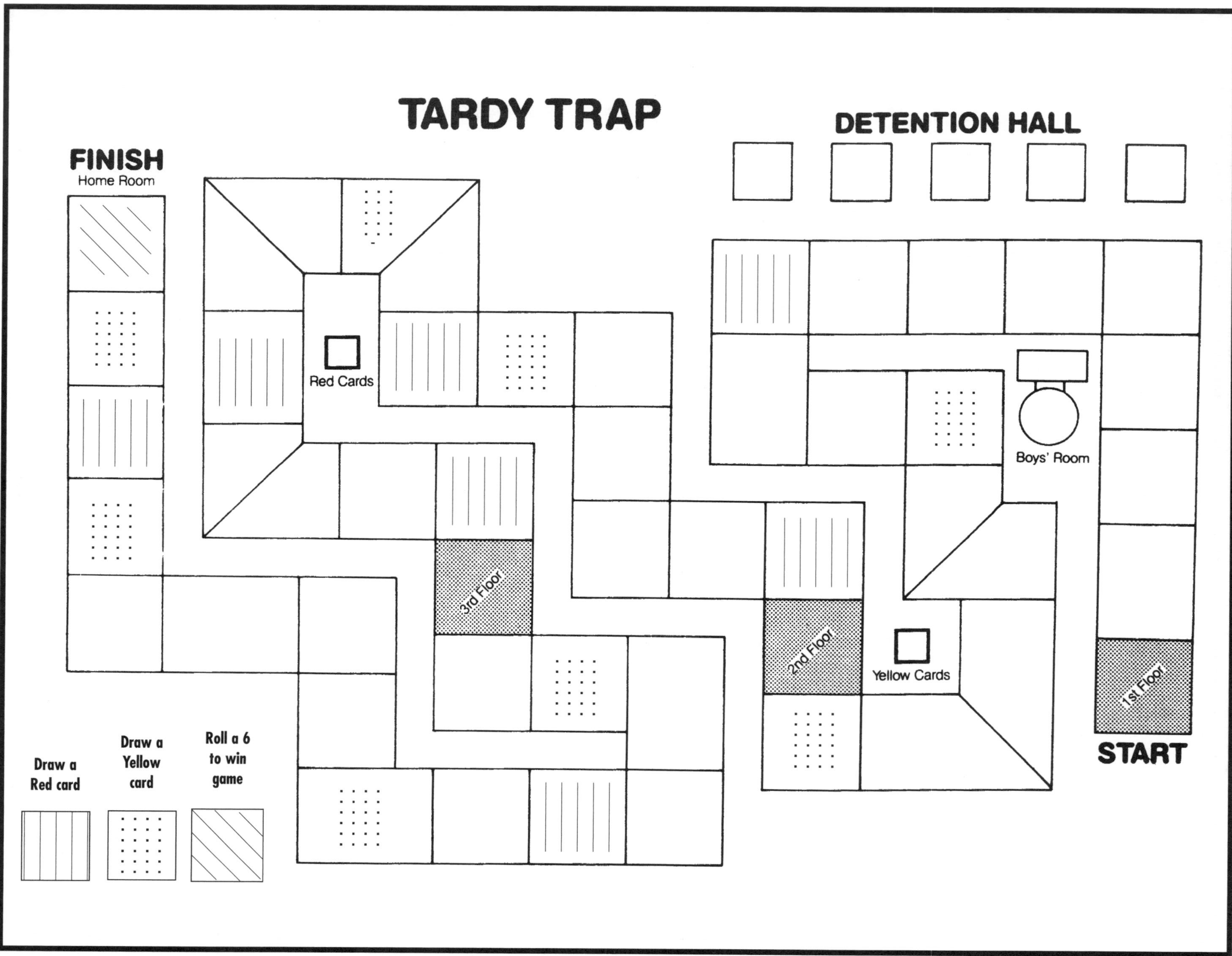
TARDY TRAP
DETENTION HALL
FINISH
Home Room
Red Cards
3rd Floor
Boys' Room
2nd Floor
Yellow Cards
1st Floor
START
Draw a Red card
Draw a Yellow card
Roll a 6 to win game

TARDY TRAP GAME CARDS

RED

The principal is waiting for you at the door! **YOU'RE CAUGHT! GO TO DETENTION HALL.**

Sharky Johnson deals in counterfeit hall passes. Meet him in Boys' Room. **LOSE ONE TURN! GO TO THE BOYS' ROOM.**

You were just spotted by a Hall Monitor, but you play it cool and show him your counterfeit hall pass. Does he believe you? **ARE YOU KIDDING? GO TO DETENTION HALL.**

BLAME SOMEONE ELSE–Mrs. Aulfulitch, the Home Ec. teacher, caught you in the hall. She demands your name for Detention Hall. You give her someone else's. **BLAME SOMEONE! SEND THEM TO D.H. FOR ONE TURN.**

Elmo Nerdo sees you sneaking around in the hall. He has a hall pass, but you don't and he knows it, 'cause he knows everything and reports you to the principal. **YOU'RE CAUGHT! GO TO DETENTION HALL.**

You were just spotted by a Hall Monitor, but you play it cool and show him your counterfeit pass. Will he pass you?! **YES, BUT...THE PASS IS FOR THE BOYS' ROOM.**

You were just spotted by the Hall Monitor, but you play it cool and show her your counterfeit pass. Will she pass you? **YES!! YOU LUCKY DOG!**

A Hall Monitor suddenly pops out of nowhere. The only place to hide is the Boys' Room. **LOSE ONE TURN! GO TO THE BOYS' ROOM.**

The Hall Monitor was hiding in a locker! **YOU'RE CAUGHT! GO TO DETENTION HALL.**

You hear footsteps coming, so you quickly jump into a locker. It was only the janitor, but the locker locked and you're stuck! **LOSE ONE TURN!**

TARDY TRAP GAME CARDS

YELLOW

GO TO THE NEAREST STARTING FLOOR	MOVE BACK 2 BLOCKS
MOVE BACK 3 BLOCKS	GO BACK TO YOUR STARTING FLOOR BLOCK
GO BACK 3 BLOCKS	GO BACK 2 BLOCKS
GO BACK 1 BLOCK	GO FORWARD 3 BLOCKS
GO FORWARD 2 BLOCKS	GO TO THE NEAREST RED BLOCK

TARDY Trap
The game

Your Situation: As usual, you are late for school. The situation is desperate—one more tardy slip, and you're on detention. Fortunately for you, your homeroom teacher is Mrs. Ima Blindbatt, who wears glasses made from Coke bottle bottoms. If you can get to homeroom without getting caught, you'll be safe. Unfortunately, getting to homeroom is not all that easy because it's on the third floor at the far end of the building. Each floor is infested with tattletale, nerdo hall monitors (seeking whom they may devour), and sadistic detention-crazed teachers (who slap detention slips on roaches if they're caught in the halls during class period).

But you've got a fighting chance. You can hide in lockers, purchase counterfeit hall passes, and find refuge in the Boys' Room. Be careful, though, because just when you think it's safe to go back into the hall…

The Rules:

- Each player moves forward by the roll of the dice.
- As a player lands on the red or yellow mark, he must do as indicated by the corresponding game card.
- To get out of Detention Hall, you must roll an even number on your turn, up to three turns. Three detentions and you're out of the game.
- If another player is sent to the Boys' Room while you are occupying that position, you are automatically "relieved" and may go back to the starting floor you left.
- Two players cannot occupy the same space (except for the = sign just before entering homeroom). If a player lands on a space already occupied, a pillow duel decides who stays. The loser must go back to the starting floor. The duel is fought by two players standing on only one leg, holding the other leg off the ground with one hand, and wielding the pillow with the other hand. The winner is the first one to make his or her opponent lose balance and fall over.
- To enter homeroom, you must roll a 6 on your die.

TARDY Trap
The game

Your Situation: As usual, you are late for school. The situation is desperate—one more tardy slip, and you're on detention. Fortunately for you, your homeroom teacher is Mrs. Ima Blindbatt, who wears glasses made from Coke bottle bottoms. If you can get to homeroom without getting caught, you'll be safe. Unfortunately, getting to homeroom is not all that easy because it's on the third floor at the far end of the building. Each floor is infested with tattletale, nerdo hall monitors (seeking whom they may devour), and sadistic detention-crazed teachers (who slap detention slips on roaches if they're caught in the halls during class period).

But you've got a fighting chance. You can hide in lockers, purchase counterfeit hall passes, and find refuge in the Boys' Room. Be careful, though, because just when you think it's safe to go back into the hall…

The Rules:

- Each player moves forward by the roll of the dice.
- As a player lands on the red or yellow mark, he must do as indicated by the corresponding game card.
- To get out of Detention Hall, you must roll an even number on your turn, up to three turns. Three detentions and you're out of the game.
- If another player is sent to the Boys' Room while you are occupying that position, you are automatically "relieved" and may go back to the starting floor you left.
- Two players cannot occupy the same space (except for the = sign just before entering homeroom). If a player lands on a space already occupied, a pillow duel decides who stays. The loser must go back to the starting floor. The duel is fought by two players standing on only one leg, holding the other leg off the ground with one hand, and wielding the pillow with the other hand. The winner is the first one to make his or her opponent lose balance and fall over.
- To enter homeroom, you must roll a 6 on your die.

marks. The die or dice can be made from a square box painted white with black dots or from foam rubber. Some toy stores sell oversized dice.

For the "Boys' Room," find an old toilet that the kids must sit on. (It's really funny to see the kids' reactions when they're sent to the Boys' Room.) You'll also need to provide pillows for the duel that is required when two players are occupying the same space.

You'll need to photocopy and cut out the game cards on pages 85-86. On page 87 is a master of the rules for you to photocopy and distribute to your students. *Dale DeNeal*

GARGLE A TUNE

Give everyone a small paper cup full of water and instruct them to gargle several different tunes on command ("Mary Had a Little Lamb," "Jingle Bells," "Row, Row, Row Your Boat," and so on). Make a contest to see who can guess what tune a person (or small group of people) is gargling. Have plenty of towels handy to clean up the mess that is sure to be made on this one. *Michael Capps*

GO FLY A KITE!

For a March fling any time of year, bring a window fan and some yarn, and ask the kids to bring materials to make kites—paper, straws, Popsicle sticks, glue, Scotch tape. Announce a kite-flying contest, but tell everyone to bring what they need to make a kite. (Don't let them bring already-made kites.) The ones the group will fly must be several times smaller than regular kites because they'll be flown with the help of the yarn and the window fan.

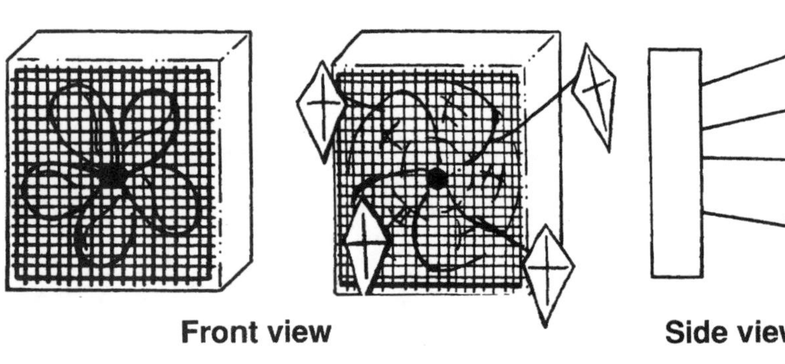

Front view

Side view

Give the kids a set time to create small kites, using whatever materials they wish, just so long as the kite can stay up whenever the fan is blown at full blast (see diagram).

The best kites are those made in the traditional diamond shape. After everyone has made a kite, begin tying them to the fan one at a time with about three to four feet of yarn (shorter lengths if the yarn is heavy), and turn the fan on full blast, facing away from the house or into the center of the room. Add more kites and see how many you can fly without tangling them up together. This activity works well with a small youth group or study group. *Michael Capps*

KOOL-AID TASTE-OFF

Ask three volunteers to sit in chairs facing the rest of the group. On a signal they each open a different flavored packet of Kool-Aid. Volunteers then lick just one finger and dip it into the packet. The person who in that manner can eat all of the Kool-Aid in the packet first wins. It's hilarious because they do not anticipate it being so sour, and they usually end up with it all over their lips. *Amy Zuberbuhler*

LETTER SEARCH

Do you want to impress on your kids a key word or short phrase in an upcoming study or lesson? Write the word, letter by letter, on inch squares of paper. Then tape these squares in obscure places in the building—under the fire extinguisher, on the doorknob to the pastor's office, etc.

When the meeting begins, give each of the teens a pencil and 3x5-inch card—then tell them that they're looking for a word, the letters of which are scattered throughout the building. Tell them also the specific number of letters they're looking for. After they've found all the letters, they must unscramble them to form a word or phrase—though they don't have to wait until they've found all the letters in order to take a guess at the word. Warn them to be subtle as they're hunting so they don't give away to others the location of letters they've already found.

Award two prizes: one for the student who finds the most letters, and one for the student who first figures out the word or phrase. *Howard B. Chapman*

Pew Crawl

Play this game in your church sanctuary—if you can get away with it. Divide into two teams (more if you have a large sanctuary with several sections of pews). Each team begins the game by standing behind the pew farthest from the front of the auditorium. Their team captain and a team referee is at the front of the auditorium.

On "Go!" each team captain randomly opens a hymnbook. The captains yell out the last digit on the right hand page, and all the team members hit the floor to crawl under that many pews before standing up again. Let's say a team captain opens to page 352 in the hymnal—he yells "Two!" and teammates must crawl under two pews, then stand up in front of the second pew (counting, remember, from the back). Moving toward the front of the sanctuary this way, the first team to reach the front wins the game.

A captain cannot yell out the next number until his or her entire team is standing up again in front of the correct pew. (No need to wait for the other team, however—this is a race!) As soon as the last member of a team is up, their captain yells out a new number, and the team hits the floor again, crawling as fast as they can.

The referees ensure that everyone abides by only two rules: The hymnbook must be opened randomly, and the entire team must be standing before the next number is called.

- **Pew Jump.** In this variation, all the contestants sit along the middle pew, equal distance from front and back. Give each one a penny, which they flip on signal. Whoever gets heads hops (or dives) forward a row; those with tails go back a row. Play continues in this way, as quickly as players want to move, but they must flip in order to move each time. Players who reach the back row must stay there until they flip a heads. The winner is the first one to reach the front row, and then get one more heads. *Larry Stoess and Randy Wheeler*

Pop Fly! Ground Ball!

The object of this indoor game for 25 or so players is to be the first of four teams to successfully throw or roll a colored Nerf ball among all its members and then back to the captain.

First arrange the chairs in a square, divide the group into four equal teams, and instruct members of each team to sit opposite their teammates—like this:

Next, give each team a different-colored Nerf ball. Volunteer one person on each team as captain; captains should sit at one of the ends of their team, and the four captains should sit at the same positions relative to their teams.

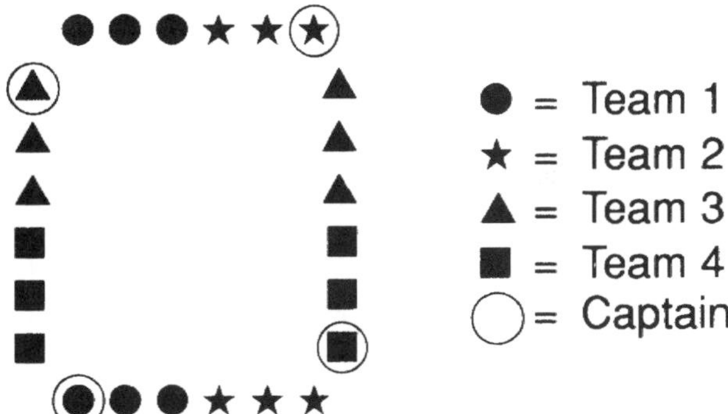

Here's how the game is played. Each captain tosses the team's Nerf ball across the square to a teammate opposite him. That player then tosses the ball back across the square to the player seated next to the captain—and so on.

You can imagine the delightful chaos of four teams of teenagers all trying to pass Nerf balls through the same confined area. The last person on the team to receive the ball tosses it back to the captain, after which everyone on that team stands up and yells—thus letting everyone else know they've finished.

Now here's what makes it fun: At any time the youth leader can yell "Ground ball!" At this signal all teams must immediately begin rolling their balls across the floor instead of throwing them. And when they hear "Pop fly!" they return to tossing the

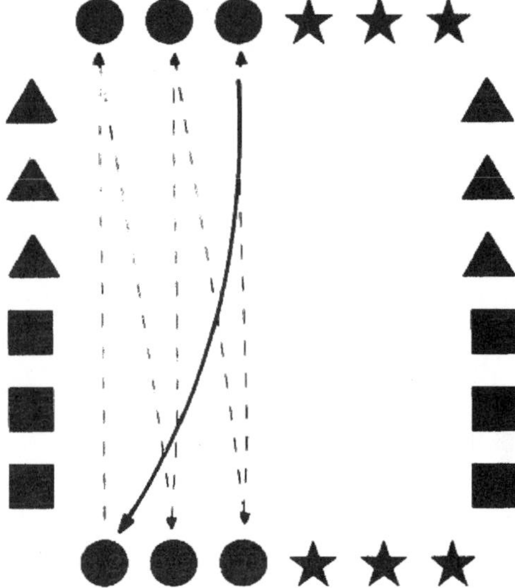

balls. It is legal for the leader to yell the same signal several times in succession—just to keep the kids guessing! *Michael W. Capps*

Shooting Gallery

Blindfold three or four adult leaders and give them kazoos, party noisemakers, or something similar. They are the "ducks" in this shooting gallery, moving back and forth and bobbing up and down behind a wall or board that's five feet high or so, making "duck" noises all the while.

From about 10 feet away, kids have five throws of a beach ball at the "ducks." Most hits wins; carnival-type prizes are appropriate. *John Krueger*

Q-Tip War

Divide your kids into two teams, separate them by a line down the middle of the room, give each team five or 10 Q-Tips per person and each person a straw—and open fire! The object for them is to blow-gun as many Q-Tips across the line onto the enemy's side of the room as possible before time runs out. Students can reload with Q-Tips shot over onto their side.

After the shooting ends, objective volunteers count the Q-Tips on each side, and the team with the lesser number wins. *Todd Ladd*

Four-Way Q-Tip War

After dividing your kids into two to four teams, give the groups several minutes to form walls by placing folding tables on their sides. Each team's bulwark should be within 15 to 20 feet of the other team's defenses. Give each player a drinking straw and each team an equal number of Q-Tips.

At the signal all teams use their straws to shoot Q-Tips over the tables to one of the other teams. You will truly be amazed at how far Q-Tips can travel this way! Teams should send their original pile of Q-Tips and also try to keep up with sending back those that are blown over their defensive wall. After five to 10 minutes, signal an end to the game. Count each team's pile of Q-Tips. The team with the fewest Q-Tips behind its bulwark is declared the winner. *Leif A. Ford*

Spitfire

Give each player a Styrofoam cup, a straw, and about 20 Q-Tips. Then pair off everyone.

Pairs sit facing each other with their Styrofoam cups on their heads. The aim of Spitfire is to shoot your partner's cup off his head by using the straw as a blowgun and the Q-Tips as ammunition.

You can score it any number of ways—for example, the winner can be one who shoots the cup off a partner's head the most times in one minute in the winner. Or play elimination-style until only one player is left. *Jim Ramos*

Super Combat Tape Heads

The object of this game is to stick as many Q-Tips to a volunteer as possible, with drinking straws as blow-guns.

Before the meeting gather the following:

- Hundreds of cotton swabs.
- Drinking straws for each player (straws from McDonald's work best).
- Wide masking tape—a roll at least two inches wide, one roll for each team.
- One pair of safety glasses for each team.
- A hat for each team.

Divide into teams of six to 12 players. Pick one victim per team to be the targets. Targets tuck their hair into a hat and put on the safety glasses. Teammates then wrap their targets thoroughly with masking tape, sticky side out. At this point distribute the straws and Q-Tips to the rest of the players, who then line up 10 feet away from the living targets. At a signal the kids start firing away, blowing the Q-Tips through the straws at their own team's target until time is called.

Award points as follows:

- 5 points for every Q-Tip stuck to the head
- 2 points for every Q-Tip stuck from the neck to the waist
- 1 point for every Q-Tip stuck from the waist down

Or try this more competitive variation. Shooters shoot at the other team's target, who is free to move to avoid getting hit. The team with the most hits on the enemy target wins. Each team may equip one member with safety goggles and a tennis racquet, with which he may defend his team's target. *Matt Klein*

In Your Face

- **Peanut-Butter Makeover.** Create several girl-guy pairs. Give the guys a large scoop of peanut butter (either crunchy or smooth works great). The race begins with the guys spreading the peanut butter all over their partners' faces.

When the Maybelline women are sufficiently made up, they get down on all fours and crawl along a line of large and lightweight objects (egg cartons, milk cartons, shoe boxes, paper plates, slices of bread, etc.) and pick up these objects with their peanut-buttery faces. The guys walk alongside with bags, into which the girls drop the objects.

Peanut butter, by the way, is said to work better than Crisco or Vaseline.

- **Dip and Stick.** Now it's the girls' turn. Each girl is given a pack of Lifesavers—the fruit-flavored ones, not the minty ones. On "Go!" each girl rips open her pack, then dips the Lifesavers in a glass of water and sticks them to her partner's face. If one falls off, she can pick it up and dip it and stick it on again. First pair to have the entire pack sticking to the guy's face wins. Or give teams a time limit; then if more than one pair gets their entire packs on the guys' faces, judge the winner by how long beyond the time limit the Lifesavers stay stuck to a face.

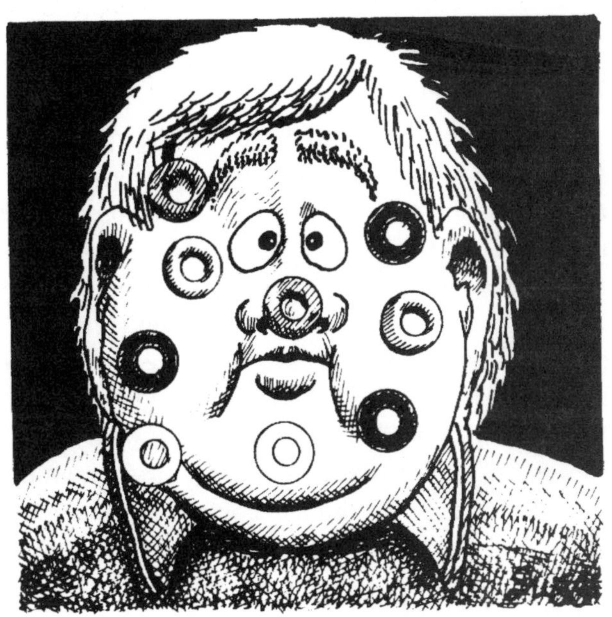

For ultimate stickiness, girls should put all the Lifesavers in the water at once, then pull them out to stick them on their partners' faces. *Steve Bridges and Rodney Oxford*

No-Fly Zone

Welcome to a battle between paper airplanes and Q-Tip missiles.

Set up one chair at each end of the room. Using masking tape, mark a large circle around each to establish the team's territory. Collect straws, cotton swabs such as Q-Tips, a pile of copier paper in two colors, and two pairs of safety glasses.

Give one color of copy paper to each team.

Have everyone make a paper airplane while you pass out one straw and one cotton swab to each player. Resupply the ammo after each airplane launch to avoid stray missile attacks on the adult leaders. Now for the game: Each team picks a player to sit in the chair to launch an airplane. All the other teens sit outside the tape-marked territory in the no-fly zone waiting to attack with their missile launchers and missiles. At the signal, the airplane is launched and the missiles are fired in an attempt to down the airplane before it lands in the opposing territory.

The first team that lands 10 planes within the circle wins.

Collect all the straws and cotton swabs after the game so you don't get shot during your talk. *Matt Klein*

RING TOSS

This is just like the traditional carnival game—except that students are the bottles (perhaps with traffic cones on their heads) and Hula Hoops are the rings. Arrange the game to fit your group or your event. Have teams of two take turns tossing the hoops over each other, after each toss taking a step backward to increase the distance between them. Or have students one at a time step up to a line and face a group of bottles, and give each thrower three tries to ring a peer (the bottles further away from the throwing line are worth more points). *Michael Capps*

TEAM NINTENDO

Borrow or rent a big screen TV and the latest Nintendo offering (or other computer game popular among your students) for two teams of kids to battle for the video-game championship.

Start the game with one person from each team at the controls and the rest of the team standing 10 feet behind the players. Players have 30 seconds at the controls—you manage the stopwatch—while their teams cheer them on. After 30 seconds the next two players run up to the controls and take over, hopefully without missing a shot. When all members of the teams have taken their turn playing, round one is over and the score is recorded.

Play as long as enthusiasm lasts and promise a stupendous prize to the team with the most points. *Jeff Koch*

PAPER AIRPLANE DERBY

Provide plenty of paper, paint, glue, and markers so that everyone can make a paper airplane. Give awards for the best looking airplane, the one that can fly the farthest, and the plane that stays in the air the longest.

PAPER SHUFFLE

Give each person two pieces of paper (newspaper works fine). At the starting line, players try to race to the finish line. However, they are only allowed to take a step when they step on their pieces of paper. So they must constantly pick the papers up and put them down as they make their way to the finish line (one step per piece of paper). Whoever reaches the finish line first with both papers intact wins.

BANANA RELAY

This is a good indoor relay game that requires very little space. Divide the group into four equal teams and arrange chairs in a square, each team being one side of the square. There is a chair in the center, but no one sits in it. The first player at the left end of his line is given a banana (the first player on each team). At the signal, the first player runs to the center around the center chair without touching it and back to the right end of his own line. In the meantime, all of his team members have moved up one seat toward the head on the line leaving a vacant

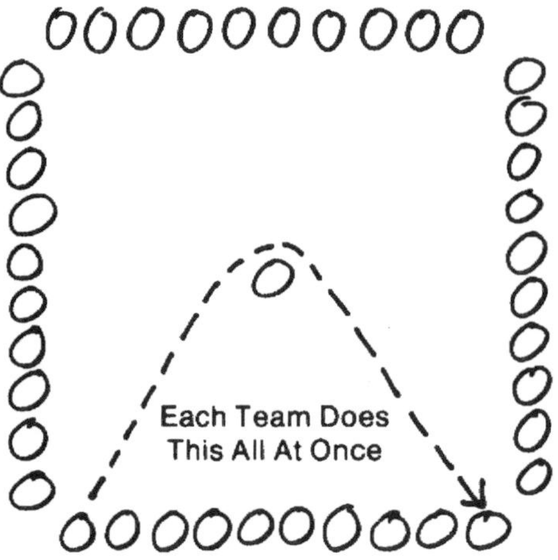

chair at the right end. After taking the vacant chair, first player passes the banana up the line. When the end player receives it, she repeats the run around center and comes to the end, taking the vacant chair. Each team attempts to be the first to have all players circle center chair and get back in original position. Original first player must eat the banana when his team is finished, and his team wins.

SWITCHER

Here's an indoors musical-chairs-type game ideal for retreats. Arrange the 36 chairs in a hexagon (or as few as 24), divide kids into six teams of six each, assign each team a number (one through six), and give the captain of each team a sign or large card with his or her team number on it. Have the players sit as teams, in numeric order, clockwise (see diagram).

Now call out the first number pattern: "1-3, 2-6, 5-4—switch!" This means that, when you yell "Switch!" teams one and three must exchange places, teams two and six must exchange places, and teams five and four must exchange places. (You should list lots of number patterns ahead of time and simply read them off during the game.) Each captain's sign should help get everybody to the proper section, but it's still mayhem.

Here's the competitive angle: the last person seated is out (the chair, however, is left in). If the captain is out, she gives the team-number sign to a teammate. Then you call out the next number pattern: "4-2, 1-5, 3-6—switch!"—and so on, until only one player is left. An interesting variation is eliminating players down to the last person on each team only, then letting these few play the final rounds.

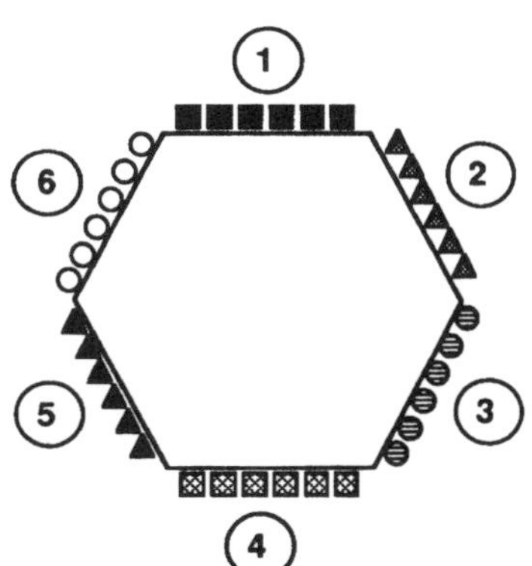

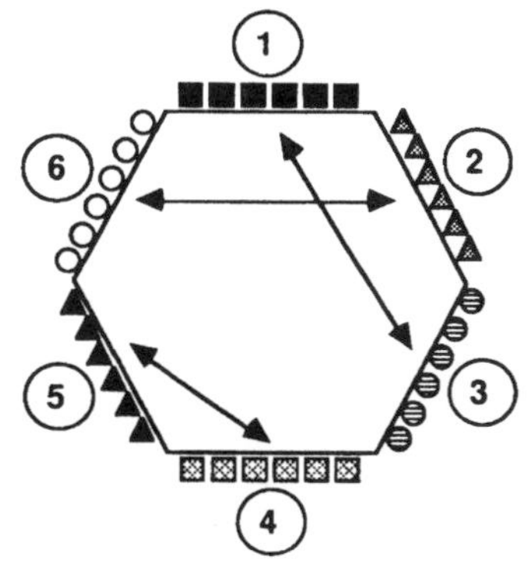

Michael W. Capps

MOTHER GOOSE CHARADES

Divide the group into two teams. Have each team select from memory a Mother Goose rhyme to act out for the other team, without actually telling the other team which rhyme it is. The object is to get the other team to guess the rhyme correctly. If the game is to be a contest, divide the group into three teams, and have the third team be the audience, trying to guess which rhymes are being acted out. Each acting team must portray a rhyme selected by the opposing team. The team whose rhyme is guessed correctly in the shortest time wins. *John Bristow*

FEET-BALL

This is an active game that requires real teamwork. Divide the group into two teams and seat them (in chairs) in two lines, facing each other. The object is for the teams, using only their feet, to move a volleyball-like ball toward and through their goals: The left end of the line, as each team looks to its left.

TEAM A

□ □ □ □ □ □ □

Team B's goal 2 rows of chairs, facing each other **Team A's goal**

□ □ □ □ □ □ □

TEAM B

Players must keep their arms behind the chairs to keep from touching the ball, which is a penalty. To begin the game, drop the ball between the two teams in the middle.

If the teams are especially aggressive, you may want them to remove their shoes to avoid bruised shins. Also make sure the two rows of chairs are just far enough apart that their feet barely touch when legs are extended on both sides. *Mike Weaver*

JINGLE JANGLE

Using old magazines, cut out two different ads for a product, collecting ads for all sorts of products, e.g. Bold detergent. Individually take people into a back room (or whatever is available) and pin an ad to their back. Have the people then match up with the other person who has on their back the same product. Next, they should get together and make up a two-line or four-line jingle advertising that product. Give each couple a chance to "sell" the product. *Vivian Worsham*

STRAW CONTEST

This contest looks easier than it really is. Each contestant receives two straws and a cup filled with water. One straw is to be put in the cup of water, the other is not. However, both straws are to be inserted in the contestant's mouths. As the contestants race to empty their cups, they won't realize that they will be slowed down by the straw which is only sucking air. *Kathie Taylor*

APRIL FOOL'S GAME

At the beginning of a party or special event, give everyone in the room a card with an instruction written on it. The instruction is an April Fool's trick that kids must play on someone before the event is over. For example, it might say "Tell someone that his fly is open" or "Tell someone that there is a phone call for her," and so on. If the person falls for it (looks down, goes to the phone, etc.) then that person has been officially fooled and is out of the game.

The idea is to try to avoid being fooled and to eliminate as many of the others as you possibly can by faking them out. This works best when there is plenty of time (while other things are going on as well). Check at the end of the party or event how many people were fooled, who fooled the most people, and so on. It's fun!

STRENGTH TEST

Here's a good stunt you could use on contest night. All you need is a flat, ordinary bathroom scale. Each person holds the scale with two hands and squeezes it, pressing as hard as possible to register the highest weight on the scale. Or you could have two people, one holding the scale and the other pushing, attempt to register their highest score.

Kathie Taylor

REVIVAL!

These games can be used to promote church attendance with your kids. Tell them that in order for them to know how to attend a church service, they need to practice certain church-going skills. Then play games like these (you may be able to make up a few of your own):

- **Find a Seat.** Just in case there is a standing-room-only crowd at the next church service, they had better practice getting a seat. Play musical chairs.
- **Pass the Plate.** It takes skill to pass the offering plate! Play any relay game here (like the Banana Relay, page 92), but use an offering plate to pass along.
- **Name That Hymn.** It's time to sing! Play Charades with titles of hymns. As soon as the guessing team knows the name of the hymn, they must sing a few bars.
- **Memory Verse.** This is practice for listening to the

reading of the Scripture for the day. Play the Gossip game, using a verse of Scripture. Kids line up, and the verse is whispered in the ear of the first person, who whispers it to the second, and so on down the line. The last person must quote the verse correctly.

• **Sermon Cheers.** Kids need to practice responding to good points in the sermon, right? Distribute on slips of paper words and phrases like "Amen!" "Hallelujah!" "Preach it, Brother!" "Glory!" and other enthusiastic responses, with several slips for each expression. On a signal players must find everyone else in the room who is yelling out the same thing they are. The first group to get together wins. *Alan C. Wilder*

MAC ATTACK

A guy and a girl make up a team in this hamburger-eating race. Boys are seated, girls stand behind them and feed them a Big Mac. This model hamburger has plenty of drippy sauce and lettuce and all, and makes a delightful mess, especially when the girl uses just one hand to feed the boy and keeps the other in her pocket or behind her back. Boys aren't allowed to use their hands to help.

Award winners gift certificates to (burp!) McDonald's. *Randy Trotter*

TRIP TRIVIA

Here's another Trivial Pursuit spinoff. On your next extended outing, put someone in charge of gathering little bits of trivia, like "What cabin number did the sponsors sleep in?" or "What is the first letter on the church bus license plate?" or "What was the last word the youth director said before he was thrown into the pool?" Use your imagination—nothing is too far out. Then put all the questions together and during your next meeting, see who can be the Youth Trip Trivia Champ. This is an excellent way to reminisce and to set the stage for an evaluation time for any activity or trip. *Rod Rummel*

PSYCHO

Prime your group for this game by showing Alfred Hitchcock's classic *Psycho* at your next lock-in. Also in advance of the game, select five students—one to play the psycho, four to play detectives. Keep their identities secret from each other and from the group at large. Only you know their identities, and they are to tell no one who they are.

After the movie announce that a psycho is in your midst—the individual looks perfectly normal and could be anyone. Fortunately, there are four undercover detectives on the job to catch the psycho—but they must catch him *in the act*.

The psycho must wear a wig at the time of attack and must mark the victims with a felt-tip marker. (Hide the wig and marker prior to the game and let the psycho know where to retrieve them when the game begins.) Provide pocket New Testaments to your four detectives as badges and proof of their identities. The detectives can make an arrest only if they catch the psycho in the act, wig and all.

Release everyone to go and hide from the psycho throughout the darkened building. But warn them to be careful—the psycho might be hiding with them! Once the psycho marks a victim, that person must return to the youth room to await the outcome of the game.

This game ends one of two ways: either a detective catches the psycho in the act, or the psycho attacks and gets rid of all the detectives before any of the four can apprehend the psycho. *Jason McClelland and David Moss*

SPIN THE COMPLIMENT

Like the old favorite Spin the Bottle, this game

needs a Coke or Pepsi bottle and a circle of kids willing to affirm each other with words of appreciation. The spinner lays not a smacker, but a compliment or word of encouragement on whomever the bottle points to at the end of its spin. *Marti Lambert*

SCARED STIFF

For this hair-raiser, choose several long-haired guys as contestants. Each guy chooses two girls to be on his team. Give the girls a full bottle of super-hold hair spray, a blow dryer, and a brush, then tell them the objective: to style the guys' hair in five minutes. The winner is the guy whose hair is sticking up and out the farthest. Award consolation prizes for "do's" that are especially funky. *Stephen Troglio.*

LEGOLYMPICS

Buy several small Lego sets—race car, airplane, spaceship—(or ask your students' younger brothers if you can borrow them) and create races that require the students to assemble the sets under some limitation. You'll discover that youths of all ages love putting Lego sets together. Create your own Lego Olympic events. Some suggestions:

- **Blindfold Sprint.** Two players work together. One player can do nothing but read the instructions. The other player is blindfolded and must construct the item solely from verbal directions from the teammate.
- **100 Yard Dash.** A pure speed contest—who can assemble a Lego figure the fastest?
- **Relays.** Teams take turns adding pieces to build the item.
- **Hurdles.** Place pieces of the Lego set around the room. The player must move around the room to find the pieces needed to finish the item in the fastest time.
- **Awards Ceremony.** At an awards ceremony following the event, give Lego sets to the team or individual with the most wins. Play a tape recording of you or some students singing each winner's high school alma mater or fight song.

Mark Schwartz

YOU LOOK GREAT TONIGHT!

This revealing games goes over most effectively at a dressy event that the kids attend with their dates. Select several male volunteers to leave the room for a few moments. They return one at a time, blindfolded, and each one hears this:

> **Thank you for taking part, [name]. You were recommended to be one of our contestants on the basis of your highly developed ability of observing girls' styles. Don't you agree that our girls always come out nicely dressed? Great. I'm sure you'll have no trouble giving us a full description of the style and colors of the clothes your date is wearing tonight.**

After a few moments of vague mumbling, desperate fabrication, or sometimes brilliant improv, bring the next guy in. *Fred Swallow*

CHOCO-STARE DOWN

Have players pair up and sit facing each other. Each person places a chocolate miniature candy bar on the other partner's tongue, which should be sticking out. The winner is the one who can keep the piece of chocolate on his tongue the longest without biting it, dropping it, touching it with hands or lips, or having it completely melt. This game will cause tons of salivating, so be prepared. *Duane Steiner*

SCRABBLE SCRAMBLE

Give several sheets of construction paper and markers to each of two or more equal-numbered teams. Assign each team a word, one letter per team member. Then the kids write one letter per sheet of paper in large bold print for all to see easily.

The object of the game is to stump the other teams. For example, members of a team that is assigned the word Nazareth may stand up and hold their letters in this order:

The team that guesses the correct word in the shortest time wins the round.

Scrabble Scramble is easily adapted to any topical, biblical, or seasonal lesson or study by simply using words that are pertinent to the topic, passage, or season.

Or try this variation:

1. Beforehand, write out the letters of a word (or short phrase) on separate sheets of paper. Make as many sets of the word as there are teams.
2. Shuffle the letters in each set so they're out of order.
3. At the meeting, give a set of scrambled letters to each team.
4. On a signal each team tries to be the first to unscramble the word, each player lining up in order with his or her letter.

Michael Capps

TABLOID GAME

The object of this game is to distinguish between actual and contrived tabloid headlines.

1. Purchase several supermarket tabloids, skim them, and write the best headlines on index cards (one headline per card). Write up 10 to 20 of them.
2. Label the back of each card with a letter—A, B, C, etc.
3. Now compose some tabloid-type headlines of your own—write twice as many fakes as you have actual headlines. (Recruit a few students or sponsors to help you write the bogus headlines.) Keep a master list of correct headlines for yourself or the emcee.
4. On the backs of two fake headlines cards, write the letter A; on the backs of another two fakes, write B; etc. What you're doing is making triads: each triad has an actual tabloid headline and two made-up ones.

5. To start the game, choose three youth panelists (perhaps the ones who helped you write the headlines); each of them will read one of the three cards in a triad.
6. Divide the other students into teams of three to eight or so, depending on the size of your group.
7. Give an A card to each of the three panelists. Each panelist reads the headline on his or her index card.
8. Allow a minute for teams to confer and guess which of the three headlines is the actual one. Award points to each team guessing the correct headline.

Or you can buy Tabloids, the commercial form of the same game (Pressman, about $25). *David A. Narigon*

ASSAULT

Adapt the assault game of TV's "American Gladiators" to your church hall or youth room. Set up the playing area with four barriers, such as tables and desks, for runners to hide behind. Set aside a small area for the gladiators to stay in, and designate a finish area. Provide 50 or more tennis balls for the gladiators to use. Supply safety gear—goggles, head gear, knee pads, etc.—for runners to use while running the course.

Give each runner one minute to run the course: from the start area to each of the barriers, trying to finish the course as quickly as possible—despite the barrage of tennis balls thrown by a pair of gladiators. Runners hit by a tennis ball are out.

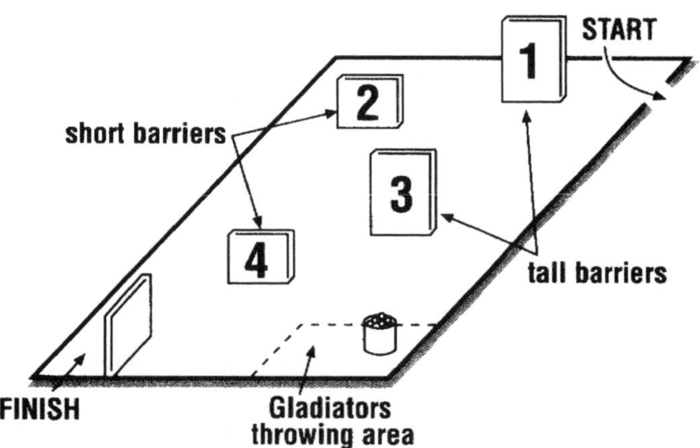

Heighten the competition by placing an eight-foot-high target on the wall behind the gladiators. Then place a tennis ball behind each barrier. A runner successfully reaching a barrier may throw the tennis ball there. Players who hit the target win the round.

Record the times of those who finish the course, and reward the fastest times with an American Gladiator T-shirt or similar prize. *Bruce Smith*

PICK A PIC

Fill a basket or sack with pictures cut out of newspapers and magazines. Divide your group into at least two teams, each of which sends a person to the basket to pull out a picture. The teams then have 30 seconds to start a story, in writing, about the illustration.

After 30 seconds, teams send another person for another picture; each group continues the story, but somehow including the new picture. This continues until all teens have chosen pictures. Judges determine the team with the most creative story.

Paste the pictures on paper and intersperse them with pages from the stories. The end result is a book the teens can read.

WHISTLE SPRINT

Have some teenagers in your group who are full of hot air? Give each student a playing card and a whistle (cheap plastic whistles work great). On a starting line, line up teenagers (on their knees, whistles in mouths) and their cards (on the ground in front of them), point out the finish line, and let 'em go! Players must blow their cards—through their whistles—to the finish line.

If the noise gets to you, you can always replace the whistles with straws. *Rob Ely*

TONGUE TISSUE RACE

All you need for this game is two boxes of Kleenex-type tissues. The kind that don't pop up work best. Place the box at one end of the room and designate a starting location at the other. The first two participants run to a box, put their faces in, and—using their saliva only—stick as many tissues as they can onto their tongues. Use of hands or teeth is not allowed. With tissues on tongue, each kid runs back to the starting line, where another person removes the tissues; judges keep a tally of each player's tissues. (Run the race twice, each time letting half the kids be players, half judges.)

After time is called, the player who has brought back the most tissues is declared the winner. Try playing the game as a team relay, too. *Bret Luallen*

RUBBER BAND DANCE

Divide players into at least two teams. Line them up, relay fashion. Give each team a giant rubber band (or four XXL ones from your office supply). When the whistle blows, each team's first player pulls the rubber band over his entire body head to toe, passing it on to the teammate behind him. The first team done wins.

Plan to have a videocam ready: videotape the kids as they're gyrating, trying to get the rubber band over their heads and down around their waists. Play the videotape back to Glenn Miller's "In the Mood," and viewers will swear that the kids are doing some crazy, strange dance. *Jim Mitchell*

HULA BALL

Tape a large Hula Hoop to the seat of two chairs to use as a goal. With masking tape, mark off a five-by-seven-foot rectangle surrounding the goal. Also mark off a semi-circle around the goal with a 24-foot diameter. Add a foul line about 15 feet out from the goal. Set up an identical goal at the other end of the playing field. You will also need a beach ball or four-square ball. Sideline boundaries are not recommended—the bigger the playing area the better. Play the ball off walls and ceilings if possible.

Now to play the game. Divide the group into two teams. The goal is to win by scoring five goals first. Players may bounce, dribble, roll, or pass the ball to other members of the team. They may not run with it, or possession will be awarded to the other team. Each basket is worth one point. If a foul occurs, the violator must remain frozen until a goal is scored. Each team has a goalie, playing on his knees, inside its own semi-circle to protect the goal; no other players may enter the semi-circular area. The goalie must stay out of the five-by-seven box in front around the goal. Foul shots are granted to the opposing team when infractions occur. For larger groups, divide each team into two squads, and rotate them every three minutes. *Bob Early*

SHRINK-WRAP GAMES

A 24-inch-wide roll of shrink-wrap (also known as pallet wrap) is a way of creating lots of variations to otherwise stale games. Consider it a must-have in your supply cabinet.

• **Mad Banana-Eating Caterpillars.** Wrap 10 contestants—hands at their sides—in shrink-wrap from the neck down. (For reasons of safety and in case of emergencies, do not wrap them so tightly that they are completely immobile. And be prepared and equipped to strip off the wrap at a moment's notice.) Carefully lay them down on the floor at the opposite end of the room from 10 unpeeled bananas. Place people as obstacles between the "caterpillars" and the bananas.

After inching and squirming across the floor in a caterpillar fashion, players eat their bananas and return to the starting point. The first one to finish is the winner.

• **Siamese Twin Olympic Games.** Siamese twin games are a great way to encourage teens to work together. Join two players by wrapping them—or parts of them—together with shrink-wrap.

Now play games like touch football, soccer, and volleyball—but with shrink-wrapped pairs of players, instead of with individuals. *Matt Klein*

Hula Ball

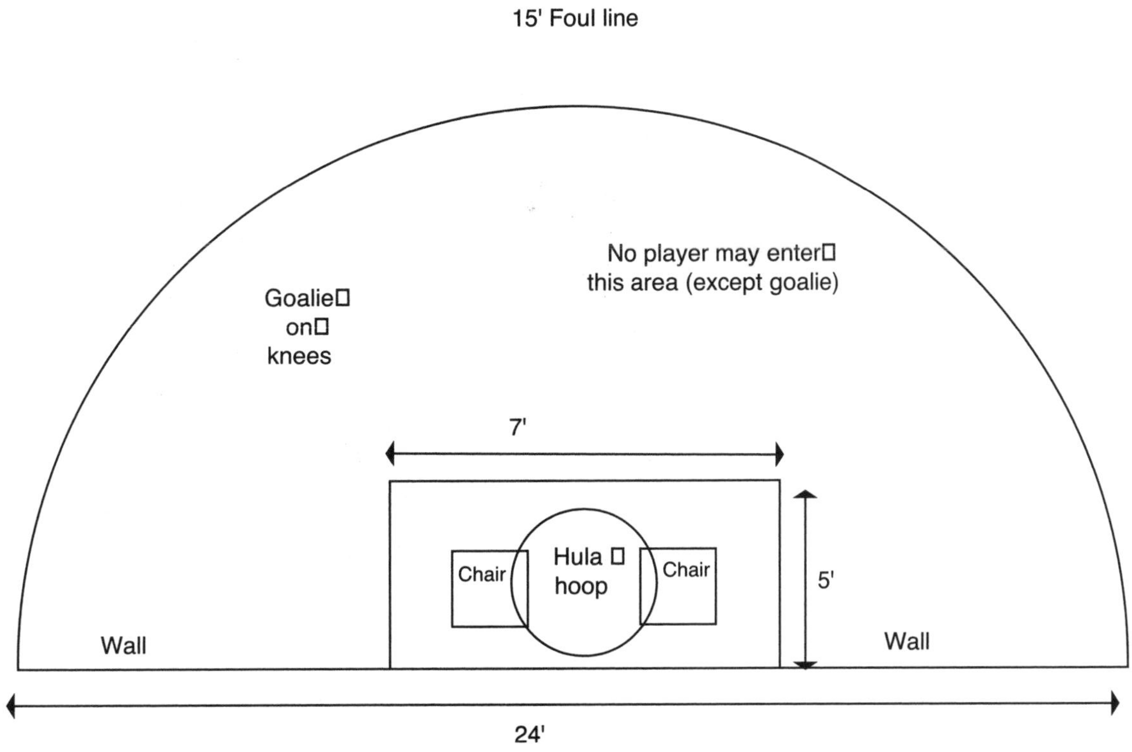

Ninja

For this game you need 10 soft foam rings (or five-inch circles cut from cardboard), a piano bench (or step stool), and masking tape to mark the "danger zone"—a strip running the full width across the center of the room (see diagram).

Select one person to be the Ninja. Give her the rings and stand her on the piano bench, where she must stay during play.

Line up the rest of your group at one end of the room. On "Go!" they try to run past the Ninja without being killed (hit by a ring); because runners may not feel the rings hitting them, officials determine who is hit. Players who are killed must remain in the danger zone for the rest of the game.

Once they are confined to the danger zone, however, dead players work for the Ninja by trying to slow down live players from leaving the danger zone, but without holding onto them. Dead players can also retrieve rings for the Ninja. Live runners keep passing back and forth through the danger zone until only one is left: the next Ninja. *Doug Partin*

No-Snow Snowman Race

Collect the Styrofoam and shredded paper packing material you receive until you have a very large plastic bag of it. Divide the kids into small groups, and have each choose a volunteer to be the snowman (or snowwoman, as the case may be). On a signal the volunteer is wrapped with packing tape sticky side out. The team members carry Styrofoam and shredded paper from the opposite side of the room to the snowperson and stick it on him. After the allotted time, a judge selects the best looking snowman. *David Overholt*

Magnet Darts

You'll need a refrigerator (or other large surface that a magnet will adhere to). Draw or attach a large archery or dart-board target on it. Make the concentric circles or the wedges on the target worth not merely 10 or 20 points, but thousands and millions of points. (Just don't use permanent ink on the church kitchen's Irma Wagner Memorial Refrigerator.)

Tape a line on the floor eight to 10 feet away from the target. Tell your kids ahead of time to bring four or five refrigerator magnets each.

To play Magnet Darts, divide the group into four teams, let the kids choose a team name, and fill in the beginning of a tournament chart. Let players throw three magnets for each turn. Whichever team reaches a predetermined total first is the winner and progresses through the tournament until a champion team emerges. *Mark Simone*

Sock Wars

Sock Wars is best when played inside a building with lots of corners, doors, hallways, and hiding places—or a playing area outside with similar features.

Divide into two teams. Give each player the following:

- Three tickets—one color to one team, another color to the other team.
- Three socks, knotted for better throwing.

The teams gather at opposite ends of the playing area, the lights are turned out, and the game begins. The object: to get tickets by hitting opponents with socks. A hit player must surrender a ticket to the player who hit him; while the "shooter" is getting the ticket due her as well as her sock back, both players are safe from getting hit by others.

When a player runs out of tickets, he can't throw any more socks—until, that is, he is given a ticket by a teammate. This game can last as long as you want. *Mark Miller*

Sock Attack

Split the group into pairs of students, and give each pair a pair of socks. You will need a different color pair for every team (five colors for five teams). Players may knot their socks if they wish, which makes them fly better.

Teams are sent to separate corners or areas of the room. When the whistle sounds, players try to eliminate the other teams by throwing their socks to hit them. After throwing a sock, players must either retrieve it or the partner's sock to continue throwing. Team members may throw only their own socks. There are no boundaries so players are free to go anywhere in the room. When students are hit by a sock, they must immediately be seated and remain still for the rest of the round. The team who has the last person standing wins the round.

Each round is usually over in about 20 to 30 seconds. Play for an established period of time. The team winning the most rounds is declared the winner.

For additional excitement, add a pair of wild socks, a pair of socks not assigned to any team. Anyone may throw one of these as his own at any time. *Mark Thieret*

GIANT FOUR SQUARE

In a large room or racquetball court, mark the floor into quadrants and provide a giant ball. Use normal four-square rules with the following additions:

- Players can bounce the ball off any of the walls.
- The ball can touch the floor only once in a square before being passed to another square.
- The ball cannot be returned to the same square that it came from.
- Numerous players can be in each square.

This game requires teamwork and cooperation.

Duane Steiner

HUMAN TWISTERS

First number each player:

- **Up to six players:** Number them one through six. (The roll of the die will indicate which kid plays that turn.)
- **Seven to 11 players:** Number them two through 12. (The total of the roll of a pair of dice will indicate which player plays that turn.)
- **12 to 21 players:** Number them according to possible combinations of a pair of dice: 1:1, 1:2, 1:3, etc. Sally, for instance, is 1:3; Bill is 2:5; Mark is 4:6. Let the smaller number come first: a 5 and a 2 is 25, not 52.

Next, number body parts. For example, the right ear is 1, the left ear 2, the right hand 3, the left hand 4, the right foot 5, and the left foot 6.

Your first roll is for the person; the second roll, for his or her body part. Say you're playing with 12 players or more. Your first roll is a 4:6 (that indicates which player—Mark, in this case) and your second role is a 2 (that indicates Mark's left ear). The next pair of rolls is a 2:5 and a 3, which indicate Bill's right hand—so Mark places his left ear against Bill's right hand. The next thing you know, every person in the youth group is attached in one giant puzzle.

Whether you play this game competitively or just for laughs, it's still a lot of fun. This might be a good game to capture on film. Hang the less embarrassing photos in the youth room. *Dik LaPine*

OVER AND BACK

All you need for this high-action game is dice (just one die, actually), a whistle, a watch, two scorekeepers, a timekeeper, and a room divided by a masking-tape line on the floor.

Split your students into two teams, placing the teams on opposite sides of the room. One team is the Odd Team; the other, the Even Team. The timekeeper stands on the sideline and begins play by rolling a die. Depending on the roll, he then calls out "Odd!" or "Even!" The team whose name he calls immediately crosses into enemy territory and tries to pull other team members across the line. They get a point for every opposing player they can pull across.

Meanwhile, the die is rolled every five seconds. If the roll changes from odd to even, the whistle is blown and the task of the players changes. Those who are in enemy territory must exit without getting tagged; otherwise, the other team gets a point.

At the end of one minute, the round ends with three short whistle blasts. The scorekeeper announces the scores for the round. Play resumes with a 0-0 score for each round. Winners are announced as the best of five rounds. *Frank Riley*

Office Chair Dodgeball

Junior highers love this. A person sits on a revolving, rolling office chair in the center of a circle of players, who throw a ball at the chair. The sitter, meanwhile, attempts to block shots against her chair. Whoever hits the chair with the ball becomes the new sitter.

With a little practice, a sitter becomes pretty good at spinning, rolling, and twisting as she dodges the ball. The back of the chair, on the other hand, makes a great target for throwers. *Steve Smoker*

Centipede Wars

Make several centipedes—each centipede is five (or so) students, standing in a line, with their hands on the shoulders of the person in front of them.

The first person of each centipede is the striker, who attempts to eliminate segments (individuals) in other centipedes by throwing a ball at a rival centipede's rear segment. (Balls must strike the players below the neck.) When a centipede's hindmost segment is struck by a ball, that person drops out of the game. A centipede remains alive until the segment behind the striker is hit. Centipedes can maneuver anywhere in the playing area, but must remain attached at all times.

After a couple rounds, your teens will develop their own strategies for protecting the rear section while maneuvering to attack other centipedes. *Tom Lytle*

Mannequin

The goal is to dress the team's mannequin with the items on the list, using what players have on or with them. Direct the teams to form a circle and choose one person to be the mannequin in the center. Give each group the following list.

Baseball hat	**Headband**
Hair comb	**Barrette**
Ponytail holder	**Earring**
Red lipstick	**Necklace**
Watch	**Bracelet**
Ring	**Sweatshirt**
Vest	**Coat or sweater**
Belt	**Knee sock**
Sandal	**Gym shoe**
Nail polish	

The team using the most items from the list wins. *Cindy Allen*

Hungry Fish

Have youths compete against the clock in a race to eat gummy worms hanging from the ceiling.

Gather clothespins, strong string, and lots of gummy worms. Cut various lengths of string, attach one end to the ceiling and one end to a clothespin, and clamp gummy worms in each clothespin. Kids run from string to string and, using only their mouths, snatch and eat the gummy worms. The winner is whoever eats all the worms in the shortest amount of time. *Matt Klein*

GAMES

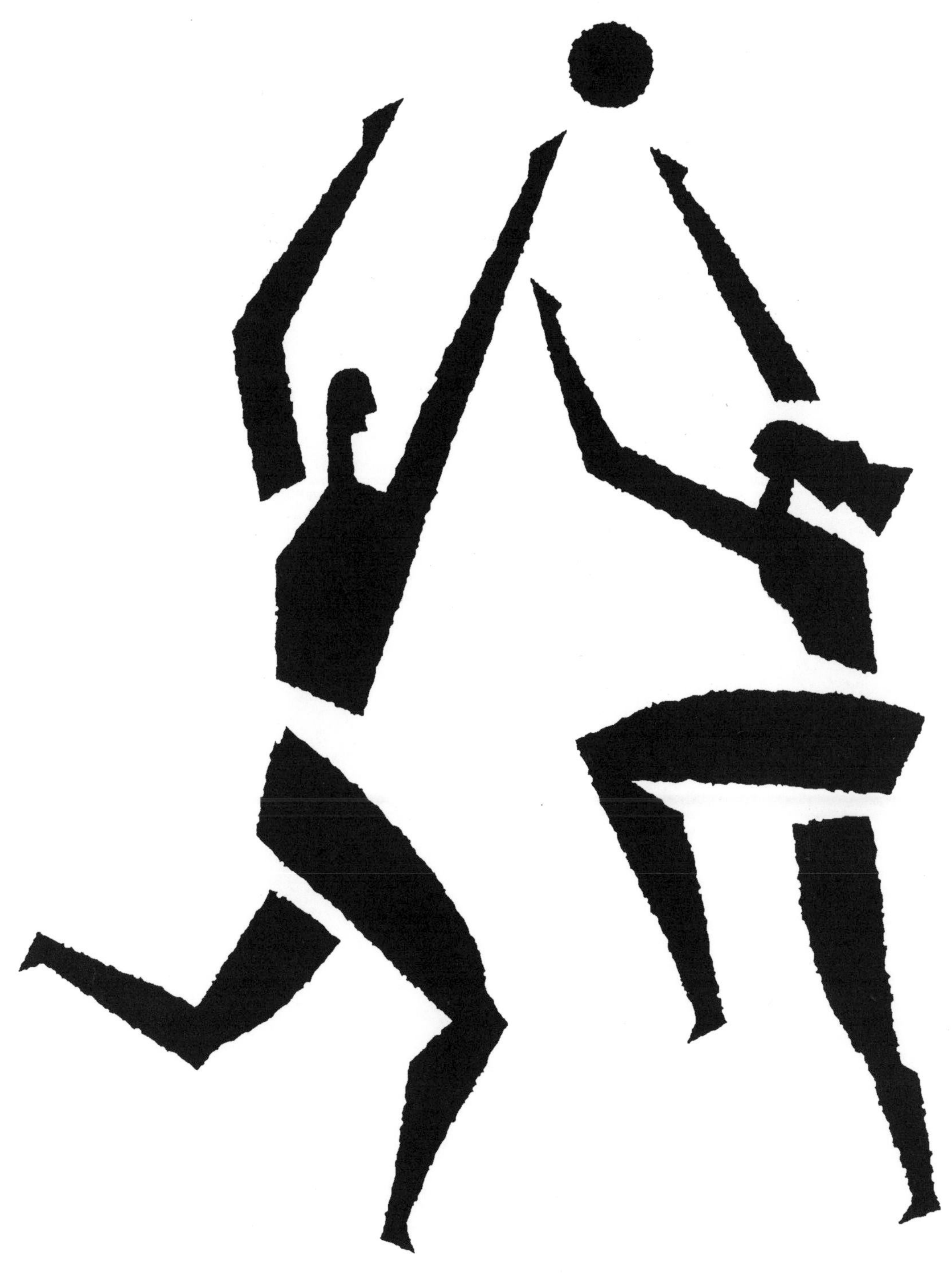

LIVING ROOM GAMES

No access to a fellowship hall or gymnasium? Then try some of these games, all of which can be played in a living room. They're great for informal gatherings, parties, or anytime you've got a roomful of people just sitting around. Some are quiet games that involve little action, others require some moving around. No need to limit yourself to living rooms, of course, for you can play many of these games practically anywhere—on road trips, during those long arena waits before a concert begins, etc.

GRAPEFRUIT PASS

Divide into teams and give each team one grapefruit. Players line up. Their goal is to move a grapefruit down the line by passing it along under their chins. No hands are allowed. If the grapefruit is dropped, it must be started at the beginning of the line again. The first team to successfully pass the grapefruit the length of the team wins.

ASSASSINATION

Here's a good "thinking" game that is a lot of fun. You will need two leaders or referees. The leaders first of all divide the group into two teams, and explain that each team represents a country. In each country everyone will be loyal citizens, except for one person on each team who will secretly be a spy for the opposing enemy country.

The two countries then move into separate rooms, where they cannot be heard by the enemy country. There they must choose from among their own members a ruler, who will be unknown by the enemies. After choosing a ruler, a spy will also be chosen from among the other members of the country by a secret drawing of cards, so that the members will not know which one among them is the enemy spy. This can be accomplished by the leader having all members of one country (except the ruler) draw slips of paper from a bowl, look at their slips, then return the slips to the leader so he, too, can see them. All the slips (except one) will have LOYAL written on them. The one other slip will read SPY. This way only the spy and the leader will know his or her identity. The other leader does the same with the other country.

Then, while the countries are still separated, the two leaders switch rooms, telling each country the name of their spy on the other team, but not telling them the name of the other country's ruler. After this the two countries are brought into the same room. The object is for each country to find out from their spy on the other team who that country's ruler is, and to then assassinate that ruler. Assassination is done by stabbing the enemy with one's finger, in his or her back (only!). You can come up with another method if you wish.)

Each team knows who on the other team is their

spy, but they do not know which of their own members is really an enemy spy for the other team. If they find out, they can then assassinate this spy. If they are mistaken, however, and assassinate one of their loyal members, then they lose the game. Also, if they assassinate one of the members of the other team who is not in fact that country's ruler, they lose the game.

The spies may use any method they wish to tell their friends on the other team who the ruler is in the country in which they are spies. But the spies should be subtle, lest they give away their identity to their country's members and be assassinated. Likewise, the country members should be careful not to give away to the other team who is the ruler among them, lest they assassinate him. The country to assassinate the othe's ruler first, without assassinating anyone by mistake, is the winner. *John Bristow*

BLIND TAG

Conjure up something with a circumference of about 20 feet, such as two tables pushed together or rope wrapped around four chairs. Blindfold two people and put them on opposite sides of this object. Both must always be touching it. Choose which one will try to tag the other. The bystanders may shout to their favorite which way to go to catch or avoid being caught by the other. Beware of high-speed collisions. One variation is to have everyone remain silent and let them listen for each other. This won't work on a carpet. *Rogers E. George III*

BUZZ

This is a good indoor game. Players sit in a circle and begin counting around the circle from one to 100. Whenever someone comes to a number containing seven or a multiple of seven, he or she says "Buzz." (Example: 1, 2, 3, 4, 5, 6, BUZZ, 8, 9, 10, 11, 12, 13, BUZZ, 15, 16, BUZZ, 18, 19, etc.) Anyone who makes a mistake or pauses longer than an agreed upon number of seconds is out.

Make the game easier for younger kids by using the number five and multiples of five, and saying "Fizz" instead of "Buzz." To complicate things, play a combination of Buzz/Fizz, using sevens and fives and their multiples.

COLOR CRAZY

On a poster board, have several colored areas (red, blue, green, etc.). On each colored area write the name of a color, but not the actual color of that area of the poster. Then for a gag, have the kids try to name the colors on the poster as you point to them (not the words written, but the actual color). It is not easy. *Rita Hollis*

CUT THE CAKE

Pack flour in a big bowl and turn it upside down on a tray or baking sheet removing the bowl. It is a mold now; put cherry on top. Everyone in the circle around the cake must cut off some part (be it large or small) of the cake and then the knife is passed around the circle. The more the cake is cut, the closer you get to the cherry in the center. Whoever cuts the cake and the cherry "falls" has to pick it up with his teeth with hands behind his back, and eat the cherry. *Gary Wrisberg*

DO I KNOW THAT PERSON?

Divide young people into four groups. Have each group select one person and list six to eight facts about him or her. Then have the recorder of the group read the facts to the other three groups. The object is to guess who the facts describe as soon as possible. The group that guesses the correct person with the least amount of clues is the winner. *William C. Moore*

EARTH, AIR, FIRE, WATER

Kids form a circle with one player in the middle. That player throws a ball to someone in the circle, and quickly says either "earth," "air," "fire," or "water," and then counts rapidly to 10. The person who receives the ball must say the name of an animal (earth), bird (air), fish (water), or say nothing (fire) before the thrower finishes counting. The receiver takes the thrower's place if he or she responds incorrectly. Players can't reuse names that have been previously used. Each answer must be an original.

Map Game

Obtain several road maps (all identical) of your state (or any state, for that matter) and before the game draw a large number, letter, or symbol, such as a number 8, on one of the maps with a pencil. Make a

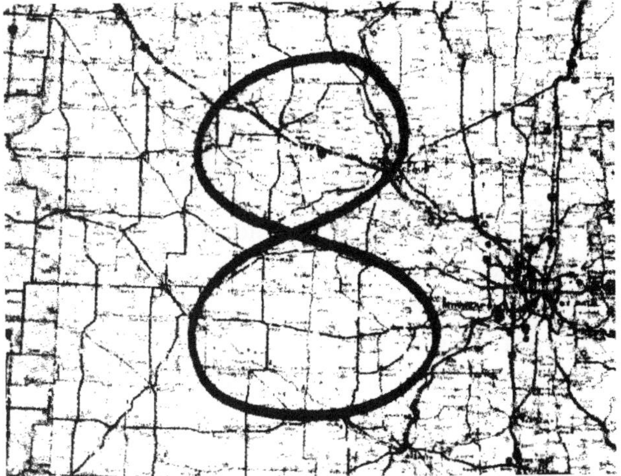

list of all the towns that your pencil line crosses or comes near. Have the kids divide up into small groups and give each group a clean map and the list of towns. On a signal they must locate the towns on the map and figure out what the number or letter is that the towns form when connected with a line. No guessing allowed (a wrong guess disqualifies them), and the first group to come up with the correct answer wins. *Don Snider*

Elephant, Rhino, and Rabbit

The players sit in a tight circle with "It" in the middle. "It" points to someone in the circle and says either *elephant*, *rhino*, or *rabbit*. The person that "It" points to must either put his hands behind his back for the *rabbit*, or put his hands in a fist in front of each other in front of his nose for the *elephant*, or he must put both fists on his nose with the two index fingers pointing upward for the *rhino*. The two people on either side of the player pointed to must put an open hand facing "It" to the first player's head for *elephant*. For *rhino* they must put a fist to the person's head. For *rabbit* they must put a fist to his head with one finger pointing upward. All of this must be done before the count of 10. If any one of the three people fail to do his part, he then becomes "It." *K. David Oldfield*

Hide the Loot

Make two counterfeit one-million-dollar bank notes on slips of paper, and hand one each to members of two teams. After one team leaves the room, have the other select a place to hide the counterfeit note. The other team members, who are now treasury agents, are then invited back in and allowed to ask questions. The questions may be about the act of hiding the note, what the note is touching in its hiding place (wood, paper, leather, skin, etc.), and so on. For instance, an agent may ask, "Did the person who hid the note have to stand on tiptoes or on a chair in order to reach the hiding place?" Or, "Is the note lying directly under something?" The agents may not move around during the interrogation and may only ask yes or no questions. The questions cannot be about specific areas of the room, and each question must be directed at a specific individual among the counterfeiters team, who must always answer the questions truthfully. Each treasury agent is allowed to ask as many questions as he wishes, but whenever an agent decides to guess a specific location as the hiding place, he must announce that he is doing so. If he guesses wrong, he is eliminated from the game. After the hiding place is discovered, the first team leaves the room, and the other team hides their bank note, and the process is repeated with the teams switching roles.

The object of the game is either to eliminate all of the agents, or else keep them asking questions. If one team is able to eliminate all the agents, and the other cannot (when the roles are switched), then the first team is the winner. Otherwise, the team which forces the other to ask the most number of questions before the hiding place is discovered is the winner. *John Bristow*

Mind Stopper

Form a circle. In the middle stands the person who is "It." She quickly points to someone in the circle and says, "This is my toe." At the same time she points to her chin with her other hand. The person pointed to must grab his toe and say, "This is my chin" before "It" counts to five. If the person pointed to goofs or doesn't make it by five, he becomes "It."

Kleenex Blow

Give each team a Kleenex tissue. Teams must toss the tissue into the air and keep it aloft by blowing it without touching it. Time each team one at a time. The team with the longest time wins.

Mad Ads

Give each team one copy of the same issue of the same magazine. Also have each team appoint a runner. While a leader describes an ad from the magazine, each team must search for it, rip it out, and have the team runner deliver it to the leader. The team with the most wins is the victor.

Clothespin Challenge

Two contestants are selected and seated in chairs facing each other with their knees touching. Each is shown a large pile of clothespins at the right of their chairs. Each is blindfolded and given two minutes to pin as many clothespins as possible on the pant legs of the other contestant. *William Moore*

People Machines

Divide up into groups of seven or eight. Each group has the task of becoming a machine, such as a washing machine, a tape recorder, a fan, etc. Each individual must be a working part with a suitable sound (electric cord with a hum, etc.). Each machine is then presented to the rest of the group for them to guess what is being portrayed. *Senior High Fellowship, First Congregational Church, Webster Groves, Mo.*

My Ship Sails

Players sit in a circle. The leader begins the game by holding up a towel with a knot in it (or a ball) and says, "My ship sails with— " (and names something that begins with his initials). For example, if his name is John Doe, he would say, "My ship sails with juicy donuts" (or jumping ducks, jolly doctors, etc.).

He then throws the towel or ball to another player in the circle (who may not know how to play). She too must say "My ship sails with—" If she knows how to play, she'll say something that begins with her initials.

Have players throw the towel back to you if they need another clue from you. Complete your sentence using two different words than your original statement. Give players this hint if necessary: Almost everyone's ship sails with something different, and they must listen carefully to the item you identify.

Open or Closed

This is a great game for small informal meetings in which kids sit around in a circle and pass around a book or a pair of scissors. When the object is passed, each person must announce whether he is passing it "open" or "closed." For example, he might say, "I received it (open or closed) and I am passing it (open or closed)." The leader then tells the person whether they are right or wrong, and if they are wrong, they must sit on the floor or stand up (anything to look conspicuous). The idea is to learn what the secret is, namely this: If your legs are crossed, you must pass the object closed. If your legs are open (uncrossed), you must pass the object open. It sounds simple, but it really is tough to figure it out, and it makes for a real fun game. *Darlene Landan*

Third Degree

The leader divides the group into two teams, one composed of FBI agents, the other of spies. Each spy is given a card bearing one of the instructions listed below, with each spy receiving a different instruction. The FBI agents then take turns asking questions of specific spies, calling out the name of each spy before asking the question. The FBI agents may ask as many questions of as many or few spies as they wish, and may ask any questions they wish (except about the instructions the spies were given). Each spy must answer each question asked him, but always in the manner described on his card. Whenever a spy's instruction is guessed correctly by an FBI agent, he is eliminated from the game. The questions continue until all the spies' instructions are guessed correctly. If a spy gives an answer without following his instructions, he is eliminated.

Scores are kept on individuals rather than

teams. The winning spy is the one who has the most questions asked her before her instructions are guessed correctly. The winning FBI agent is the one who guesses correctly the most number of instructions. (An FBI agent may make a guess at any time, whether it is his turn to ask a question or not.)

Some sample instructions:

1. Lie during every answer.
2. Answer each question as though you were (name of adult leader).
3. Try to start an argument with each answer you give.
4. Always state the name of some color in each answer.
5. Always use a number in your answers.
6. Be evasive; never actually answer a question.
7. Always answer a question with a question.
8. Always exaggerate your answers.
9. Always pretend to misunderstand the question by your answer.
10. Always scratch during your answers.
11. Always insult the questioner.
12. Always begin each answer with a cough.
13. Always mention some kind of food during each answer.
14. Always mention the name of a group member during your answers.

This game can also be played without teams. Give everyone in the group an instruction like those listed above. Then just go around the room with each person answering questions from the entire group until someone can guess her secret instructions. Each new question asked without the instruction being guessed is worth a point. *John Bristow*

THE POINT GAME

Give everyone a score card, then read a list similar to the one below. Everyone keeps track of personal points as specified. The person with the most points wins. Make up you own list with about 30 items like these:

- 10 points if you are wearing red.
- 10 points for every penny you have in your pocket.
- 10 points if you have a white comb.
- Your shoe size in points. Half sizes get next highest points.
- 15 points if your birthday is on a holiday.
- 10 points if you have ridden on a train.
- 10 points if you have a ballpoint pen with you; 25 points if it has red ink.
- 10 points if you are wearing an earring.
- Minus 10 points if you have a nose ring.

Lee Breedon

COOTIE

Here's a fast moving game that has kids meeting and having fun with almost everyone in their youth group by the time the game is over.

Cootie Score Sheet		
	Number on Dice — Points 1 — Head = 1 2 — Body = 2 3 — Eyes = 6 4 — Ears = 8 5 — Tail = 5 6 — Legs = 36	

Have a number of card tables set up with one pair of dice per table, a good supply of score sheets (see example), and four pencils. Before everyone arrives, arrange the tables in a large circle or pattern which will allow movement from a lower number table to the next higher number table. The tables should be numbered consecutively with the number 1 table considered the highest numbered table. When the group arrives make sure all the tables are full and remove any extras. Give each person a score sheet and have them write their name on the upper right hand corner of the sheet.

The game is 10 rounds long. At the beginning of each round, the people sitting across from each other are automatically partners for that round only. The partners then trade score sheets at the beginning of each round to "draw the cootie" for the other while he or she rolls the dice.

The game begins and every table starts at the same time. Each person takes a turn rolling the die as rapidly as possible. Each number on the die corresponds to a part of the cootie's body (see score sheet). A 2 must be rolled first before any other part of the body can be drawn. If a person rolls a number they can use, they keep rolling until they roll a number they can't use. Then they pass the die to the next person. When one person has rolled all the numbers needed to finish their cootie, then they may use their turn to roll for their partner. When both partners have completed their cooties, they shout "Cootie!" and the round is over. Play stops at all tables, regardless of how far along everyone else is.

All partners then trade score sheets and have 60 seconds to add up their score and move to a new table, if necessary. Movement between rounds is as follows: The people with the highest score at each table move to the next highest numbered table (e.g., from number 4 to number 3). People with the lower scores at each table remain at that table. (Exception: the winners at the number 1 table remain and the losers at the number 1 table move to the last table.) No one can play with the partner they had in the previous round. The winner (the "Great Cootie") is the person with the highest total score for all 10 rounds. *Dave Zehring*

Ring on a String

Have a group sit in a circle on chairs. Take a piece of string and have every person hold the string with both hands, except for one person who stands in the middle. Tie the string at both ends so it is one big circle with a ring (a large one is better) on the string that can slide all the way around. Have the group members slide their hands along the string and pass the ring along as they try to hide it from the person in the middle. She tries to guess who has the ring by going around the circle (from the inside) and tapping different people's hands. When a person's hand is tapped, he opens his hands to reveal whether he has the ring or not. When the person in the middle taps someone with the ring, they switch places. This can be used with small groups of eight to 20 kids. *John Simmons*

What Flavor Ice Cream?

On large paper or cardboard compile two lists. The first list contains the names of five people or characters. The names can be fictional or real, living or historical. But they should be names most people are familiar with— George Washington, Mae West, Moses, Superman, etc. The second list should include the following: What flavor ice cream? What kind of tree? What type of fabric? What make of car? What kind of building? What kind of bird? What color?

Make copies of these two lists to match the number of teams you have determined. Each team is asked to spend 15 minutes in choosing one name from the list of characters and then attempting to match that character's personality or attributes to the second list of categories. At the end of 15 minutes each team reports back by reading down the list of categories what attributes they have agreed on, e.g., tutti frutti ice cream, weeping willow, etc. The other teams must then guess which of the five characters this particular team is describing. *Glenn Miller*

French Charades

This version of Charades works best with older teens.

Divide into teams of five to seven people. Have the members of one team leave the room while the others think of a situation that can be acted out without words. Then bring in one person from the team that was sent out of the room. Explain the situation he or she will be acting out.

Now bring in a second person from that team. Without saying a word, Player 1 must act out the assigned plot for Player 2. Player 2 may or may not understand the charade, but she must subsequently act out the same situation for a third member of the team. Player 3 performs the charade for Player 4, and so on. The last person must guess the original story line.

Remember, all this is done in complete silence. Even the simplest charade can undergo a thorough metamorphosis after being passed down several times. If the last person cannot guess the charade, Player 1 should perform it again and let the last person guess once more.

Here are a couple of classic French Charade situations to spur your creativity.

- **You are a high school beauty pageant contestant, anxiously awaiting the announcement of the winner. Suddenly, you hear your name! You now step forward to receive your crown and roses. Then comes your victory walk down the aisle. As you proceed down the aisle, waving to the crowd, you encounter several misfortunes. First, you are allergic to roses so you begin to sneeze, but you keep on going, waving and sneezing to the crowd. Then, on the way back up the aisle, your high heel breaks and you finish the walk with one heel missing!**

- **You are a pregnant mama bird about to give birth! You must fly around the room gathering materials for your nest. Once you make your nest, you lay your egg. Then finish the charade by hatching the egg and finding a worm to feed your new baby.**

ARTIST CHARADES

Here's a guaranteed, live-wire indoor game. Unlike other Charade games, this one is great for shy people. The game works best in a building that has three, four, or five separate rooms available for use.

Divide the group into four or five small groups. Each group should have at least five members. Ask each group to select an initial representative to start off the relay. Give each of the starting representatives a pencil and a large sheet of butcher paper. The large sheet of paper should be placed on a hard surface that will not be damaged by drawing.

The leader makes up a list of 15 common words—things, persons, and places which can be drawn or sketched without the use of letters or numbers (Moses, avocado, mascara, Statue of Liberty, etc.). You should be prepared for two or three rounds and should have two or three lists on hand, gauging the difficulty of the list to the level of the crowd. You will need a thick piece of paper or thin cardboard to cover up the words on your list. The list itself should be on a narrow strip of paper such as an 8½x11 inch sheet of typing paper folded length wise and the words should be spelled out clearly in capital letters. You are to station yourself with your list in a reasonably central location so that all may reach you. You will need to have more than one monitor placed at strategic spots if you have a huge crowd with many small groups. In that case, each monitor would have lists which are identical with yours.

Instruct all the participants on the rules of the game before you excuse them to their assigned rooms. All the drawings are to be drawn on one side of the paper for the entire round. That way, the reverse side is available for the second round. No spelling with letters or numbers is permitted. All participants are not permitted to speak, mime, or act out the words when it is their turn to draw. Each artist is allowed to indicate how many words are involved and to show by a nod or shaking of the head if the group is hot or cold while they are guessing. The groups should be cautioned not to shout out their answers too loudly or another group may hear their correct answers, unless, of course, the group wishes to deliberately throw off the other groups.

The game starts when the leader calls the starting representatives over and shows them the first word on the list. The reps then run back to their groups and attempt to draw a picture representing the word shown to them. The first person in the group with the correct answer is given the pencil and rushes to the leader, whispers the correct word to them, and receives the next word. This procedure continues until a group successfully identifies all 15 words on the list. After each round is completed, each group will then have an incredible piece of modern art. You may want to give awards for the most artistic rendition of the evening, etc.

As a variation all the words in the list can have a theme—song titles, Bible stories, animals, etc.

Once the kids catch on, Artist Charades will constantly be in demand. Be prepared to have a second or even a third round to break any ties. Another suggestion: rearrange members of the small groups constantly to keep the same groups from winning all the time. *Alan G. Stones*

Hip Charades

This is a great game for casual get-togethers. It is played just like Charades except that team members spell out words with their hips instead of using pantomime or hand signals. Each contestant tries to get their team to guess the words they are spelling out by standing with their back to the team and moving their hips to form (write) the letters in the air. The team shouts out each letter as they recognize it and attempt to guess the correct title in the fastest time possible. The results are hilarious. *Lorne H. Belden*

Pictionary Charades

You'll want to play this game often. Divide your group into two teams and, using the cards and timer from a Pictionary game, play Charades.

One member of Team 1 chooses a Pictionary card and scans the words listed. When the timer is started, that player must act out for her teammates each of the words or phrases on the chosen card in any order. (Do the easy ones first.) Teammates try to guess the word or phrase being acted out. Once a word is guessed, the acting player can go on to another word on the chosen card, acting out as many words as possible within the time limit.

The team receives one point for every correct guess within the time limit. If a team guesses all five words or phrases on the chosen card, it receives two bonus points. Team 2 then chooses a card and repeats the process. *Sheridan Lehman*

A Strobe Situation

Can you imagine Charades illuminated with a strobe light? Then you begin to get the idea of this game. Be careful, though—it can be as thought-provoking as it is hilarious.

Before the meeting, write on slips of paper situations that the group can role play—a family confrontation, spectators at a sports event, a dance, impressions of the congregation on Sunday morning, the choir and director, a church conference.

Form groups of four or five kids, then hand out your prewritten situations. Allow five minutes for the groups to plan their presentations. They can use actions only—no words. Each group performs for the other groups, who try to guess the situation being acted out.

The surprise element is that when the acting starts, the lights go out and the strobe goes on until the performance is concluded. Customize the situations to your own group. Discussion following the strobe situation may be appropriate. *Sondra Edwards*

Ha Ha Ha

This is a crazy game that's good for a lot of laughs. One person lies down on the floor (on his back) and the next person lies down with his head on the first person's stomach, and the next person lies down with his head on the second person's stomach and so on.

After everyone is down on the floor, the first person says "Ha," the second says "Ha, Ha," and the third says "Ha, Ha, Ha," and so on with each person adding another "Ha." It is to be done "seriously," and if anyone goofs, the group must start over. It's hilarious.

Aunt Sally

This game is not only fun to play but entertaining to watch. Line up six to eight chairs side by side. Choose five kids to sit in the chairs with the leader on the end. The leader starts by saying, "Aunt Sally went to town." The person next to the leader replies, "Really? What did she buy?" The leader responds, "Some knitting needles" (makes motions of knitting).

The dialogues and actions are repeated until the last one in line repeats the dialogue to the leader.

While everyone is making the motions of knitting, the leader begins the dialogue again: "Aunt Sally went to town."

The person next to the leader: "Really? What did she buy?"

Leader: "A rocking chair" (begins rocking on chair while still knitting).

Continue down the line again. This game can continue as long as you can think of things that Aunt Sally buys. Here are some suggestions:

- A stand up machine (stand up and down)
- A Hula Hoop (pantomime Hula Hooping)
- A bicycle (jump up and pedal in the air)

After you have enough actions, you can end with this:

"Aunt Sally went to town."

"Really? What did she buy?"

"Nothing, she died."

B. McKinney

CASSETTE GAMES

Here are some ways to use a cassette tape recorder as a game resource:

- **Name That Ad.** Record current television commercials on a cassette tape. Do not allow the name of the product to be mentioned on your tape. Play these commercials to your group. The first one to blurt out the name of the product being referred to scores for his team or himself.
- **Name That Star.** Same as above, only record the voices of current television or movie stars. Score one point for the name of the star and one point for the name of the show or movie.
- **Name That Sound.** Record various sounds from a sound effects record. (Special effects records may be borrowed from a public library.)
- **Name That Tune.** Record current popular songs while playing them at a speed which is either too fast or too slow. Score one point for the song title and one point for the recording artist.
- **Name That Oldie.** Same as above except in some cases it is unnecessary to vary the speed at which the recording is played.
- **Name That Noise.** Use all of the above ideas in one tape. This tape is a greater challenge because the kids are always off-guard.
- **Miscellaneous Noises.** Other topics that could be used include theme songs from TV shows, theme songs from movies, voices of people from your church, school teachers, radio disc jockeys, voices of people in your youth group, voices of children in your church, the opening lines of Bible stories, Aesop's fables, children's stories, children's songs, and church hymns.

Bill Calvin

FUNNY BUNNY

This is a great travel game that can be used to make those long miles on youth trips go by at a rapid pace. Everyone can participate at the same time, either by giving clues for the game or trying to guess the answer. The game goes like this—someone begins by giving a two-word clue, like "distant light," and then it's up to the rest of the participants to guess the answer. The answer must be two rhyming words. In the case of this illustration, the answer to "distant light" would be "far star." The game continues with everyone participating until you arrive at your destination, run out of two-word phrases, or just simply go out of your mind. There are literally hundreds of combinations, but here are just a few to get you started.

Clue	Answer
distant light	far star
chef's delight	okay souffl é
royal hawk	regal eagle
white spike	pale nail
pig chaser	hog dog
bench fur	chair hair
log cover	wood hood
distant auto	far car
tnjoyable jog	fun run
tiny insect	wee flea
bed plunder	bunk junk
street frog	road toad
sack label	bag tag
important path	main lane
lemon dessert	yellow Jell-o
thin coin	skinny penny
tidy chair	neat seat
branch notch	stick nick
false pond	fake lake
mop closet	broom room
ski-slope rake	snow hoe
pale watercolors	faint paint
old antler	worn horn
chubby insect	fat gnat
sliced acorn	cut nut
dark plunge	dim swim
thin spear	narrow arrow
wet postage	damp stamp
cap tap	hat pat
ordinary locomotive	plain train
correct evening	right night
letter bucket	mail pail
pokey pull	slow tow

lengthy melody	long song
ranch siren	farm alarm
tire noise	wheel squeal
poster sentence	sign line
plain board	blank plank
path wind	trail gale
mountain fall	hill spill
cookie bag	snack sack
attractive outfit	cute suit
dish-cloth shovel	towel trowel
lettuce song	salad ballad
blender repairer	mixer fixer
specific drapes	certain curtain
satellite faint	moon swoon
center violin	middle fiddle
burning wheel	tire fire
snow hoe	flake rake

McIlvain and Martha Sager

GEIGER COUNTER

In this party game everyone is seated in the room. The leader selects a volunteer to leave the room. While he is away, the group agrees on a hiding place for a random object, which the leader hides. The person returns and tries to find the object, not knowing what it is. The rest of the group, much like a geiger-counter tick-tick-tick-ticks slower as he moves away from the object and faster as he moves closer, until he finds it. Volunteers may compete for the fastest time. *Steve Illum*

GIFT GRABBER

This idea works best with 15 to 20 people. Everyone gets a wrapped gift to begin with. (They should be joke gifts and absolutely worthless, if possible, like an old shoe, an old motel key, etc.) After the gifts are distributed, deal out an entire deck of playing cards, so that everyone has an equal number of cards. The leader should have a second deck of cards that he keeps. When everyone has a gift and some cards, the leader shuffles his deck, draws one card and announces what it is. Whoever has that card (from the first deck) gives the leader that identical card and then gets to help himself to any other person's gift that he'd like. Then, the next card is announced by the leader and the possessor of that identical card gets his turn to help himself to someone else's gift, and so on until the whole deck of cards is used up.

It is a scream to see how the gifts go back and forth. One person at first might accumulate several but as his cards are exhausted, the momentum shifts. Of course, whoever has the gifts at the end of the game gets to unwrap them and keep them. Sometimes seeing what actually was the content of some of the packages that were most furiously sought after produces as much fun as the game itself.

As a variation use this procedure with gifts at Christmas. *Douglas Whallon*

MATCH GAME

This is an indoor game that is quite simple and easy to play. Distribute the list on page 115 to each person. Then ask players to find the clue for each item. Of course, earlier you planted the following clues around the room (the numbers correspond to the items on page 115):

1. The letter "o" on a card
2. Kernel of corn
3. Rubber band
4. Ruler
5. Pillow
6. Spoon
7. Letter "r"
8. Two banana peels
9. Writing pen
10. Old ribbon bow
11. Pair of scissors
12. Dictionary
13. Tacks on tea bags
14. Blotter or sponge
15. Mirror
16. Umbrella
17. Alarm clock
18. Pitcher
19. Penny (one sent)
20. Match
21. Nail
22. Shoe polish
23. Rice
24. Dirt

You can think of many more besides these. The winner is the person who can correctly match up all the items in the fastest time. To make the game harder, place twice as many items on the table than you have clues for. *Steve Stricklen and Bob Fakkema*

BITE THE BAG

Stand an open grocery bag in the middle of the floor and ask everyone to sit in a wide circle around it. One at a time each person must come to the bag and try to pick it up with just her teeth, then return to a standing position. Nothing but the bottoms of players' feet are ever allowed to touch the floor. As

Match Game

Check off an item when
you discover its clue.

___ 1. A letter from home

___ 2. The colonel

___ 3. A famous band

___ 4. Looks like a foot

___ 5. Headquarters

___ 6. A stirring event

___ 7. The end of winter

___ 8. A pair of slippers

___ 9. Pig's retreat

___10. An old beau of mine

___11. The peace maker

___12. There love is found

___13. Cause of the Revolution

___14. An absorbing article

___15. A place for reflection

___16. The reigning favorite

___17. A morning caller

___18. Seen at the ball game

___19. Messenger

___20. Fire when ready

___21. Drive through the wood

___22. Bound to shine

Match Game

Check off an item when
you discover its clue.

___ 1. A letter from home

___ 2. The colonel

___ 3. A famous band

___ 4. Looks like a foot

___ 5. Headquarters

___ 6. A stirring event

___ 7. The end of winter

___ 8. A pair of slippers

___ 9. Pig's retreat

___10. An old beau of mine

___11. The peace maker

___12. There love is found

___13. Cause of the Revolution

___14. An absorbing article

___15. A place for reflection

___16. The reigning favorite

___17. A morning caller

___18. Seen at the ball game

___19. Messenger

___20. Fire when ready

___21. Drive through the wood

___22. Bound to shine

you go around the circle you will observe that almost everyone can do this. After everyone has a turn, cut off or fold down an inch or two of the bag. Go around again. With each round, shorten the bag more. When a person is no longer able to pick up the bag and stand again, she is out. The winner is the one who can pick it up without falling when no one else can. *Jim Walton*

LIAR

Here's a good game for parties or small groups that's fun and helps people get to know each other a lot better. Each person gets a sheet of paper and a pencil. At the top of the page, he or she writes down four statements about himself or herself. One of the statements must be true. The other three must be false. The true statement should be a little-known fact that no one would know until now.

Then the game really begins. One at a time each person reads those four statements, and everyone else tries to guess which one is true. When it is your turn, you score one point for every incorrect guess (the correct answer is not given until everyone has guessed each time). When you are guessing on someone else's statements, you get one point if you make a correct guess. At the end of the game, whoever has the most points is the winner. Each person should keep his or her own score. *R.D. Birdwell*

MATCH UP

This is a variation of the old television game show "The Match Game." Divide into two or more teams of equal number. Have each team choose a team captain who goes to the front of the room with the other team captains. Everyone, including the team captains, should have several sheets of paper and pencils.

The leader then asks the entire group a question, such as "Who is going to win the World Series this year?" Everyone, without any discussion, writes his or her answer down on one slip of paper, and passes it in to the team captain, who has also written down an answer. When ready, the team captains announce their answers, and a point is awarded to each team for every answer from that team which matches the team captain's. In other words, if the team captain answered, "The Dodgers," then his or her team would get a point for every answer from that team which also was "The Dodgers."

Some sample questions, or make up your own:

1. If you were going to repaint this room, what color would you do it in?
2. What country in the world would you most like to visit?
3. What is your favorite TV show?
4. Pick a number between one and five.
5. What book of the Bible has the most to say about good works?
6. What's the best way to have fun in this town?
7. What's the funniest word you can think of?
8. How many kids do you think you will have?

Rick McPeak

ONE FOOT STAND

Here's a game that sounds very simple, but isn't. All each individual has to do is stand on one foot while holding the other, with his eyes closed. The one who can do it the longest is the winner. It is doubtful anyone will be able to do this for more than 30 seconds. *Ron Erber*

NAME SIX

Players all sit in a circle with the exception of one person who sits in the center of the room and closes her eyes. An object (it can be anything—a ball, book, shoe) is then passed around the circle until the person in the center of the circle claps her hands. The person in the circle who is holding the object waits until the person in the center assigns a letter from the alphabet. The object is then passed around the circle while the person who was caught with the object tries to name six objects that begin with the assigned letter before the item being passed once again reaches him. If unsuccessful, that person must change places with the person in the center of the circle. The second time a person is unsuccessful at naming six objects, he is out of the game and the circle gets smaller. *Robert Schnitzer*

SLIDE STORIES

Divide the group into teams of five to 10 each. Provide each team with 20 or more slides of various things: people, objects, travel, nature, whatever you can throw in. Each team must make up a story using as many of the slides as possible. Set a time limit and have each team project their "slide story" for the rest of the group. The most creative, funny, longest, etc., wins. *Don Snider*

NATIONAL GEOGRAPHIC

Give everyone an old National Geographic or other magazine with pictures. Everyone starts with the magazine closed. The leader says "Find a picture of...(any object)" and everyone races to find it and earn a point. Rotate the magazines once in a while. For ideas, have them look for things such as a flag, a sailing ship, a guy with a mustache, a fish out of water, lightning, a particular word, a Kodak ad, a map, a purple Cadillac on Park Avenue, etc. *David Coppedge*

OJII-SAN TO OBAA-SAN

In this Japanese game, the players sit in a circle, and two rolled-up kerchiefs are given to any two players in the circle who are seated some distance apart. One kerchief represents the grandmother (Ojii-san) and the other kerchief represents the grandfather (Obaa-san). The game is built around the idea that the grandmother is chasing the grandfather.

When the game starts, the players who have the kerchiefs put them around their necks, tie a simple overhand knot, give their hands one clap, then pull the kerchief off and pass it to the right.The players on the right repeat the same process. This continues until someone gets caught with the grandmother kerchief before passing the grandfather kerchief on to the next player. Whoever gets caught receives a penalty of some kind. *Burrell Pennings*

ANIMAL RUMMY

Here's an enjoyable game if you don't want much physical activity, but still want to have some fun. Give everybody a piece of paper and a pencil. Then have each person write someone's name at the top of a sheet of paper, each letter to head up a column, like so:

H	U	B	E	R	T

Everyone should use the same name.

The leader now calls "Animal" and each player writes the names of as many animals as he or she can in each column—the animal names must begin with the letter heading that particular column. Set a time limit of about two minutes or so. Then the leader should ask for all the animals listed in each column and make a master list. Players receive points for each animal they have listed on their own sheet, plus each animal is given a bonus point value based on the number of players who did not have that particular animal listed.

This game can also be played with flowers, vegetables, trees, cities, or any other category you can think of. It's a lot of fun. *J. Russell Matzke*

SPOONS

This classic knuckle bruiser is much like musical chairs except you use spoons and a deck of cards. For each player there are four cards of one kind (four kings, four tens, etc.). Spoons are placed on the table equal to the number of players minus one. The cards are mixed up and four cards are dealt to each player.

After the players have had a chance to look at their cards, they start passing one card from their hand to the player sitting on their right. They keep passing the cards until one player has four of a kind in his hand. That player then grabs a spoon and everyone tries to make sure they have one after all the fighting is over. If the player who first reaches for the spoon does it quietly, then it is a while before the others notice a spoon missing. *Bill Thompson*

TAKING A TRIP

Here's an indoor or travel game that taxes everyone's concentration. The leader starts by saying "I'm taking a trip and I'm bringing _________." He can bring anything as long as it is only one word. The second person repeats the sentence and adds one item to the list. The third person adds another, and the game continues as long as the list is repeated correctly in order. If a person forgets an item or gets them out of order, he is eliminated. *Kit Hoag*

STORY LINE

The group is divided into two or more teams. Each team elects a spokesperson for the group. Each group then gets a card with a daffy sentence typed on it. (Create your own; the daffier the better. Example: "Fourteen yellow elephants driving polka-dotted Volkswagens converged on the Halloween party.") The spokesperson from each group then comes forward with the card.

The leader explains that she will begin telling a story; at a certain point, she will stop and point to one of the spokespersons, who will have to pick up the story line and keep it going. Every minute or so a whistle will sound and that person must stop talking and the next spokesperson must pick up the story line. This continues for about 10 minutes.

Now here's the object: to work the story line around so that you get the sentence you have been given into the story in such a way that the other groups cannot tell that you have done so.

At the end of the story, each group must decide whether the spokespeople for the other groups were able to get their sentences into the story—and if so, what it was. Points may be awarded for getting in the sentence, guessing whether or not it got in, and what the sentence was.

Here's how a story line can start, for example:

Dudley Do-Right and Priscilla Pure were rowing in the middle of the lake one fine summer day. Dudley as infatuated with Priscilla and longed to hold her fair, soft hand. When no one was around, he pulled his oar in and reached for Priscilla's smooth fingers. He was inches away when suddenly . . .

Keith Geckeler

FARKLE

The object of this game, also known as Zilch, is to score as much over 5000 points as possible by throwing six dice. Points are scored in this manner:

Any three of a kind or large straight must be rolled in one roll, not accumulated in more than one roll.

The player starts by rolling all six dice. After rolling, she has the option of ending her turn and adding the score of her dice to her accumulated game score; or putting aside one or more of her dice that score, and rolling the remaining dice. She may continue to do this until she either decides to stop, or scores nothing on the dice she rolls. Any time a player rolls dice and scores nothing on the dice she

Farkle

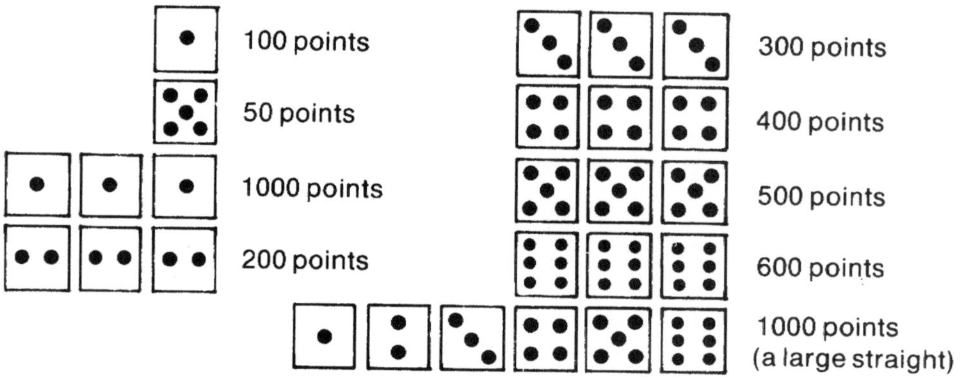

100 points
50 points
1000 points
200 points
300 points
400 points
500 points
600 points
1000 points (a large straight)

rolled, she immediately loses her turn and all points accumulated on that turn. This is known as a "Farkle." Whenever she ends up with all six dice scoring points, whether in one turn or in several, she has "turned them over," in which case she may pick up all six dice up and roll them again, adding to her accumulated score on that turn, including those before she turned them over. Thus, a player's score is not added until she chooses to stop. Once a player sets aside scoring dice, she may not roll them again until she turns over all six dice.

To begin the game, a player's first score must be at least 500 on that turn. If she doesn't score 500 points before she Farkles, she must try again on her next turn. Play goes around the circle until a player accumulates 5000 or more points. At this point, her game is over, and everyone else has only one more turn—a last chance to pass her. Whoever ends then with the highest score wins.

Farkle is a good party game because any number can play. It's simple, and it promotes conversation. It also tests the balance between a player's greed and good judgment! *David Oakes*

TOSS THE RAG

Tie a rag or sock into a tight knot. Everyone is seated in a circle with "It" in the middle. "It" tosses the rag to someone and shouts some category (such as soft drinks, washing machines, presidents, birds, theologians, books of the Bible, etc.). He then counts to 10 rapidly. If he reaches 10 before the other person names an example of that category (Coke, Kenmore, Lincoln, sapsucker, Kierkegaard, Ezekiel, etc.), then that person takes his place in the center. The category named should be a common noun, while the examples given are normally proper nouns. *Richard Bond*

WHO SIR, ME SIR?

Here's an exciting indoor game, best with groups of between five and 20 kids. The object of the game is to work your way up to the head chair and stay there. Seat everyone in a semicircle of chairs or benches. Let the group count off; players keep their number for the whole game no matter where they sit.

The leader begins the action by saying,

The Prince of Paris lost his hat, and number eight (or any number) knows where it is. Eight, go foot.

Now before the leader says "go foot," number eight has to shout out "Who sir, me sir?" (or "Who ma'am" or "Who miss" or "Who Trish" or "Who Bob"—whatever's right for you and your group). Otherwise he must leave his seat and go to the end chair (at the leader's right); everyone moves up a seat to fill in his spot.

If he says "Who sir, me sir?" in time, there is a short conversation between the leader and him, like this:

Leader: "Yes sir, you sir."
Number eight: "No sir, not I, sir."
Leader: "Who then, sir?"
Number eight: "Four, sir" (or any other number).

The leader then quickly says, "Four, go foot." and number four has to say "Who sir, me sir?" before he does, then the process repeats. Any time someone loses, the leader starts over with "The Prince of Paris lost his hat" etc.

Teach the group how to play, then start out slowly, allowing one mistake each before making anyone "go foot." But then gradually speed up; the faster you go, the more exciting the game gets. Believe it or not, once they get the hang of it teenagers have a lot of fun with this game.

In case of a tie between the leader and the victim, let the group vote on whether the victim should keep his seat or go foot. With good players you can penalize those who say "Who sir, me sir" at the wrong time. Players try to get the ones higher than them out, so they can move up toward the head chair. Work for a humorous atmosphere so no one is too embarrassed about going to the foot of the line. *David Coppedge*

CRAZY BRIDGE

Crazy Bridge is actually not like Bridge at all, but can be played with regular cards or Rook cards. It is a simple game that anyone can play and anyone can win. Older youths, college age, and adults should enjoy it. It is recommended as a good way for leaders to get together with sponsors and enjoy an evening without the kids!

You can adapt the game to almost any situation, but it is designed for mixed couples. Set up several card tables and play partners, four to a table. After each game losers move down a table and winners move up a table, and all change partners.

Photocopy the instructions and score sheet (page 121) for all players. There are 16 rounds or hands, and each is played by different rules. But in all of them, you deal out the whole deck and play for tricks. High card takes the trick, or trump will take anything. You can play trump only when you do not have a particular suit in your hand. Whoever takes a trick then takes the lead and plays the next card. In this way it is similar to games like Pitch and Hearts.

Each person is on his or her own, and the one with the highest point total wins. You use a lot of time for visiting because it is an easy game, plus you get to be with different people constantly. Have plenty of food on hand between rounds. If there is an odd number of people, work them in at the last table.

The Instruction and Score Sheet should be given to each participant. *Larry Jansen*

FINGERS UP PLAYOFFS

Have the entire group pair off and play the game Fingers Up. Two people face each other with their hands behind their backs. On the count of three, they bring out both hands in front of them with a certain number of fingers on each hand held up. They should hold their hands and fingers right in front of their face so the other person can see them. A closed fist means a zero on that hand. The first person to give the total number of fingers up on all four hands wins the game. Each pair should go for the best two out of three. The game requires quick thinking and is a lot of fun to play.

After everyone has played two out of three, all of the losers sit down on the floor, and all the winners pair off again and play the game amongst themselves, with the losers each time sitting down and the winners pairing off. It should wind down to a championship match with two people. Give the winner a pair of gloves, some hand cream, or some crazy prize that has to do with fingers. *Glen G. Davis*

GUESS THE MENU

Copy the ingredients from a few common items from your pantry or refrigerator. Pass this list around to your kids and have them guess what each item is. Here are a few examples:

1. Soybean oil, eggs, vinegar, water, salt, sugar, and lemon juice (mayonnaise)
2. Tomatoes, vinegar, corn sweetener, salt, onion powder, and spice (catsup)

Kathie Taylor

HOW'S YOURS?

Here's a simple living room game that's good for a lot of laughs. Everyone gathers in a circle while one person is sent out of the room. The group then chooses a noun (such as shoe or job). When the person comes back into the room he must ask "How's yours?" Each person he asks must then answer with an adjective that describes the noun chosen by the group. "It" must guess after each response and continue around the circle until he can guess the noun chosen. The last person to give an adjective before "It" guesses the correct noun becomes the next "It." *Glenn Tombaugh*

HELP YOUR NEIGHBOR

Here's a simple card game that kids like to play. You need a minimum of four people to play and there is no maximum. If you have lots of kids, get lots of games going at once. You will need one deck of regular playing cards (or some other kind of numbered cards) for each four people who play. If you have more than four people, you'll need more cards.

Everyone gets one suit (hearts, spades, etc.) from the deck—numbers two through 12 (Jack is 11 and Queen is 12). The King and Ace are not used. The cards should be spread out in front of each person so that they can be seen (face up).

The first person in the group (it doesn't matter who starts) takes a pair of dice and rolls them. Whatever number is rolled, the player then turns over the corresponding card. For example, if the dice total comes to seven, then the player turns over his number seven card. If the number total is 11, then

Name ____________________

CRAZY BRIDGE
INSTRUCTION AND SCORE SHEET

1. No bidding, no dummy, no honors counted.
2. Player to left of dealer leads.
3. Each trick counts as 10 (do not score as in Bridge).
4. Play partners. The side taking the most tricks is the winner.
5. After each game change tables (winners move up, losers move down) and partners.
6. High score after 16 rounds wins.

Round 1	Spades are trumps.	________
Round 2	No trump. Winners add 100.	________
Round 3	Clubs are trumps. Winners and losers trade scores.	________
Round 4	Hearts are trumps. Don't look at your hand; play from table.	________
Round 5	Spades are trumps. Losers subtract 10 from score.	________
Round 6	Clubs are trumps. Winners add 300 to their score.	________
Round 7	No trumps. Winners take all.	________
Round 8	Diamonds are trumps. Winners and losers trade scores.	________
Round 9	Hearts are trumps. Winners take all.	________
Round 10	Cut for trump. Winners add 50.	________
Round 11	Clubs are trumps. Don't look at your hand; play from table.	________
Round 12	No trump. Loser takes all.	________
Round 13	Spades are trumps. Winners add 50 to score.	________
Round 14	Diamonds are trumps. Winners add 100 to their score.	________
Round 15	Spades are trumps. Winners and losers trade scores.	________
Round 16	Hearts are trumps. Winners double score.	________
	Total Score	________

the Jack is turned over, etc.

The player keeps going so long as he has cards to turn over. He can, however, also turn over the player to his left's cards in order to keep his turn alive. (That's when you help your neighbor). In other words, if a second seven is rolled, then you check your neighbor's cards to see if he has a seven still showing. If so, then you can turn it over and keep going. Your turn continues until you can no longer turn over any cards from either your hand or your neighbor's. The game ends when one person has turned over all of his cards. *Malcolm McQueen*

SOUND SWEEPSTAKES

Here's a fun and simple game. All you need is a tape recorder. Before your meeting go out and record the sounds of 20 various things, such as a light switch, a car starting, the spraying of a deodorant can, and so forth. Try to record sounds that most people would be familiar with.

At your meeting pass out paper and pencils and play back the sounds allowing time in between for the students to record their guesses. You can play with teams, by having the groups try to agree on the sound and come up with the list. At the conclusion, play back all of the sounds and review the answers. Award points for each correct guess. *Mike Shields*

TEAM CROSSWORD

Here's a good indoor game that requires some quick thinking. Get a book of crossword puzzles and select one that would be about the right difficulty for your group. Reproduce the crossword puzzle on a large piece of butcher paper, or project it on the wall with an overhead projector. Divide your group into two or more teams.

After you read the clue, the first team to shout out the right answer gets a point for every blank letter space filled. The team with the correct answer then gets to select which clue is read next, and so forth. It's usually a good idea to have one person read the clues and have another person fill in the correct responses and keep score. If one team gets too far ahead, give triple point value on the last few words to give the teams that are behind a chance to catch up. *Dan H. Prout*

IRONGUT

If you have some daring kids in your group, try this contest. Prepare a concoction using ingredients found in any kitchen, and carefully list all the ingredients you use. (Fifteen to 25 are needed.) At your meeting, call for some volunteers to be the Irongut. If teams are already formed, choose one or two from each team.

Those who are brave enough to accept the challenge take turns tasting a cup of the potion, which is usually a yucky brown color and thick. The winner is the person who can write down the most correctly-identified ingredients in the brew.
Some suggested ingredients:

Catsup	**Mustard**	**Horseradish**
Cinnamon	**Nutmeg**	**Garlic**
Milk	**Salad Dressing**	**Pickle Juice**
Onion Salt	**Vinegar**	**Orange Juice**
Tartar Sauce	**Paprika**	**Oregano**
Soda	**Salt**	**Hot Sauce**
Pepper	**Worcestershire Sauce**	

Keep a careful watch on the kid who asks for seconds! *Byron Harvey*

BUNKO

Here's a longtime favorite party game. Twelve or more players (in multiples of four) are needed, plus lots of dice. Set up small card tables with four chairs

PERSONAL SCORE CARD

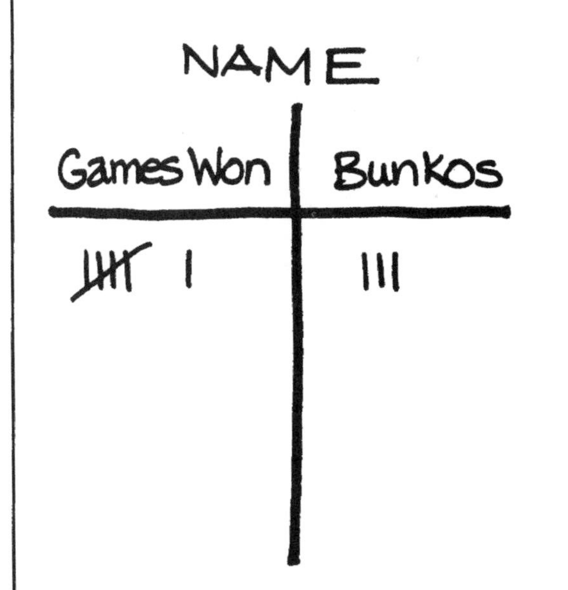

TABLE SCORE CARDS

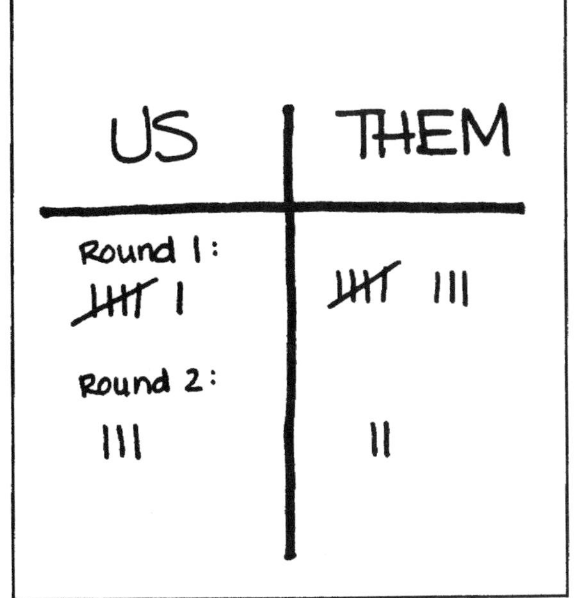

at each, two apiece on opposite sides of the table. Tables should be numbered, with Table 1 designated as the head table.

Each player chooses a partner, who sits directly across the table from him or her. Players are given their own personal score cards which they take with them wherever they play. Each table is provided with three dice, a pencil, and a score card, which stay at that table.

The object of the game is to win more points in each round of play than the opposing team at your table, so that you and your partner can move toward the head table and attempt to stay there. Play begins when the head table rings the bell. Partners at the head table attempt to win 21 points in each round, while teams at all other tables win as many points as they can. When a team at the head table reaches 21 points, they ring the bell, and the round ends immediately at all tables.

To score: Players take turns throwing all three dice at once, with teams alternating turns. If the player rolls a one in the first round, his or her team earns a point, and the player rolls again. Every one rolled in that round earns a point; but if no ones are rolled, a player on the other team takes a turn. Team scores are recorded on the table score cards.

When the head table rings the bell to end the first round, each team calculates its score for that round on the card. The first team at the head table to reach 21 wins the round at Table 1; at all other tables, the team with the higher score wins. If there is a tie when the bell rings, teams roll again until someone wins (sudden death).

The winning team at the head table remains there for the next round, while the losers go to the last table. Winners at each of the other tables advance to the next table (Table 3 winners go to Table 2, Table 2 to Table 1, and so on) while losers remain in their seats. Before the next round, players at the new table must swap partners; no player should have the same partner twice in a row.

In the second round (begun by the bell at the head table), players earn one point for their team with each two they roll. In the third round, threes earn points, and so on. Rounds continue up through six and then back down to one again for a total of 11 rounds.

Points can also be earned by two other types of throws. A throw of three of a kind that are not the number for the round (for example, three 4s in round two) earns six points, and the player keeps rolling. A throw of three of a kind that are the number for the round (three 5s in round five) is called a Bunko, and earns an automatic 21 points (an automatic win at the head table). The player who throws a Bunko yells "Bunko!" and records it on his or her personal score card. Personal cards should also record each game won by the player's team.

At the end of the game (11 rounds) three prizes are awarded:

1. To the last team to win at the head table.
2. To the player with the most (personal) Bunkos.
3. To the player with the most wins.

Dick Gibson

TANGLE

This game allows for lots of close contact and cooperation among the group members.

Using an even number of people (between six and 20), have them get into a close circle. Have all players put their right hands into the circle and grab someone else's right hand, though not the person's next to them.

Now have them put their left hands into the circle and take someone else's left hand, though not the person next to them or the person with whom they've joined right hands.

Now, without letting go of hands, everyone must maneuver into one large circle by twisting, turning, going under, and going over each other. It can be done and it's a lot of fun to try. You might want to have two groups going at once to see who can finish first. *Murray Wilding*

CAN YOU PICTURE THAT?

How well do your kids really know your town, your church, their schools? Having eyes, do they not see? Shoot a roll of film of places the kids see every day—but take the photos from unusual perspectives. For example, take a picture from inside the local pizza place, looking out. Look for some obscure places to shoot. Throw in a few easy ones.

Line up the photos on a table and number each one. Give the kids some paper, and let them guess what each shot is of and where it was snapped from. Give a prize to the winner, and have a Polaroid camera on hand to get a shot of winner, prize, and group.

Brad Davis

LICENSE PLATES

Here's a variation of a time-honored road game that just about everyone's played. Divide your group into teams, then hand out copies of page 125—one copy per team, or one copy per person. (For an easier game, use the matching version on page 126 instead.)

Give students a time limit to fill in (or match) the names of the 32 states. Here are the answers:

1. The Aloha State (Hawaii)
2. America's Dairyland (Wisconsin)
3. The Bay State (Massachusetts)
4. The Bluegrass State (Kentucky)
5. The Centennial State (Colorado)
6. The Constitution State (Connecticut)
7. The Empire State (New York)
8. First in Flight (North Carolina)
9. The First State (Delaware)
10. The Garden State (New Jersey)
11. The Golden State (California)
12. The Grand Canyon State (Arizona)
13. The Great Lake State (Michigan)
14. The Hawkeye State (Iowa)
15. The Heart of Dixie (Alabama)
16. The Hoosier State (Indiana)
17. The Keystone State (Pennsylvania)
18. Land of 10,000 Lakes (Minnesota)
19. The Land of Enchantment (New Mexico)
20. Land of Lincoln (Illinois)
21. Land of Opportunity (Arkansas)
22. The Lone Star State (Texas)
23. The Magnolia State (Mississippi)
24. The Ocean State (Rhode Island)
25. The Peach State (Georgia)
26. The Show-Me State (Missouri)
27. The Silver State (Nevada)
28. The Sportsman's State (Louisiana)
29. The Sunflower State (Kansas)
30. The Sunshine State (Florida)
31. The Vacation State (Maine)
32. The Volunteer State (Tennessee)

Bill Williamson

THE LITTER GAME

The next time you (or someone in your group) has a pregnant cat, make a contest out of it. Give the kids a list of questions like the ones below, and award a prize to whoever has the most correct guesses.
1. On what day do you think she'll have her kittens? (Hint: it looks like it'll be within two weeks.)
2. How many kittens will she have? (Please, God, let

License Plates

Fill in the blank with correct state name.

1. The Aloha State ______
2. America's Dairyland ______
3. The Bay State ______
4. The Bluegrass State ______
5. The Centennial State ______
6. The Constitution State ______
7. The Empire State ______
8. First in Flight ______
9. The First State ______
10. The Garden State ______
11. The Golden State ______
12. The Grand Canyon State ______
13. The Great Lake State ______
14. The Hawkeye State ______
15. The Heart of Dixie ______
16. The Hoosier State ______
17. The Keystone State ______
18. Land of 10,000 Lakes ______
19. The Land of Enchantment ______
20. Land of Lincoln ______
21. Land of Opportunity ______
22. The Lone Star State ______
23. The Magnolia State ______
24. The Ocean State ______
25. The Peach State ______
26. The Show-Me State ______
27. The Silver State ______
28. The Sportsman's State ______
29. The Sunflower State ______
30. The Sunshine State ______
31. The Vacation State ______
32. The Volunteer State ______

Match the state with the license plate phrase by writing the name of the state on the appropriate line.

1. The Aloha State ____________________
2. America's Dairyland ____________________
3. The Bay State ____________________
4. The Bluegrass State ____________________
5. The Centennial State ____________________
6. The Constitution State ____________________
7. The Empire State ____________________
8. First in Flight ____________________
9. The First State ____________________
10. The Garden State ____________________
11. The Golden State ____________________
12. The Grand Canyon State ____________________
13. The Great Lake State ____________________
14. The Hawkeye State ____________________
15. The Heart of Dixie ____________________
16. The Hoosier State ____________________
17. The Keystone State ____________________
18. Land of 10,000 Lakes ____________________
19. The Land of Enchantment ____________________
20. Land of Lincoln ____________________
21. Land of Opportunity ____________________
22. The Lone Star State ____________________
23. The Magnolia State ____________________
24. The Ocean State ____________________
25. The Peach State ____________________
26. The Show-Me State ____________________
27. The Silver State ____________________
28. The Sportsman's State ____________________
29. The Sunflower State ____________________
30. The Sunshine State ____________________
31. The Vacation State ____________________
32. The Volunteer State ____________________

Alabama
Arizona
Arkansas
California
Colorado
Connecticut
Delaware
Florida
Georgia
Hawaii
Illinois
Indiana
Iowa
Kansas
Kentucky
Louisiana
Maine
Massachusetts
Michigan
Minnesota
Mississippi
Missouri
Nevada
New Jersey
New Mexico
New York
North Carolina
Rhode Island
Pennsylvania
Tennessee
Texas
Wisconsin

it be just one!)
3. Where in the house will she have them? (If you guess "On the living room couch," your guess is automatically disqualified—and you get the cleaner's bill if you're right!)
4. What color will the runt be?
5. During what time of day will they arrive? (Circle one)
Morning Afternoon Evening Late night
6. Which of the three children in the home will see them first?
7. Would you like to own a kitten of your own? (Extra credit for a yes answer here.)
Kurt Staeuble

IDENTITY CRISIS

Though you can play this game anytime, it's especially appropriate at the end of a food event.

A few hours before the event, put a half dozen different fruits and vegetables (bananas, grapefruits, eggplants, etc.) in a food processor, grind them all up some, let them sit until the end of the party, then bring out the mess and let representatives of each team poke through it—or taste it—and try to guess what's what. *Mark Ziehr*

PEOPLE TRIVIA

To help your group get better acquainted with one another, try this variation of the popular trivia games. Distribute a questionnaire to your kids with questions they must answer about themselves. Make the questions correspond to the categories in the trivia game you plan to use. For example, for "Entertainment" you can ask for the person's favorite TV show; for history, you can ask for his or her birthplace. Also use miscellaneous questions such as "What was the most embarrassing moment of your life?"

Next, prepare question cards for the game that combine the "official" questions with questions about your group members, such as "Who was born in Hogsback Mountain, Montana?" "Whose favorite TV show is Lawrence Welk?"

Play the game otherwise as usual—and prepare for some fascinating "trivial" revelations about your group. *Bob Machovec*

PIN THE COLLAR ON THE PASTOR

If you have a big shopping mall near you, chances are good that it has a place which makes life-sized computer photos from a snapshot. Have one made of your pastor's face (from the shoulders up), and play Pin the Collar (or necktie) on the Pastor. Your kids will love it! *Gary McCluskey*

THE RULE GAME

Players sit in circles of three to six people each in order to play this laugher. The game's only rule is that players take turns devising rules—and the rules must be followed for the duration of the game.

For example, a player might say in her turn, "If you use a word that begins with T, you must stand up and take a bow." Or, "If you touch your hand to your face, you must run around your chair three times." Or, "Every time you break a rule, everyone must point at you and cough." And the game cannot end without—can you guess?—someone making it a rule.

You can adapt this game for long bus trips or use it as a discussion starter about keeping God's rules.
Tawn Bueltmann

STATES

Everyone sits in a circle and takes the name of a state (Tennessee, Oregon, etc.). One person chosen to begin the game stands in the middle of the circle with a rolled-up newspaper (not too thick). When the newspaper-wielder calls out the name of a state, the person who represents that state must stand up and call out the name of another state before the newspaper-wielder can whack him (below the neck) with the newspaper. The round continues until the whacker in the center actually whacks a state-person below the neck before the latter calls out another state. The whackee then becomes the whacker, and accordingly takes his or her place in the center, rolled newspaper in hand.

Just a few guidelines:

- You must call the name of a state that's represented in the group.
- You cannot call the state that just called you.

• You cannot call the state of the person in the middle.

Action can get fast and furious between just a few states, so occasionally redistribute the states among the players so that everyone participates. *Lynn H. Pryor*

TRAVELING MURDER MYSTERY

To encourage kids to get to know the kids outside their immediate circle of friends, try this whodunit patterned after the board game Clue. It's also a great game to dispel the monotony of a long bus ride. Everyone is given a master sheet listing all students (you provide this), and another sheet with all the roles (though without telling what role a kid is playing—that's for each individual only to know), the

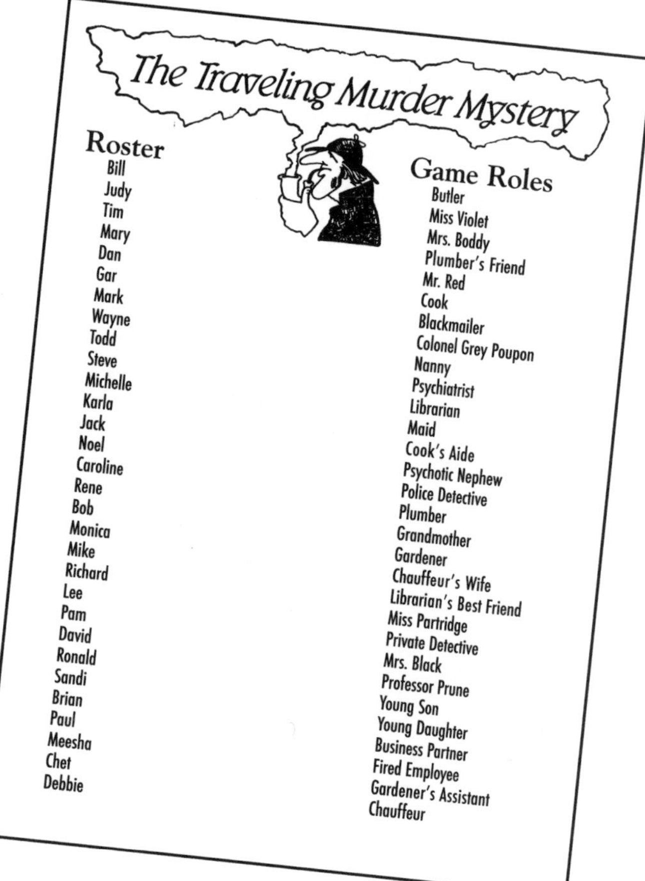

game's instructions, and the floor plan of Murder Manor (page 129). Each player is also given a slip of paper explaining his or her own role, testimony, and particular nervous trait (pages 130-132, cut apart). Each person spends five minutes with every other person in the game, asking questions that will help solve the three aspects of the plot. At the end of five minutes, before moving to the next person, players give one additional fact that has yet been undiscovered about their characters. *Dick Gibson*

UP JENKINS

This game of concealment and feint is best played by small, even groups of six to 12 players. All that's needed is a long table, chairs for all players, and a quarter. Divide people into two teams; teams sit on opposite sides of the table. Each team elects a captain.

The game begins with one team secretly passing the quarter back and forth among its players underneath the table. When the captain of the opposing team says "Up Jenkins!" all the players on the quarter-passing team close their fists, lift their arms, and place their elbows on the table. In one of the fists, of course, is the quarter. Then the opposing captain says "Down Jenkins!" and all the players simultaneously slam their hands down on the table. If it's done well, the other team won't be able to hear the quarter.

The object then is for the guessing team to eliminate all the hands that do not have the quarter, leaving at last the one hand with the quarter under it. So the opposing captain chooses people to lift a hand, one hand at a time. The team with the quarter can respond to the captain only; lifting a hand in response to anyone else on the opposing team means forfeiture of the quarter. One of the goals of the opposing team, therefore, is to persuade people to lift their hands in response to someone other than their captain. If the opposing team's captain successfully lifts all the hands except the one covering the quarter, his or her team wins and takes possession of the quarter. If, however, the captain uncovers the quarter before the last hand, the quarter-passing team retains possession and a new round begins.

Once the kids get the hang of it, they'll develop all sorts of strategies—how to make your hand "look guilty" when you don't have the quarter, etc. *Dave Sherwood*

The Traveling Murder Mystery

GAME ROLES

Butler
Miss Violet
Mrs. Boddy
Plumber's Friend
Mr. Red
Cook
Blackmailer
Colonel Grey Poupon
Nanny
Psychiatrist
Librarian
Maid
Cook's Aide
Psychotic Nephew
Police Detective
Plumber
Grandmother
Gardener
Chauffeur's Wife
Librarian's Best Friend
Miss Partridge
Private Detective
Mrs. Black
Professor Prune
Young Son
Young Daughter
Business Partner
Fired Employee
Gardener's Assistant
Chauffeur

INSTRUCTIONS: This game has several plots that will demand your attention and a discerning eye. Mr. Boddy, master of Murder Manor, has been found dead at the foot of the stairs. He is lying on his back, his body badly broken, with a red face. In his hand he clutches a single feather. You are to discover the following things:

- Who murdered Mr. Boddy, where the murder was committed, and how he was killed
- The game roles of all those playing
- The location of each person at the time of the murder

To assist you in discovering the truth, all characters have a nervous habit or trait that they do whenever they lie while answering a question. If you find someone with the same nervous habit as you, you must confide to that person all your information.

Let the game begin!

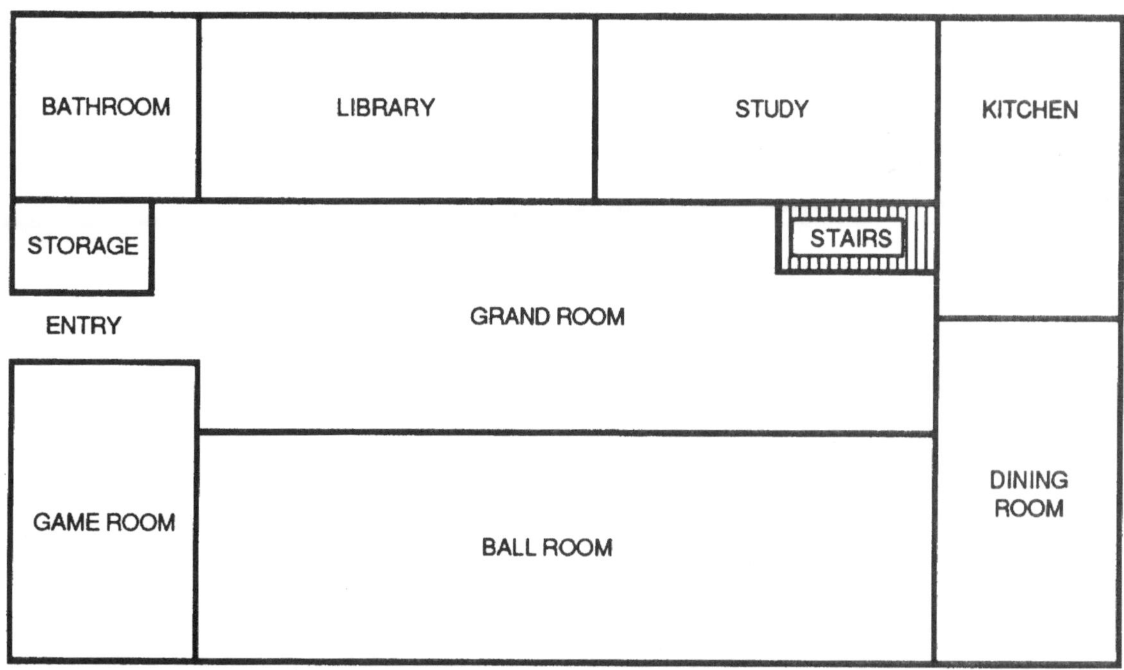

Your role: **COOK'S AIDE**
Your testimony: You came with the Cook to Murder Manor and spend all of your time in the Kitchen. You have no motive for killing Boddy, but are covered with blood. The Cook had no time to help you clean up after the murder was committed.
Your nervous trait: Bite nails

Your role: **MR. RED**
Your testimony: You are a convicted murderer sent to prison by the POLICE DETECTIVE. While in jail you worked in the prison infirmary and picked up enough medical knowledge to get a job as an Emergency Medical Technician after you were released. You were in the GAME ROOM when the murder was committed but checked the body to declare BODDY dead.
Your nervous trait: Bite nails

Your role: **PSYCHOTIC NEPHEW**
Your testimony: You have fried your brain with drugs and have no touch with reality. Your driving passion is to kill your uncle. Nothing that you say is the truth.
Your nervous trait: Pick any

Your role: **PLUMBER'S FRIEND**
Your testimony: You are a silent witness and accessory to the murder of MR. BODDY, which took place in the BATHROOM. You have no motive.
Your nervous trait: Touch hands to face

Your role: **MRS. BODDY**
Your testimony: You have never been in love with your husband and married him only for his money. For some time now you have been creating household problems as an excuse to cover your rendezvous with your real love, the PLUMBER. He wants you to run away with him, but you can't bear the thought of being poor. You were in the DINING ROOM with the guests at the time of the murder.
Your nervous trait: Run hands through hair

Your role: **PLUMBER**
Your testimony: You have been to the manor an unusual number of times over the past few months, but not to fix the plumbing. You killed MR. BODDY because you wanted to run away with MRS. BODDY, and he would not divorce her.
Your nervous habit: Lick lips

Your role: **GRANDMOTHER**
Your testimony: You are blind and deaf. You were caught "in the act" at the scene of the crime, but did not commit the murder.
Nervous trait: Run hands through hair

Your role: **POLICE DETECTIVE**
Your testimony: You have been called in to investigate the murder of MR. BODDY. Upon arriving, you discover that one of the guests is a former murderer that you sent to prison 10 years ago.
You are the LIBRARIAN'S ex-husband.
Your nervous trait: Rub eyes

Your role: **LIBRARIAN**
Testimony: Although prim and proper by day, you lead the life of a swinging single at night, hitting all the hot spots in a neighboring town. That is where you got addicted to drugs, supplied to you by MR. BODDY. You are now deeply in debt and BODDY has threatened to cut off your supply if he does not get paid.
Nervous trait: Rub ear

Your role: **BUTLER**
Your testimony: You are secretly married to the maid. MR. BODDY has been making improper advances toward her for some time now, which has made you extremely jealous. He came upon the two of you embracing in the DINING ROOM before the guests arrived and has threatened to fire you.
Your nervous trait: Cross legs

Your role: **MAID**

Your testimony: You are an illegal alien in this country and secretly married to the BUTLER. MR. BODDY knows and has threatened to expose you unless you play along with him. As he made a pass at you, he missed, grabbing your feather duster instead, falling down the stairs into the GRAND ROOM. Frightened, you run off to join the guests in the DINING ROOM.

Your nervous trait: Cross legs

Your role: **COLONEL GREY POUPON**

Your testimony: You are a retired Army hero and war buddy of MR. BODDY. He has been blackmailing you for years to keep secret the fact that you were, in reality, a coward and ran from battle. You have been invited to the home for dinner, and BODDY has threatened to expose you. You were in the LIBRARY when the murder was committed.

Your nervous trait: Tap pencil

Your role: **YOUNG DAUGHTER**

Your testimony: You were with your brother when the murder was committed. All you remember is being awakened by a suction sound followed by a dragging sound.

Your nervous trait: Scratch head

Your role: **YOUNG SON**

Your testimony: Your father has mistreated you and your sister for quite some time now. Through this, you have grown to hate him, often expressing that you wished he were dead. Your father locked you in the STORAGE ROOM before the party began. You heard a scream, a fall, and the sound of something being dragged before getting tired and falling to sleep.

Nervous trait: Rub eyes

Your role: **NANNY**

Your testimony: You are a longtime employee of the family and even raised MR. BODDY when he was a child. He was a very devious brat, doing several things that almost cost you your job. Lately he's been mistreating the children, but telling MRS. BODDY that you are at fault. You are close to retirement age, but too old to get a job elsewhere. You were with the COOK when the murder was committed.

Your nervous trait: Touch hands to face

Your role: **BUSINESS PARTNER**

Your testimony: MR. BODDY talked you into investing with him in a new computer company. He said that it was a can't-lose opportunity, but you have yet to receive a return on your money. You think that BODDY has swindled you and have come to confront him about it. You are with PROFESSOR PRUNE when the murder is committed.

Your nervous trait: Bite nails

Your role: **FIRED EMPLOYEE**

Your testimony: You call MR. BODDY to tell him that his out-of town BUSINESS PARTNER came by for a surprise audit of the company books—which showed that most of the assets had been embezzled. BODDY blames you and fires you immediately. You have come to explain and are out with the GARDENER'S ASSISTANT when the murder is committed.

Your nervous trait: Rub ear

Your role: **PROFESSOR PRUNE**

Your testimony: You teach at a prestigious eastern college and went to graduate school with MR. BODDY. He knows that you cheated on your final college board exams and has threatened to expose you. You were with PRIVATE DETECTIVE as the murder was committed.

Your nervous trait: Tap foot

Your role: **GARDENER'S ASSISTANT**

Your testimony: You have no formal education and have to be pushed to get things done. From your work, you are covered with red clay and can only look in from outside the house.

Your nervous trait: Scratch head

Your role: **PSYCHIATRIST**

Your testimony: You have hated MR. BODDY since the day he fired your mother and she committed suicide. After being hired to care for the PSYCHOTIC NEPHEW, you have been training him to kill his uncle. You were in the STUDY when the murder took place.

Your nervous trait: Tap foot

Your role: **MISS PARTRIDGE**
Your testimony: You are a schoolteacher in town and the secret love of MR. BODDY. He has promised to marry you, but fears a messy divorce settlement. You are being blackmailed by a former boyfriend who knows about you and BODDY. You were in the GAME ROOM when the murder was committed.
Your nervous trait: Lick lips

Your role: **LIBRARIAN'S BEST FRIEND**
Your testimony: You are rather old, dressed in red, and you never left the LIBRARY on the night of the murder. You have no motive to kill MR. BODDY and heard nothing, even though the murder was committed in the next room.
Your nervous trait: Lick lips

Your role: **BLACKMAILER**
Your testimony: After being jilted by MISS PARTRIDGE, you have been acquiring suggestive photographs of her and MR. BODDY and have been using these to blackmail both of them. You have come for your weekly collection and were hit on the head in the KITCHEN. You awake with the murder weapon in your hand.
Your nervous trait: Rub eyes

Your role: **COOK**
Your testimony: You are the newest employee of Murder Manor, having served in various places over the past few years. The only one on the house staff to befriend you is the NANNY. You are aware of BODDY'S efforts to have her dismissed and promise to do what you can to help. You were in the KITCHEN when BODDY was killed.
Your nervous trait: Tap pencil

Your role: **GARDENER**
Your testimony: In replanting roses around the manor, you discover a shallow grave containing the decomposing body of a man. From identification in his wallet, you find out that he is a PRIVATE INVESTIGATOR hired by MR. BODDY to follow his wife. In his hand is the broken handle of a plumber's helper. You rush to your room to clean up before telling MR. BODDY, and come down the stairs to discover him dead.
Your nervous trait: Run hands through hair

Your role: **CHAUFFEUR**
Your testimony: You have called the PRIVATE DETECTIVE to give him information about MR. BODDY'S lover, which the PRIVATE DETECTIVE promises to pay you well for. The BLACKMAILER discovers this and threatens to kill you. You come upon him in the KITCHEN, hitting him on the head with the COOK'S AIDE, and leave the house.
Your nervous trait: Tap foot

Your role: **CHAUFFEUR'S WIFE**
Your testimony: Aware that the BLACKMAILER is after your husband, you come upon him unconscious in the KITCHEN. Rushing to the bathroom, you grab the murder weapon and leave it in his hand.
Your nervous trait: Scratch head

Your role: **PRIVATE DETECTIVE**
Your testimony: You were hired by MRS. BODDY to follow her husband to see if he was having an affair as she suspected. You are called by a secret informant and given vital information that you come to share with MRS. BODDY. You are in the BALLROOM when the murder is discovered.
Your nervous trait: Rub ear

Your role: **MR. BLACK**
Your testimony: While searching for your date, MISS VIOLET, you find the PLUMBER, who has just discovered the murdered body. You rush off to call the police.
Your nervous trait: Cross legs

Your role: **MISS VIOLET**
Your testimony: You're in real trouble! Invited to this dinner party by your boyfriend, MR. BLACK, you discover that another boyfriend of yours, the GARDENER, is also present. Both are insanely jealous and unaware of the other. Your solution to the problem is to hide beneath the stairs. From this position you see the PLUMBER drag MR. BODDY from the bottom of the staircase, but you hear someone approaching and must return to hiding. When you look again, BODDY is back at the foot of the stairs.
Your nervous trait: Tap pencil

WRDS

The imaginations, vocabulary, and teamwork of your youth group will get a workout with this one. Give each team a list with several letter combinations on it—PMR, for example, and RTS and SPF. Each team attempts to make a word that keeps the letters in their order. From PMR a team might make ProMpteR; from RTS, ReTreatS. The team with the longest word wins that round—ReTreatS, for example, beats CRYing.

The winner of the most rounds wins the game. Variations? Require that words be proper nouns, foreign words, biblical words, etc. *Tim Gerarden*

Drawing in the Dark

In a dark room or with tightly closed eyes, participants must make a pencil drawing of a scene you describe to them.

Give every student a sheet of paper and a pencil. The idea is to direct them to draw portions of the entire picture in the dark so they can only guess at the accurate position to place an object.

Turn out the lights, then tell them to draw, say, a house in the middle of the paper. Then ask them to place a tree to the left of the house. Then add a snowman to the right. Now put a chimney on the roof of the house. Draw a mailbox by the door. Draw a boy by the snowman. Put a scarf on the boy. Put smoke coming out of the chimney. Draw a dog by the tree. Put curtains in the window, a hat on the snowman, a nest in the tree, a flag on the mailbox, and so on.

Post the masterpieces at the end of the game. *Lyn Wargny*

Hidden in Plain Sight

In a relatively cluttered room, hide about 20 small items where they can be seen without having to open drawers or move other items. A shoelace can be wrapped around a chair leg, a dollar bill can be folded up and wrapped around a book spine, a pen can be placed atop a door frame with only the end showing, a button can be taped to a doorknob. Write out and photocopy a list of the things you've hidden—a pen, a bobby pin, a clothespin, a match—and then place a duplicate of each hidden item on a tray beside the lists.

When the kids are ready to play, give them each a copy of the list of hidden items, and leave the tray of duplicate items out for comparison. Set a time limit for the players to search the room to find each of the listed items. They are not to remove the items; they are only to note the location of each item. The winner is the player who finds the most items within the time limit. *Lyn Wargny*

Candy Quiz

Hand out the quiz on page 134 as an individual challenge or a small-group project. Each phrase is a clue to the name of a candy bar.

Candy quiz answers:

1. Musketeers
2. Twix
3. Mounds
4. Milky Way
5. Red Hots
6. Mars
7. Hollywood
8. O'Henry
9. Snickers
10. Butterfinger
11. M & M's
12. Clark Bar
13. Baby Ruth
14. 5th Avenue
15. Kiss
16. Payday
17. Slow Poke
18. Black Cow
19. Junior Mints
20. Milk Duds
21. Bit-o-Honey
22. Almond Joy
23. Reese's Pieces
24. Sweet Tarts
25. Rolos

Roger Haas

Hovercraft Drag Races

Set out 8½x11-inch sheets of paper and crayons, pencils, or markers. Instruct your students to design their own sports car—a flat, two-dimensional dream machine, colored from a bird's-eye view. Encourage them to use their imaginations—to name their cars, cover them with "sponsors'" names and logos, and number them. Remind them to distinguish the front from the rear.

The drag strip is a table; provide start and finish lines. Owners of the hovercraft dragsters puff lightly on the rear of the vehicles to "float" them down the strip and across the finish line. Leaving the strip (falling off the table) and spin-outs (when the rear

Candy Quiz

1. A famous swashbuckling trio of old: ____________________
2. Elmer Fudd's sleight-of-hand or magical maneuvers: ____________________
3. Places of interring enemies of those who tend and drive cattle and who are usually mounted on domesticated, large solid-hoofed, herbivorous mammals: ____________________
4. A broad, luminous, irregular band of astral lights that encompasses the stellar sphere: ____________________
5. Crimson-colored libidinous cravings: ____________________
6. A celestial body fourth in order from the sun, conspicuous for the redness of its light; its planetary symbol is: ____________________
7. The hard, fibrous xylem substance produced by the Aquifoliaceae family of shrubs and trees, characterized by their thick, glossy, spiny-margined leaves and usually bright red berries: ____________________
8. Author William Sidney Porter's pseudonym: ____________________
9. Multiple expressions of mirth, joy, or scorn in a covert or suppressed manner: ____________________
10. An idiom, used here singularly, employed to describe one whose dexterous deficiency denies proficiency in getting a grip on goods: ____________________
11. Possessive clone alphabetical characters: ____________________
12. A saloon named after the newspaper-reporter alias of a superhero: ____________________
13. Childhood name of a former renowned baseball player whose strike-out record is recondite: ____________________
14. Celebrated street in the Big Apple: ____________________
15. Labial massage: ____________________
16. The 24-hour part of the week set aside to compensate for labor or toil: ____________________
17. A sluggish jab: ____________________
18. Ebony-colored country critter: ____________________
19. Subordinate spices or seasonings: ____________________
20. Lactic flops: ____________________
21. A morsel of regurgitated sweet viscid material from the social and colonial hymenopterous insect: ____________________
22. The jubilant sensation of an ellipsoidal and edible nut: ____________________
23. Label on the body bag containing the remains collected after a cat named "Reese" was run over by a mower: ____________________
24. Dissonant confectionery mixture of dulcet and piquant seasonings: ____________________
25. To rotate several members of the cylindrical-shaped component of the vowel family: ____________________

of the dragster is farther down the strip than its front) disqualify the "drivers," who can race the clock or each other in time trials and tournaments.

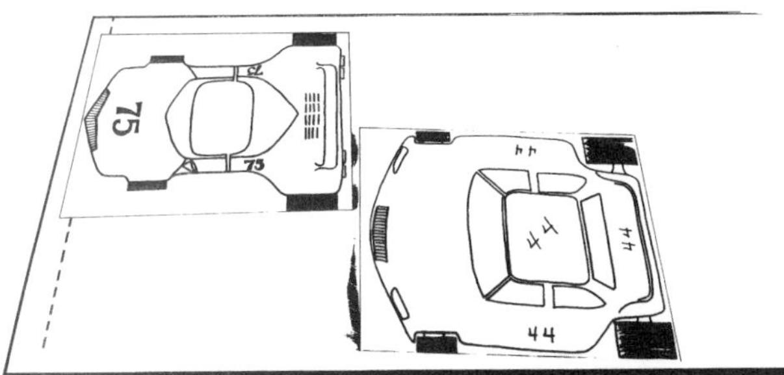

The final race can be a "Hovercraft 500." Set a square racetrack with four tables, divide your kids into teams, place some puffers on the inside of the track, then have each team race the clock and try to best each other's times. *Brett C. Wilson*

MOVIE MADNESS

Distribute one 3x5-inch card to each teenager and instruct kids to write down the name of a movie, TV program, or commercial. Players should not see what others have written. Collect the cards.

Now divide the group into teams of four or five each (involve the adult sponsors, too) and have each team draw one card from the pile you're holding. Teams then take three to five minutes to plan a scene from the movie, TV program, or commercial that they chose. After you've gathered the groups together again, let the teams act out their scenes one at a time. The other teams can guess what movie, program, or commercial the performing team is portraying only when the performing team is finished.

For extra fun, record the evening on video—then edit it and play it at your next Movie Night. *David Smith*

MY AUNT LIKES—

Here's a word game that needs no equipment. Tell your students that you will tell them some things your aunt likes, and some things she doesn't—and they have to figure out why she likes one thing and not the other. Here are examples of what you'll say:

"My aunt likes rattlers but hates snakes."
"My aunt likes sparrows but hates birds."
"My aunt likes rabbits but hates hares."
"My aunt likes weeds but hates plants."
"My aunt likes trees but hates pines."

In case you haven't figured it out yet, your aunt likes anything that is spelled with repeating letters (rattlers, sparrows, etc.) and hates words without such double letters. The kids will probably be delightfully frustrated for awhile until a sharpie in the group hits on it. *Werner von Bergen*

NAME THAT VIDEO GAME

Your video game and video arcade pros will shine at this activity, which requires kids to identify video games by their sounds. It takes a lot of prep time. Take a portable tape recorder to your local video arcade or to stores that sell video games and get the manager's permission to record the characteristic tunes and sounds of 20 or so games.

With the recorder on, preface each game's sounds with a spoken number—for example, "This is game number one." Then place the mike properly to capture that game's distinctive audio effects. After you get a minute or so of sounds, turn off the recorder and write down the number and the game's name for your own reference. Then on to another game.

Some games that are on display emit a continual pattern to attract players; take advantage of these.

With your cassette of electronic sounds in hand, walk into your youth meeting or party, let your video-game freaks be captains and choose teams. Give each team a sheet of paper and pencil. Separate the teams from each other, and announce these simple rules: As you play the mystery sounds, the teams must quietly discuss the possibilities, arrive at a consensus, and record their decision on paper. Following the playing of all the sounds, correct names are given; the team with the most correct answers wins.

The prize? Tokens to the local arcade. *Jim Johnson*

PICTURE SEARCH

Borrow a 35mm camera (or a photographer with a 35mm camera), then stroll around inside your church building, photographing both familiar and not-so-familiar objects from unusual angles. Close-up and wide-angle lenses are helpful. How many people know what the back of the pulpit looks like? How about the inside of the janitor's closet?

When the photos are printed, post them on a bulletin board with identifying numbers. Then give each of the kids a simplified copy of the floor plans of the church building. Instruct them to figure out where in the church each photo was taken, then to write the photo's number in the corresponding area of the floor plans. The student with the most correct locations wins.

Be careful—common objects can be the most difficult to identify ("Now which exit sign had the yellow paint spattered on the bottom?"). And you can make the game more challenging by using black and white film instead of color. *Howard B. Chapman*

PUCKS AND PIGSKINS

Time to put all your sports-spectating prowess to work. The object of the quizzes on page 137 (Touchdown! and On Ice!) is to identify the football teams and the hockey teams from the clues. It's especially fun to play during half-time when your group is watching a televised sporting event together.

The answers:

TOUCHDOWN!

1. Dallas Cowboys
2. Washington Redskins
3. Philadelphia Eagles
4. Arizona Cardinals
5. New York Giants
6. Minnesota Vikings
7. Chicago Bears
8. Green Bay Packers
9. Detroit Lions
10. Tampa Bay Buccaneers
11. San Francisco 49ers
12. New Orleans Saints
13. Atlanta Falcons
14. St. Louis Rams
15. Miami Dolphins
16. Indianapolis Colts
17. New England Patriots
18. New York Jets
19. Buffalo Bills
20. Pittsburgh Steelers
21. Houston Oilers
22. Baltimore Ravens
23. Cincinnati Bengals
24. Oakland Raiders
25. Denver Broncos
26. Seattle Seahawks
27. Kansas City Chiefs
28. San Diego Chargers
29. Jacksonville Jaguars
30. Carolina Panthers

ON ICE!

1. Pittsburgh Penguins
2. Hartford Whalers
3. Buffalo Sabres
4. Florida Panthers
5. Anaheim Mighty Ducks
6. Philadelphia Flyers
7. Montreal Canadiens
8. Detroit Red Wings
9. Calgary Flames
10. St. Louis Blues
11. New York Islanders
12. New York Rangers
13. Toronto Maple Leafs
14. Edmonton Oilers
15. Boston Bruins
16. Dallas Stars
17. Los Angeles Kings
18. Washington Capitals
19. Vancouver Canucks
20. Chicago Black Hawks
21. New Jersey Devils
22. Colorado Avalanche
23. San Jose Sharks
24. Phoenix Coyotes
25. Tampa Bay Lightning
26. Ottawa Senators

Phil Rankin and Terry H. Erwin

THAT'S INEDIBLE!

Here's a game-show opener for camps or activity nights. Before the event invite a half dozen or so gung-ho students to a contest you'll videotape and show at the "That's Inedible" event. Come ready with a video camera and a variety of difficult-to-get-down foods—an onion, prunes, baby food, a lemon, etc. With the camera running, interview the first student, saying something like this: "Okay, Dan,

TOUCHDOWN!

Can you recall which NFL teams go with the following clues?

__________1. Ranch hands

__________2. Cherokee, Navajo, Blackfoot, etc.

__________3. Bald birds

__________4. Catholic officials

__________5. Goliaths

__________6. Eric the Red's crew

__________7. Koala, grizzly, panda, etc.

__________8. Suitcase stuffers

__________9. Kings of the beasts

__________10. Pirates

__________11. Gold diggers

__________12. Holy ones

__________13. Swift birds of prey

__________14. Head bashers

__________15. Small whales

__________16. Young horses

__________17. Minutemen

__________18. F-15s

__________19. William Cody namesakes

__________20. Ironmen

__________21. Fossil drillers

__________22. Black crow cousin

__________23. India's cats

__________24. Vandals

__________25. Rodeo mounts

__________26. Aquatic fliers

__________27. Indian leaders

__________28. The electric company

__________29. Large tawny, spotted felines

__________30. Solid black leopards

ON ICE!

Come on, all you hockey jocks. See how many NHL teams you can name from these clues. And remember—no high-sticking!

__________1. Birds in tuxedos

__________2. "A _____ of a time!"

__________3. These are "lite" swords

__________4. Black cats

__________5. Quack, quack

__________6. Frequent ones receive bonus mileage

__________7. These guys are from the Great White North

__________8. Embarrassed parts of a bird

__________9. On fire and all ablaze

__________10. "You got me singing the ______ "

__________11. Remote inhabitants, much like Gilligan

__________12. Forest police

__________13. Falling from a syrupy tree

__________14. Well-drilled wells, not for water

__________15. Name of the bear in Reynard the Fox

__________16. "Twinkle, twinkle, little _____"

__________17. Ten, jack, queen, _____

__________18. This is a great kind of idea

__________19. French Canadian or Canadian French

__________20. A dark bird of prey

__________21. The fallen angel

__________22. Sliding snow

__________23. Jaws

__________24. Wile E. ______

__________25. ______ strikes

__________26. Elected representatives

here is your challenge. In your hand is a lemon. We'll give you two minutes to eat that lemon. Will you accept the 'That's Inedible!' challenge?"

Dan, of course, says yes. You then say, "All right, contestants, it's time for you to place your bets on whether you think Dan can eat the lemon in two minutes." (It will be at this point during the showing that you will pause the video to allow contestants to place their yes or no bets.) Then say, "Okay, Dan—eat that lemon!" Then for the next two minutes, as Dan is being videotaped, give a running commentary on his lemon-eating progress.

Repeat this with each of the students, swearing them to silence about whether or not they got their foods down.

At the "That's Inedible!" event, choose three enthusiastic contestants from the crowd, seat them in front of the TV, and explain the game's rules:

- Each contestant begins with 100 points.
- They bet any number of those points on the likelihood of their videotaped peers actually eating their food. (You may want to warn them against betting big too early in the game and perhaps losing all their points prematurely.) Then begin the videotape, pausing at the appropriate time in order for the contestants to place their bets. A scorekeeper should keep track of the numbers and do the necessary addition or subtraction at the end of each videotaped eating performance.

Tally up the points at the end, and award the winner with a Gerber's coupon or a roll of breath mints. Have a couple of jars of baby food on hand in case of a tie; first person to finish wins in sudden death. *Jack Hawkins*

TV TUNE-UPS

So your kids say they know their TV shows? Challenge them with this game! Create a list of 40 to 50 current television shows. Then, give them five minutes to guess the night of the week each of the TV programs airs. Be sure to update the list of shows every season. *David Smith*

TIC-TAC-DART

On a large bulletin board, stick strips of masking tape in order to form a big tic-tac-toe figure with 18-inch squares. Tape three or four inflated balloons inside each of the nine squares.

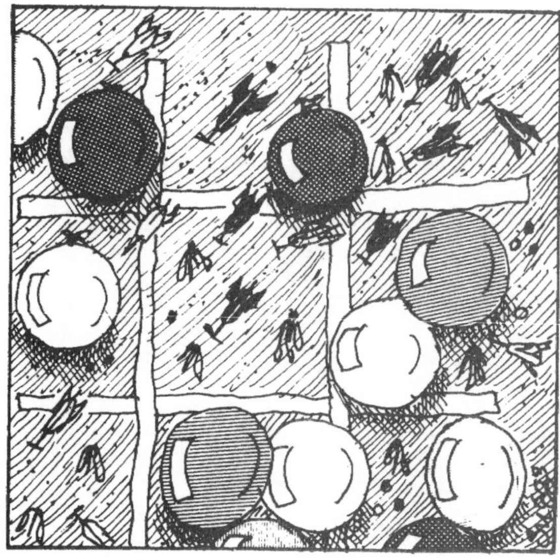

Divide your group into two teams. A player from the first team throws a single dart, trying to pop a balloon. If she succeeds, the next in line from her team attempts to pop another; if she fails, the other team sends a thrower to the line to try. The catch is this: Whichever team pops the last balloon in a square claims that square with an X or O.

You don't need darts, either—lay out the tic-tac-toe design and balloons on the floor, and drop sharpened pencils on them to pop them. *Michael W. Capps*

WHAT'S MY LINE?

In this version of the old TV game show, a contestant chooses one of several cards that describe an occupation or profession and answers yes-and-no questions put to her by a panel. Allow your panel only 10 questions or one question per panel member or some similar limitation. Contestants must answer truthfully.

Here are some suggestions for occupation cards:

Chef. A restaurant's head cook, keeps kitchen running smoothly, orders supplies, trains novices.

Piano tuner. Tools include hammer, tuning forks; repairs keyboards, replaces strings, felt; works in schools, homes, churches, studios.

Vintner. Wine maker; directs planning, growth, and pruning of vineyards; decides when to harvest, directs the crushing, pressing, and cleaning of grapes;

determines fermentation, temperature, and length of aging and blending of grapes.
Bookbinder. Sews sections of book together with hemp string or rope, covers boards with cloth or leather.
Arborist. Tree surgeon; provides supports for trees, treats diseased trees, removes hornets' nests, sprays for insects, advises how to build treehouses without killing trees.
Dry cleaner. Cleans woolens, draperies, etc., that cannot be laundered.
Tailor. Custom makes suits and other garments for men and women; takes measurements of clients and makes alterations.
Wallpaper hanger. Measures, cuts, pastes, and finishes wallpaper in homes and offices.
Chimney sweep. Cleans and repairs chimneys of fireplaces and furnaces.
Cartoonist. Often employed by a publisher; draws sketches, usually with humorous intent.
Coast Guard scuba diver. Searches for and rescues survivors (sometimes trapped) and objects from sunken ships.
Actuary. A statistician for an insurance company, who assembles and analyzes statistics to calculate probabilities of death, sickness, injury, disability, unemployment, retirement, and property loss from accidental death, theft, fire, and other hazards.
Bellhop. Carries hotel guests' luggage and ushers guests to room; ensures that guests are satisfied and informed about hotel services.
FBI special agent. Investigates bank robberies, kidnappings, white-collar crimes, thefts of government property, organized crime, espionage, sabotage, and terrorism.
Butcher. Cuts up animal carcasses into steaks, roasts, bacon, soup bones, etc.; maintains sanitary conditions; trims, wraps, and sells meat to customers in groceries or meat market.
Vending-machine repairman. Tests and repairs working parts of vending machines on site.
Len and Sheryl DiCicco

YOUTH GROUP JEOPARDY

Here's a spin-off of the TV game show "Jeopardy" that's sure to create special interaction within your group. For the answers on the board, place the names of each of your youth group members. Create some clever categories (Ripley's Believe It or Not, Claim to Fame, Most Embarrassing Moments) and plan answers that are lighthearted and fun. Pick students who are quick-witted to be participants and play just like TV's "Jeopardy."

Allow participants to "buzz in" and respond to each of the answers. If you like their response better than yours, pretend that they have the right answer. This makes for exciting and fast-paced play, and obviously works best with groups that know each other fairly well. Be prepared for some bizarre responses to the questions, though. In any case, you're bound to get better acquainted with each other playing this game. *Greg Fiebig*

BOARD GAME ROTATION

Here's a good way to have an evening of board games without being bored. Set up tables in a circle with a different two-player board game on each table. Put chairs on two sides of each table with half the chairs on the outside of the circle facing in and the other half on the inside facing out:

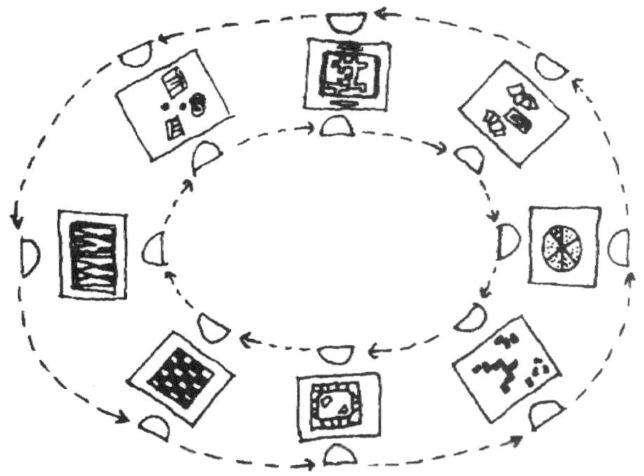

Have everyone take a seat, and begin playing the games. After five minutes, blow a whistle and instruct the youths to move one chair to their right so that each person is sitting at a different game with a different opponent. The games, however, are not reset, but the new players just take over where the last players left off. So a person might move from a winning Checkers game to a losing position in Yahtzee. Each game is worth a set amount and that "team" (inner circle or outer circle) is given credit for the win and the games are started again.

Obviously this works well as a mixer since everybody ends up playing against almost everybody else. Some other tips: large groups may split into several circles. Four-person games like Rook or Monopoly can be used, but you would need to set up a more complex rotation. Use games that everyone already knows how to play or games that are simple enough to explain and understand quickly. *Brent Baker and John McJilton*

ESKINOSE

Teams line up, alternating guys with girls. The first person in line receives a lipstick smear on the end of his or her nose. The idea is to see how far down the line players can pass the lipstick smear by rubbing noses. The team that can get it the farthest, or the team that can get it the farthest in the time limit (30 seconds, for example) is the winner. A good prize might be Eskimo Pies.

BACK SNATCHING

This is a good way to get everybody acquainted with each other. Pin a name onto each kid's back (either phony names, middle names, or real names if the kids don't know each other). At a given signal each person starts copying names off the backs of the other kids, while at the same time trying to keep people from copying the name on his own back. This results in a lot of twisting, turning, and trying to keep his back from being seen. At the end of the time limit, the person with the longest list—and most complete—wins. Have the winner identify the person with the name in order to claim his "prize," if any. *K. David Oldfield*

NAME GUESS

On slips of paper write different names of famous people and pin one to the back of each person, not letting them see who they are. Each person is to ask other group members questions that can be answered either yes or no to help him guess who he is. The first person to guess correctly wins and the last person is the loser. *Linda Wasson*

NITWITS

Contestants (or teams) play against each other by trying to solve the words in a crossword puzzle, which are clues about a person, place, or thing. Every clue word you guess in the puzzle is worth points (10 points for every letter in the word), but if you are first to guess the person, place, or thing, you get 100 bonus points, and you win that round.

To create the game, think of a person, place, or thing such as George Washington. Then think of words associated with George that could become

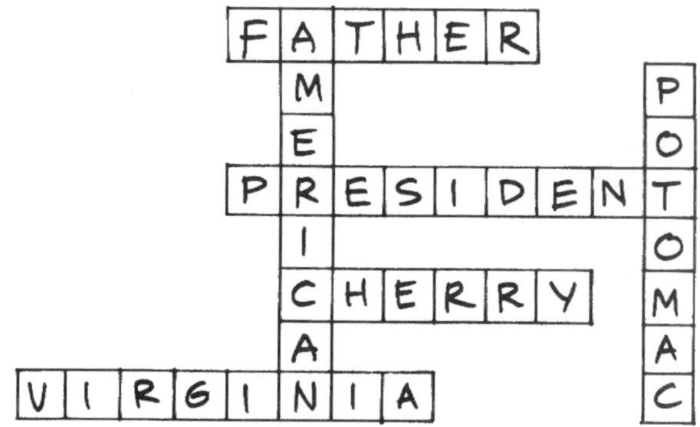

clues, such as American, president, father, cherry, Potomac, Virginia, and so on. Then put those clue words into a crossword puzzle, like so:

Then you'll need to write clues for the clue words, like:

1. What he is to his son (father)
2. A type of cheese (American)
3. The head of a company (president)
4. Sits on top of a sundae (cherry)
5. Yes, ________, there is a Santa Claus (Virginia)
6. A river (Potomac)

You'll need to create a bunch of these, as they go pretty fast. With each one, place the empty crossword puzzle up on the board or on the overhead projector. Give players on Team #1 the first clue. They get 10 seconds to come up with a guess. If it's wrong, the other team can solve that word or choose another. After each correct crossword puzzle guess, the team then gets a chance to guess the person, place, or thing when it is their turn only. *Andy Strachan*

EYE SPY

Give everyone four pieces of paper. Have kids write the word BLUE on the first piece, GREEN on the second, BROWN on the third, and GRAY on the fourth. Kids are to list everyone's name on the appropriate list according to eye color. The first person to categorize everyone correctly wins. *Jerry Summers*

First-Guess Favorite

How well do your kids really know each other? Hand out a copy of page 142 to each member of your group and find out! *Mark Skorheim*

High Roller, High Writer

Get a small group of kids around a table, and place in the middle one die and one pencil. Provide a sheet of paper for each player. Determine who plays first; then begin. The first player rolls the die once, then passes it clockwise so the next player can also roll once before passing the die on.

When a player rolls a six, she grabs the pencil and begins writing from 1 to 100—1, 2, 3, 4, 5, and so on. Meanwhile, the die is passed from player to player as before, each trying to roll a six. The writer's goal is to reach 100 before another player rolls a six, grabs the pencil from the first writer, and starts furiously scribbling numbers himself. Speed, of course, is the essence with both the number-writing and die-rolling—and the intensity builds as players get closer and closer to 100 before they're robbed of the pencil. First player to reach 100 wins. *Grant Sawatzky*

Personality Pursuit

Before you play this game, have 200 to 300 small strips of paper prepared. When the group arrives, have them write on each strip a person's name—use the name of others in your group, celebrities' names, names of people dead or alive, comic strip characters, etc., just as long as the name is well-known to most of the group. Don't worry if names are written more than once—it makes the game more fun. Then put all these strips in a pail or box.

Now divide into two teams. A player from team A dips into the pail, grabs a name, and has 30 seconds to give clues to her teammates until they can guess the name. Any verbal clue is permissible—even pointing is allowed. If her team guesses the name within 30 seconds, that strip is pocketed by the team for scoring later; if the team fails to guess the name, the strip goes back into the bucket. Then team B follows suit. Make sure clue-givers are rotated each turn.

At the end of a designated time, each team tallies up the names they've guessed, and the team with the most wins. *Pete Kenow*

Medical Mix-Up

Everyone knows teens love to play word games to make a point or get their way with parents and peers. Let your teens have fun with this play on medical words. (See page 143.) You can make up your own with any jargon or terminology.

Here are the answers to the game:

1. H	7. M	13. V	19. E
2. S	8. U	14. X	20. K
3. O	9. C	15. G	21. A
4. I	10. J	16. B	22. P
5. T	11. Q	17. R	23. L
6. D	12. F	18. N	24. W

Rob Marin

Hymn Hunt

This activity serves as a fast-paced lead-in to Bible studies or discussions on almost any subject. The objective of Hymn Hunt is to find as many hymns related to a given topic as possible in the time allowed.

Divide your students into three equal groups, and supply each team with several sheets of notepaper, pencils, and some hymnals. Working as quickly as possible, students search through the hymnal to locate any songs that relate to your topic. If the topic is love, youths are to find hymns which speak of love or contain the word love in the title or in a verse.

Details you should make known are:

- Youths may look anywhere in the hymnal.
- Record hymn titles and page numbers.
- Depending on the size of your group, one or more volunteers will need to be writing while the rest of the team calls out information.
- Limit search time to three minutes.
- Award points as follows:

Love is the first word in the title *1 point*

First-Guess Favorite

Directions: First, put a check to the left of your own favorites in each category. Then circulate around the room and guess what the favorites of others in the group are. If you guess correctly on the first try, they initial to the right of the category on your sheet. No more than two initials from the same person.

1. Favorite music ______
   - ____ Country-western
   - ____ Classical
   - ____ Rock
   - ____ Gospel
2. Favorite food ______
   - ____ Mexican
   - ____ American (meat and potatoes)
   - ____ Chinese
   - ____ Italian
3. Favorite car ______
   - ____ Luxury
   - ____ Sports
   - ____ Economy
   - ____ Truck
4. Favorite movies ______
   - ____ Adventure
   - ____ Comedy
   - ____ Mystery
   - ____ Science fiction
5. Favorite vacation ______
   - ____ Beach
   - ____ Mountains
   - ____ World travel (plane, cruise)
   - ____ Sight-seeing America (by car)
6. Favorite sweet ______
   - ____ Pie
   - ____ Cake
   - ____ Frozen (ice cream, yogurt)
   - ____ Candy
7. Favorite animal ______
   - ____ Dog
   - ____ Cat
   - ____ Bird
   - ____ Exotic
8. Favorite TV show ______
   - ____ News or news program
   - ____ Comedy
   - ____ Drama
   - ____ Soap opera
9. Favorite reading material ______
   - ____ Magazines
   - ____ Fiction books
   - ____ Nonfiction books
   - ____ Newspapers
10. Favorite spectator sport ______
    - ____ Football
    - ____ Basketball
    - ____ Baseball
    - ____ Tennis or golf
11. Favorite color ______
    - ____ Dark (black, brown, rust)
    - ____ Light (white, tan)
    - ____ Pastel (yellow, pink, baby blue)
    - ____ Bright (red, blue)
12. Favorite season ______
    - ____ Winter
    - ____ Spring
    - ____ Summer
    - ____ Fall
13. Favorite time of day ______
    - ____ Early morning
    - ____ Afternoon
    - ____ Evening
    - ____ Late night

MEDICAL MIX-UP

Instructions: Match the terms at left with their definitions at right. Be careful—some of the definitions may be a little mixed up. Example: Serology—the study of English knighthood.

1. _______ artery
2. _______ barium
3. _______ colic
4. _______ coma
5. _______ congenital
6. _______ dilate
7. _______ fester
8. _______ G.I. series
9. _______ grippe
10. _______ hangnail
11. _______ medical staff
12. _______ minor operation
13. _______ morbid
14. _______ nitrate
15. _______ node
16. _______ organic
17. _______ outpatient
18. _______ post-operative
19. _______ protein
20. _______ secretion
21. _______ tablet
22. _______ tumor
23. _______ urine
24. _______ varicose veins

A. small table
B. musical
C. a suitcase
D. to live long
E. in favor of young people
F. coal digging
G. was aware of
H. the study of fine paintings
I. a punctuation mark
J. a coat hook
K. hiding anything
L. the opposite of "you're out"
M. quicker
N. a letter carrier
O. a sheep dog
P. an extra pair
Q. a doctor's cane
R. a person who has fainted
S. what you do when CPR fails
T. friendly
U. a baseball game with teams of soldiers
V. a higher offer
W. veins that are close together
X. lower than the day rate

Love is the last word in the title *2 points*
Love is in the title but is not the first or last word *3 points*
Love is spoken of but not specifically used *3 points*
Love is in a verse but not in the title *5 points*

• The team with the most total points is declared the winner.
• *(Optional)* To make the activity more challenging for everyone, have the teams eliminate songs which are duplicated by another team.

Allow sufficient time for the groups to consolidate the songs into one list for the team. Discuss team findings and total the scores.

You may wish to provide magazines, sheet music, solos, cassette tapes, and other resources for the search. *Michael W. Capps*

DOUBLESPEAK

Doublespeak is a nonathletic game that will provide an opportunity for some of your quieter kids to really shine!

The game: Divide your group into several teams. The object of the game is to rewrite a short, simple sentence into one that is as long and elaborate as possible. For example, a junior high team changed the sentence, "See Spot run," into the monster, "Observe Spot, the friendly domestic canine, utilize his locomotor apparatus in order to achieve accelerated forward motion"! Read a sentence aloud, give them a predetermined time limit to work on the translation, and have the teams read their sentences to the group. The results are sure to surprise you and are always hilarious! The team with the longest sentence is the winner.

As a variation, give the teams different short sentences. Each team translates their sentence into a doublespeak version. One player reads the doublespeak sentence to the whole group. The other teams try to figure out what the original sentence was.

The discussion: How do our minds sometimes get in the way of understanding? In the Information Age, is more always better? Conclude with Proverbs 3:5: "Trust in the Lord with all your heart and lean not on your own understanding." Can we ask God to make things more clear? How might he do that? *John Young*

Mind Reading Games

Mind Reading Games

In the 17th century these parlor tricks could have gotten you burned at the stake, but today they're just good clean fun. These special living room games usually involve a leader and one or two other people who know the secret to a trick. The fun in these games is seeing how long it takes the rest of the group to catch on to the trick, puzzle, or clues.

Find the Mailman

Tell the kids that it's April 15 and your tax forms need to get to the post office. Hold up a fat envelope and tell them you have the tax forms, but they have to figure out who the mailman is.

Ask everyone to sit in a circle. Give one player your envelope of tax forms and ask her to wait outside of the room. Now choose another person to be the mailman, and assign him a mannerism like one of these:

Blinks a lot
Answers questions by saying "Awesome!"
Sits with legs crossed
Arms are always folded
Taps his foot
Name is Mr. Mailman
Sleepy, yawns
Ends each sentence with "...you know?"
Scratches head a lot
Laughs a lot
A Bible is on his lap
Always says "I don't know"
Hands are in a praying position
Coughs a lot
Wears someone else's jacket
Always asks if you need some stamps
Twiddles his thumbs
Licks his lips a lot
Can't talk
Shifts in his chair a lot
Puts his arm on his neighbor's chair
Smiles a lot
Ends each sentence with "Have a nice day!"
Hands have both index fingers pointing at you
Winks at you

Set a time limit (one or two or three minutes, depending on the size of your group) and a limit on how many questions the tax-envelope holder ("It") can ask each student in the circle—say, three questions per player—by which time "It" must put the envelope in the mailman's hand. When "It" returns to the room, suggest to her that she pay attention to body language as well as peculiarities in how kids answer her questions. Players must respond honestly to questions. *Mark Schwartz*

KNIFE, FORK, AND SPOON GAME

This is a simple game and yet one which can take up a good deal of time depending upon the alertness of the participants. To play you will need a knife, a fork, a spoon, and a youth group. Explain the game (secretly) to another person and begin. Have kids sit in a circle on the floor.

Send your partner out of the room and tell the kids that they should pick someone sitting in the circle. Then tell them that you will communicate with your partner by what you do so that he will know who was chosen to be "It." Place the knife, fork, and spoon in any arrangement you choose in the middle of the circle on the floor, and then pick a place in the circle to sit. The key to communicating who is "It" to your partner has nothing to do with the knife, fork, and spoon, but in the fact that you assume a sitting position which is exactly like that of "It." If "It" moves to a different position to be more comfortable, so do you.

Your partner makes a big deal about the knife, fork, and spoon, but picks up his clues from what you do, which is what you told the kids in your initial instructions. The knife, fork, and spoon are merely diversionary in that the kids assume what you do is limited to the knife, fork, and spoon. After your partner picks "It" to the total amazement of the group, the process is repeated until someone catches on. If someone feels they know the answer, they then go out of the room and become your partner. Depending on the alertness of the group, this can continue until most everyone has had a chance to figure out the key to the game. *Woody Weilage*

MIND READING GAMES

The game leader and mind reader are accomplices who know in advance how the game is played and what the code or trick is. Kids are to try to guess what the code is. As soon as someone thinks she has figured out the code, let her try to lead the game correctly. Keep going until most kids have caught on or until you decide to reveal the code.

• **Black Magic.** While the mind reader is out of the room, the audience chooses an object that the mind reader must identify. When the mind reader returns, the game leader points to a variety of objects. Surprisingly, when the leader points to the chosen object, the mind reader correctly identifies it.

Code: The game leader points to a black object just before pointing to the chosen object.

• **Book Magic.** While the mind reader is out of the room, place several books in a row. Let the kids choose one book that is to be identified by the mind reader as the chosen book. When the mind reader returns, the game leader points at random to several books. The mind reader correctly identifies the chosen book.

Code: Just before pointing to the chosen book, the game leader points to the book that is lying furthest to the right.

• **Car.** While the mind reader is out of the room, the crowd chooses three objects, one of which is to be identified by the mind reader as the chosen object. When the mind reader returns, she is shown all three objects one by one, and then identifies the correct one.

Code: When the mind reader enters the room, the leader makes a general statement that begins with one of the following three letters: C, A, or R (such as "Come in," "All right," or "Ready"). A statement that begins with a "C" indicates to the mind reader that the first object shown is the chosen one; an "A" statement identifies the second object; and an "R" statement identifies the third object.

• **The Nine Mags.** Place nine magazines on the floor in three rows of three. After the mind reader leaves the room, the crowd selects a magazine for the mind reader to identify. When the mind reader returns, the leader uses a pointer of some kind to touch the various magazines in a random order. When the chosen magazine is touched, the mind reader correctly identifies it.

Code: When the leader touches the first magazine, he appears to randomly place the pointer anywhere on the magazine.

1	2	3
4	5	6
7	8	9

However, the area that the pointer touches is significant. If the pointer touches the upper right hand corner of the magazine, the mind reader knows that the magazine in the top row on the far right is the chosen one. If the pointer touches the very center of the first magazine, the mind reader knows that the magazine in the very center of the rows is the chosen one, and so on. In other words, the leader and mind reader are to mentally divide the first magazine into nine quadrants that reflect the layout of the magazines in the three rows of three. The game leader can point to a number of magazines after the first one, before pointing to the chosen one. The mind reader will miraculously guess the correct magazine.

• **Red, White, and Blue.** This is similar to the Black Magic game; however, it is more confusing. While the mind reader is out of the room, the audience chooses an object that the mind reader must identify. When the mind reader returns, the game leader points to a variety of objects. Surprisingly, when he or she points to the chosen object, the mind reader correctly identifies it.

Code: During the first round of the game, the mind reader knows to select the object that immediately follows a red object. During the second round, she selects the object that immediately follows a white object. During the third round, she knows to select the object that immediately follows the blue object. Play numerous rounds, continuously rotating red, white, and blue objects.

SPIRIT MOVE

This is a mind reading game that will usually fool anybody. It is best played in a living room situation where everyone is casual, relaxed, and just sitting around killing time.

The mind reading is done by a leader and assistant who are in on the trick. Before the game begins the leader and assistant agree on one chair as the one in which the mystery person will sit. As the game begins, someone will be sitting in the special chair. He or she will be the first one called. Both leader and assistant will note this person as instructions are being given to the group. The group is told that everyone must change seats each time the mystery person is guessed.

The assistant leaves the room (remembering who was in the special chair). The leader has the group all move (everyone must change chairs), and informs them they must be very quiet so his assistant can get the mental message. He then calls to his assistant in an adjoining room, "Spirit moves," as he holds his hand over any person's head. The assistant answers, "Let it move." The leader continues as long (or short) as he likes. When he calls, "Spirit rests," he holds his hand over the head of the person who had been sitting in the special chair. The assistant, who remembers who was in the chair, replies, "Spirit rests over the head of [name of person]."

The assistant then enters the room appearing to be interested to see if he named the right person. The assistant looks to see who now is in the special chair for the next round.

The assistant leaves the room; the leader again has everyone move from his chair and the game continues. *Ellen Kersey*

WRITING IN THE SAND

In this mind reading game, a leader and his partner try to baffle the rest of the group. The group selects a secret word and the partner comes in and is able to guess the word correctly following a short series of clues from the leader, which the group tries to figure out.

The leader holds a stick in his or her hand, and appears to write clues in the sand. However, the writing does not appear to make sense and bears no obvious relationship to the secret word being guessed. But the partner is still able to guess the word on the first try.

Here's how it is done: The consonants in the word (let's say the secret word is light) are L, G, H, and T. These are given to the partner through a series of verbal clues after he or she enters the room. The leader might first say "Let's see if you can get this one." The first letter of that sentence is "L." That would clue in the partner that the word starts with an "L." Then, the leader draws on the floor with the stick, and at some point raps the floor one, two, three, four, or five times. These represent the vowels—A, E, I, O, U. One rap is A; five raps is U. So, in this case, the leader would tap the stick three times for I. Now the partner has two letters. The G is the next verbal clue, like "Got it yet?" As soon as the partner has enough letters to guess the word, he amazes the group, and anyone who thinks he knows how it is done may try his skill as the partner. *Glenn Davis*

PING-PONG VARIATIONS

PING-PONG VARIATIONS

Beanbags for balls, books for paddles, and bowls of water on the table—these are just some of the twisted variations we've come up with for this beloved family game. In addition to these and other wacky new versions of traditional table tennis, you'll find several ideas for using Ping-Pong balls in other sports like baseball, basketball—and, yes, even polo.

ALPHABET PONG

For this game, the group arranges itself into a circle. Each person holds a book with both hands. One player takes a Ping-Pong ball and hits it with the book across the circle, calling out A. The person on the other side then returns it to someone, calling out B, and so forth. Players in the circle work together to see how far down the alphabet they can get before they blow it. There is no particular order for hitting the ball. Anyone can hit it when it comes to them, but no one may hit the ball twice in a row. For teams, have the first team try it, and then the other, to see which one can get the farthest down the alphabet without the ball hitting the floor. It's a real challenge! *Earnie Lidell*

BASEBALL PING-PONG

To set up this game, you'll need a card table, a Ping-Pong ball, and some masking tape (for lines). On the card table, mark off lines according to the diagram pictured below. You need foul lines and lines that indicate a base hit, a double, and a triple.

To play, place the Ping-Pong ball on home plate. The team at bat rotates one by one and attempts to blow the ball across the bases to a home run. The team in the field places three players on their knees on the opposite side of the table who attempt to blow the ball off the table before it's allowed to score a base hit.

Here are some additional rules:

- The batter may blow only once.
- The fielders may not touch the table at any time.
- If the ball crosses the foul lines, that player is allowed another blow, even if it was the fielding team that blew the ball back across the foul lines.
- A ball's score is calculated at the point where it makes its farthest forward progress before being blown off the table toward the foul lines. (Example: If the batter blows the ball and it reaches the third base tape before being blown off the table, the batter is credited with a triple. Runs must be forced in.
- Outs are made by blowing the ball off the table before it reaches the first base line, so that it does not go back across the foul line.
- Home runs are made by blowing the ball off the

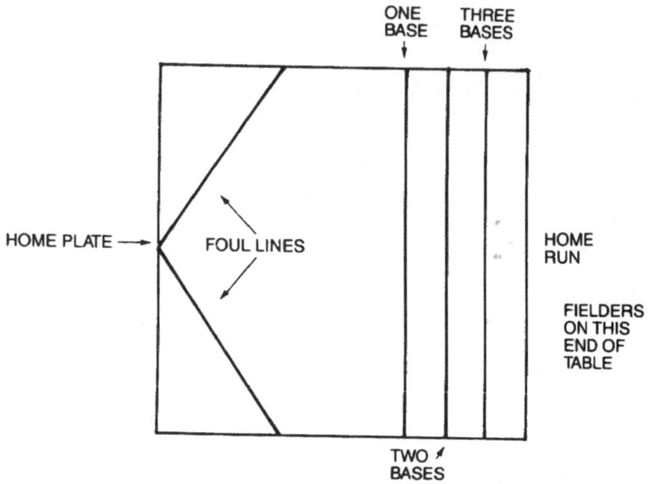

table on the opposite end from home plate, for whatever reason. Fielders need to be careful about where they're blowing the ball; they can unintentionally score for the opposing team.
Phil Blackwell

BARSTOOL BALZAC

A balzac—a fabric-covered balloon found in many toy stores—makes a great projectile for this tricky small-group game. Two players or teams pass the balzac back and forth by bouncing it off the top of a barstool placed between them, much the way tennis and Ping-Pong are played. Count the number of returns, and keep trying for higher scores. It takes perseverance to master! *Ricky Court*

BALLOON PONG

All set up for table tennis, only to find no Ping-Pong balls? Get some balloons and play this slo-mo version of Ping-Pong.

Line your kids up in two lines, one against each end of the Ping-Pong table. Players play according to regular Ping-Pong rules—except that they hit a balloon instead of a ball (weighted with a marble inside, if necessary) and play with a single paddle. After a player hits the balloon, he slides the paddle across the table under the net to the player opposite him, who grabs the paddle before the balloon arrives and returns the balloon, Ping-Pong fashion. When a player makes his shot and slides the paddle to the other player, he scoots out of the way to the back of his line as quickly as possible.

Slower players may bend the rules a bit and keep the balloon aloft with their breath if they need time to snatch the paddle.

- **Wacky Balloon Pong.** Place a ball of Silly Putty inside a seven-inch balloon and partially blow up the balloon. Clip the knot off as close as possible and you've got a durable balloon that moves in swirls. *David Washburn and Doug Partin*

KING PONG

If you have ever felt that the Ping-Pong table was just too short for your style of play, then this game could revitalize Ping-Pong for your group. Set two Ping-Pong tables end to end, and place the net as close to the middle as possible. Play regular rules or invent twists like relay-round-robin, multiple hits per side, or teams of four or more. The results are as fun to watch as they are to play. *Kevin Turner and the Camp McCullough staff*

MUSICAL PADDLES

This game is great indoors for large groups and requires a piano or cassette or CD player and several Ping-Pong paddles (or similar objects that can be passed easily). The group stands in a circle passing paddles from left to right while music plays. Players caught holding a paddle when the music abruptly stops must do certain things with every subsequent paddle they receive. For example:

- **First time caught:** All paddles from then on must be passed by the individual around his waist once before passing it on to his right.
- **Second time caught:** All paddles must be passed around the waist twice from then on.
- **Third time caught:** All paddles around the waist twice and under one leg.
- **Fourth time caught:** All paddles around the waist twice, under one leg and, under the other.
- **Fifth time caught:** All the above, then under both legs.
- **Sixth time caught:** Sing a solo.

Glenn Davis

PING BAG

Several early-bird students in a youth group came up with this idea for passing time while waiting for slower groups to finish a discussion question. Every player has a Ping-Pong paddle to toss and catch a small bean bag. You can toss the bag to anyone in the circle—it's every man for himself. If players miss the bean bag, they're out. If the toss is determined by group consensus to be uncatchable, the tosser is out. The trick is to toss the bag so that it's difficult but still possible to catch by an aggressive player. When only one player is left in the circle, everyone rejoins the circle and round two begins. *Doug Partin*

PING POOL

For a full hour of fun, try this Ping-Pong/pool table hybrid. First, borrow one of those six-foot-long fold-up tables from your kitchen or fellowship hall. Next, attach six Styrofoam cups along the edge of the table. Put one at each corner and one in the middle of each of the long sides—exactly like a pool table . Each cup should have its bottom punched out and

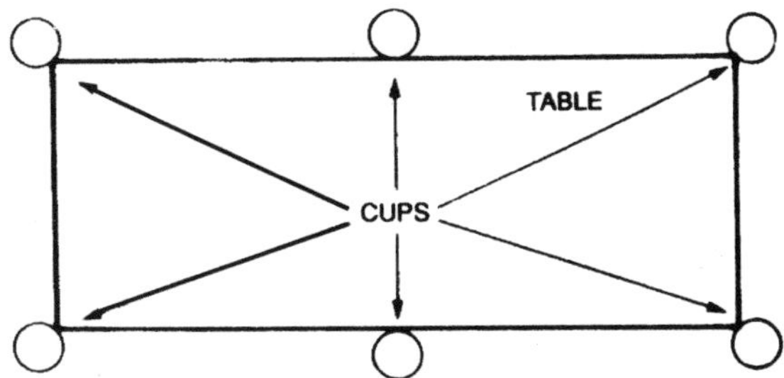

replaced by a plastic Baggie, and the cups may need part of their top edges cut back and shaped in order to fit snugly to the table.

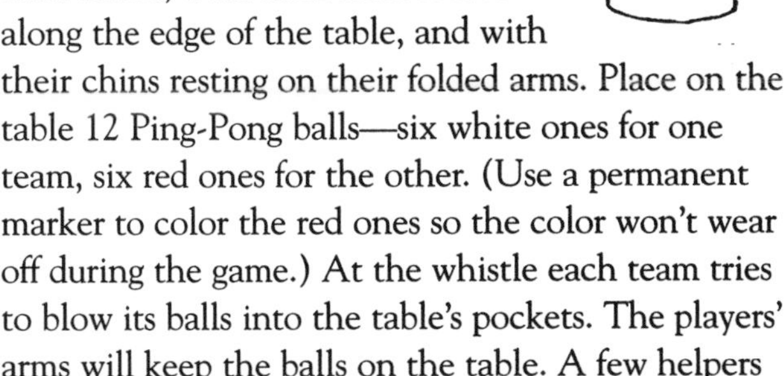

Now choose two teams of six students each and position them—on their knees, with their arms folded along the edge of the table, and with their chins resting on their folded arms. Place on the table 12 Ping-Pong balls—six white ones for one team, six red ones for the other. (Use a permanent marker to color the red ones so the color won't wear off during the game.) At the whistle each team tries to blow its balls into the table's pockets. The players' arms will keep the balls on the table. A few helpers can put balls back into play that hop the barricade of arms.

But be careful—only two balls are permitted in any pocket. A referee makes sure this rule is followed during play. The team that sinks its balls first wins.

Here are some variations:

- **Bumper Ping.** Place unopened, ice-cold cans of soda on the playing table (see below).

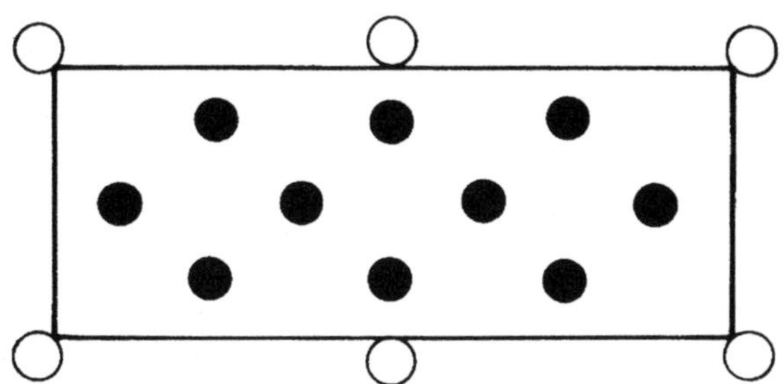

Players must blow balls around the cans of pop to sink their balls in the pockets. The winning team gets the pop!

- **Tag-Team Ping.** Only one member from each of two competing teams plays at the same time. When a person has successfully pocketed one ball, he tags a team member (those waiting for their turns sit apart from the playing table), who then represents their team at the table. The game is over when a team has pocketed all six of their balls, one ball per person.
- **Challenge Ping.** Regular Ping Pool—except that only one ball of each color may roll into each cup.
- **Pistol Pong.** After a few matches of Ping Pool, clear the plain, folding table and give a pair of kids squirt guns. Place a Ping-Pong ball in the center; the dueling players, armed with the guns, should try to squirt the ball off their opponent's end of the table. Balls that fall off the sides of the table are replaced from where they fell, and play is resumed.

For a variations, try playing doubles or set four players against each other on each side of a square table. And be prepared for the inevitable Fluid Free-For-All Finale. *Michael W. Capps and Michael Frisbie*

PING-PONG BALL IN THE CUP

This game is as fun to watch as it is to play. The only props you need are Ping-Pong balls and plastic drinking cups. And the game works best in a large room with a cement or tile floor (it gives the Ping-Pong balls maximum bounce).

Pair off teens and have them stand approximately 20 feet apart. One person is the pitcher, the other tries to catch the ball in the plastic cup. The catcher cannot use her hands and must catch the ball before it quits bouncing, which requires some patience. You could award points based on the number of bounces before the ball is caught. *Glenn G. Davis*

PING-PONG BASEBALL

Here's an exciting game that you can play indoors if you have a large playing area. All you need are Ping-Pong balls and a Ping-Pong paddle for the bat. All the usual rules of baseball apply. If the ball hits the roof on a fly, it is playable, but the walls are foul territory. It's a great game for rainy days or anytime you want to have an exciting game indoors. *Keith Robinson*

PING-PONG BASKETBALL

Have contestants bounce (at least one time; there is no limit otherwise) Ping-Pong balls into different size containers. Vary amount of points given depending upon difficulty. The smaller the container, the larger the amount of points given. *Glen Richardson*

PING-PONG BLOW

Players in this game spread themselves evenly around the edge of a large sheet, grab its edge, pull it taut (and keep it level), then attempt to blow a Ping-Pong ball off it. The players between whom the ball drops off the sheet are out, and the circle of players is gradually reduced.

Instead of a Ping-Pong ball, a balloon with a marble inside rolls around the sheet less predictably since the balloon isn't a perfect sphere. *David Washburn*

PING-PONG BLOW DRY

Here's a crazy relay game involving blow dryers (you'll need one for each team). You'll also need one large wash tub (but no water), and some Ping-Pong balls. This game is best for two or three teams.

Each team has a Ping-Pong ball in the tub (a different color Ping-Pong ball for each team). The tub containing the balls is placed 20 feet or so away from the teams. On a signal, the first person at the head of the line runs to the tub, picks up the dryer, and attempts to get their team ball out of the tub using the blow dryer to blow it out. When this is accomplished, that person puts the ball back in the tub and goes to the end of the line, and the second person repeats the procedure. When two or three people are trying to blow their Ping-Pong balls out of the tub at the same time, it's fun to watch what happens. You might want to try out the blow dryers and wash tubs, etc., before you play this game just to be sure that it works. *Steve Hopper*

PING-PONG DODGEBALL

Tape a line down the middle of the room, with half the kids on one side, half on the other. Arm each team with a box of Ping-Pong balls (10 to 20 per team for a youth group of 40).

At a signal they throw balls at the opposing team. A direct hit eliminates the player, but bounce hits and caught balls do not. Continue until all the members of one team are eliminated. Mix up the teams and play again. *Jim Ramos*

PING-PONG HOME-RUN DERBY

You can play this all-or-nothing version of baseball with just a handful of kids, a fair-sized room, a Ping-Pong ball, and a paddle (the bat). Set four or five folding tables on their sides as a playing-field fence (see diagram). Use masking tape to form a home plate and two foul lines.

Now for the rules:

- All players must play on their knees.
- There are no strikes, no balls, no base hits—just

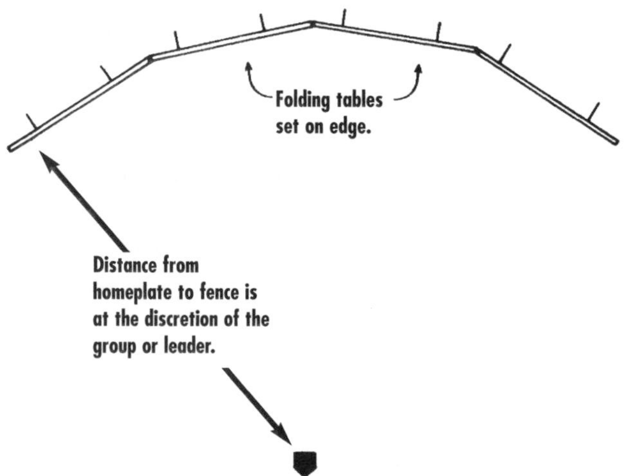
Folding tables set on edge.
Distance from homeplate to fence is at the discretion of the group or leader.

home runs or outs. The batting team tries to hit home runs. Any Ping-Pong ball that clears the fence without touching the floor or ceiling is a home run and scores a run. If a hit ball touches the floor or ceiling, or is caught or swatted down by a fielder, the batter is out. Foul balls are played over.

• The fielding team, which plays along the inside of the fence, tries to swat a hit Ping-Pong ball down before it flies over the fence.

• Each team gets three outs; play as many innings as you like. The pitcher can be a sponsor who pitches to both teams or a member of the fielding team. You may choose to have an umpire and scorekeeper.

Brett C. Wilson

PING-PONG HULA DOUBLES

Test your students' coordination and cooperation with a doubles Ping-Pong contest. Pair up a boy and a girl at each end of the table. Each player needs a paddle; each pair, a Hula Hoop.

The object of the game is to play a game of doubles Ping-Pong, with teammates restrained within a single Hula Hoop. Pairs must move together during a volley, all the time keeping the Hula Hoop off the floor. Play short games—perhaps only to 11.

Invent whatever rules fit your situation and your kids. For instance, determine if pairs can use their free hand to keep the Hula Hoop up, or whether they must keep it up without hands—only by leaning opposite directions. *Michael Capps*

PING-PONG POLO

For this exciting indoor game, have team members make their own polo sticks out of rolled-up newspaper and masking tape. Several sheets of paper should be rolled up lengthwise, then taped along the edge.

The object of the game is for team members to knock the Ping-Pong ball with the polo stick into their team's goal. An excellent way to set up goals is to lay two tables on their sides (one table per goal), with the top of the table facing into the playing area. When the ball hits the face of the table, it will make a popping noise, indicating that a goal was scored.

Each team should have one goalie who will guard the table. The goalie can use any part of his or her body to protect the table.

To make the game even more like real polo, have the kids ride broomsticks like stick horses while they play the game. It's always advisable to have a few extra Ping-Pong balls on hand. *Cindy Fairchild*

PING-PONG SOCCER

From six to 16 people can enjoy this indoor version of soccer. The rules are the same as regular soccer—except you play with a Ping-Pong ball, there are no boundaries, and the goals should be made much smaller.

Although the size of the field is small, the game plays amazingly like soccer because a well kicked Ping-Pong ball travels only 15 to 20 feet. Have plenty of Ping-Pong balls—they tend to get squashed on a blocked shot. Penalize a ball-squashing team by awarding the opposing team a free kick at the goal.

Elliott Cooke

POWER PONG

First, clear the room of all breakables. Set up the Ping-Pong table and put out at least four paddles. Start the Ping-Pong game, two (or up to six) to a team. Serving and scoring are according to standard Ping-Pong rules. Neither players nor their paddles can cross the net.

Now for the power. As in volleyball, each side is permitted as many as three hits before returning the ball across the net. A player cannot hit the ball twice consecutively. Walls, ceilings, and bodies are all in play. The ball is dead when the ball touches the floor, and the point goes to the opposition.

Like volleyball, the key is in teamwork—accurate sets, smashing returns. Better have a few extra balls for this one. *Mick Hernandez*

RETREAD REGATTA

Get some bald tires, slice them in half like a bagel, fill each half with water, and—voilà—you have your own Ping-Pong ball regatta courses! Give each team its own water-filled tire, mark starting points with chalk, and begin the race. Each team member must take turns blowing the Ping-Pong ball once around the course. The first team that has every member round the tire wins.

Variations: Use sand instead of water, blindfold

players so that they depend on their teammates' directions, or invent your own games! *Michael W. Capps*

Round Robin Ping-Pong

About 10 or so kids stand around a normal Ping-Pong table, one on each end, the rest on the sides. The first person serves the ball over the net to the person on the other end just as in regular Ping-Pong, but after he serves it, he puts the paddle down on the table (with the handle sticking over the edge) and gets in the line to his left. The next person in line (to the server's right) picks up the paddle and waits for the ball to be returned. The line keeps rotating around the table in a clockwise fashion, with each person hitting the ball once from whichever end of the table they happen to be on. If a player drops the paddle, misses the ball, or hits the ball off the table, she is eliminated. When it gets down to the last two people, they must hit the ball, put the paddle down, turn around, then pick up the paddle and hit the ball. You can vary this idea by playing on a tennis court or volleyball court with a tennis ball and old rackets. The last player left in the game wins. *Nick Wagner*

Spool Pong

Place two spools of thread, one on each side of the net, on the center line of the table about 18 inches from the ends of the table. Place an extra Ping-Pong ball on top of each. Play regular Ping-Pong, but add five points to your score if you can knock your opponent's ball off the spool. Score the game normally otherwise.

Wacky Ping-Pong

This game requires the same equipment as regulation Ping-Pong, and the game begins in the same way. But after the ball crosses the net on the serve, it must bounce at least once on the table and once on the floor before it can be returned. On the return serve, the ball has to hit the table once (it does not have to cross the net) and then bounce on the floor once before it can be returned. The ball on any return serve (once it is across the net in the beginning serve), and on all other returns, may bounce an unlimited number of times on the table, but can only be hit after it has bounced once on the floor.

The fun begins, for example, when a returned serve hits the table on the return side, takes a quick bounce off to the left or right side of the table, and bounces on the floor. It's now up to the server to get to the ball and hit it back up on the table (anywhere) after the first bounce. Here, surprise shots can cause quite a mad scramble for the ball.

Fun also enters when the table is in a room with close walls and a low ceiling. Then combination shots off the walls and ceiling add to the excitement. Here, the rule of one bounce is altered, as the ball can first bounce against the walls or ceiling before hitting the floor and after bouncing off the table, and it is still considered a fair shot.

Also, a return server can hit the ball (after the floor bounce) against the wall, carom it off the ceiling, hit the table on one or more bounces, and then continue to another wall or floor. It's then up to the other person to get that ball as soon as it leaves the first bounce on the floor. Again, quickness and practice pay off. In some games all one does is run from one end of the table to the other just to keep in the game.

Each server serves until five points are made (total) and after a total of 10 points the people switch sides. This is done since some room combinations favor one side or the other.

Increased fun can be added when teams play with mandatory alternate shots on both teams. This causes real excitement as one team member is often in the other's way, or the person who is to return the serve can be on the wrong side of the table. Fast footwork and expert combination shots are the keys to success.

If in any game, after the first serve, the ball bounces on the table, hits the net, and then goes off to the floor, it constitutes a fair shot. Also any net ball on a return shot that causes the ball to stop dead on the table can be blown off the table by the person who is supposed to hit it next. However, he must wait till it bounces once off the floor before hitting it. A team member can blow it off for you to add suspense in team competition.

WALLY PONG

Wally Pong is best played in a small room with high ceilings (but any room is adequate).

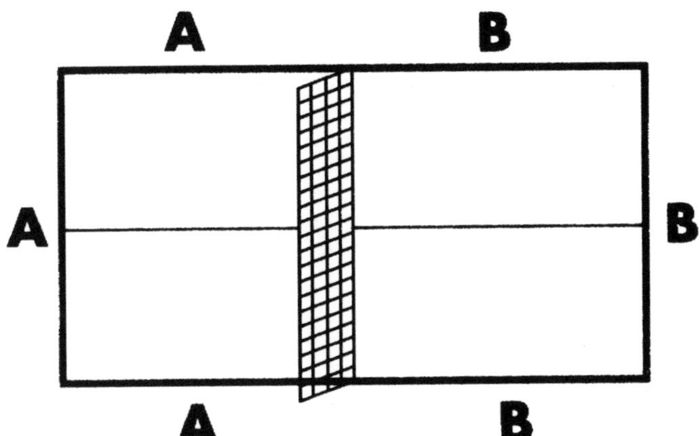

Place a Ping-Pong table in the center of the room and put three players on each side. Play and score like volleyball:

- Upon receiving the serve, players don't try to return the ball immediately, but instead set up the ball for teammates.
- Three hits per side.
- Slams (or spikes) are acceptable.
- The ball is in play until it hits the floor.
- Shots off walls, ceilings, people, etc., are playable.
- A team holds the service as long as it scores.
- Servers rotate.
- Fifteen points win the game.

Mike Vickers

WATER PONG

Fill two small saucers or shallow bowls full of water and place one on each side of the Ping-Pong net about 12 inches from the net on the center line. If a player can drop or hit the ball (in regular playing rules) in the opponent's saucer, he wins the game. Score the game normally unless it ends with a ball in the saucer.

VOLLEYBALL GAMES

What self-respecting youth group doesn't like a good volleyball game? They'll go crazy for these bizarre variations of the sport. Regardless of your group size or space limitations, you'll find several volleyball mutations that work for you!

BOOK VOLLEYBALL

This idea is another adaptation of volleyball. It's just like regular volleyball with two exceptions. First, everyone must use a hardbound book of any size instead of their hands to hit the ball. Second, a tennis ball or Nerf ball is used instead of a volleyball. *Doug Simpson*

BLACK-LIGHT VOLLEYBALL

If you can black out your gym and obtain four black lights, your kids will love this game of guesswork and strategy. With orange or green fluorescent spray paint, spray a volleyball, the top of the volleyball net, and—if they wear old shoes—your kids' shoes. Cut up old white towels or sheets for headbands, and have the kids bring either white gloves or gloves you can spray-paint. Get people to hold the black lights instead of merely standing the lights up around the volleyball court—this way the holders can dodge a wild ball and lights won't be broken.

Then turn off the white lights, turn on the black lights, and play volleyball! Since headbands, shoes, and gloves are the only clues to players' positions, the teams will develop some strategy quickly—like slipping off their shoes in order to make a spike or momentarily hiding their heads and hands to outfox the opposition. *David Washburn*

BY THE SEAT OF YOUR PANTS VOLLEYBALL

This can be an excellent indoor game for large groups, especially during rainy weather. Divide the group into two teams. Set up a volleyball net in the room so the top of the net is approximately five feet above the floor. Each player is instructed to sit down on his team's side of the net so that his legs are crossed in front of him. From this position a regular game of volleyball is played with the following changes:

- Use a beach ball-type ball or a Nerf ball.
- Use hands and head only (no feet).

• All serves must be made overhand from the center of the group. Rotation would look something like this:

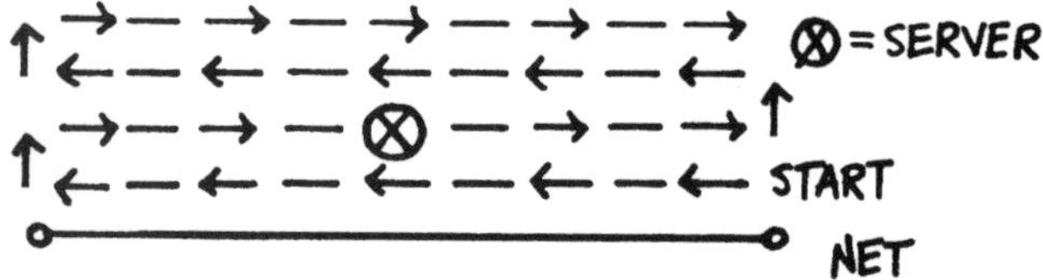

• Because of limited mobility, a large number of participants is suggested (20-25 per team).
• All other rules of volleyball apply.
• **Blind Volleyball.** The net should be a solid divider that obstructs the view of the other team, such as blankets hung over a regular volleyball net or rope. The divider should also be low enough that players cannot see under it. *Gerald Monroe and John Vincent*

CRAZY VOLLEYBALL

If you don't have quite enough kids to get up a real volleyball game, or if you have several inept players, here's a fun version of the game with a few new rules:
• Each team may hit the ball four times before hitting it over the net.
• A ball hitting the floor counts as one hit.
• A ball cannot hit the floor two bounces in succession.

These rules keep the ball in play over a much longer period of time.
• **One-Handed Crazy Volleyball.** When you have more than 18 players they can use only one hand to hit the ball.

With this rule, 24 to 30 can play. The more players you have, the further from the net you can make the back out-of-bounds line. *Dallas Elder and Samuel Hoyt*

DOUBLE-VISION VOLLEYBALL

Play volleyball with two balls. After both teams serve their balls simultaneously on the ref's command, each ball is played until it hits the floor or goes out of bounds.This means that either team can score with either ball, regardless of who served what ball. It also means that a team can score two points in a single, two-ball volley.

If you want to compensate for the power plays of stronger players, use plastic children's balls instead of standard volleyballs. *Keith King and Merle Moser*

ELIMINATION VOLLEYBALL

Divide your group into two teams, and play a regular volleyball game except that whoever makes a mistake or misses the ball is out of the game. The teams keep getting smaller and smaller, and the team that manages to survive the longest is the winner. *Judy Groen*

FOOTBALL VOLLEYBALL

A Boingo Ball (manufactured by Koosh) will add football elements—and lots of energy—to your next volleyball game. Play using the basic rules of volleyball and the following variations:
• The server kicks the ball over the net.
• The ball can bounce (but doesn't have to) between hits.
• Hits with any body part are legal.
Tommy Seth and Hannah Baker

FOUR-CORNER VOLLEYBALL

Here's a wild version of volleyball that involves four teams at once. You can set it up with four volleyball nets, or just two, depending on the size of your teams

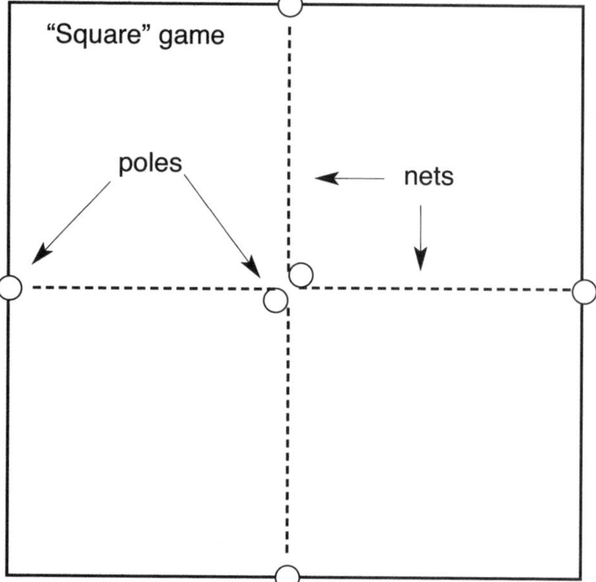

and the number of nets you have available. You'll also need five or six poles. Arrange the nets according to one of the diagrams below. If you use two nets, then you form two right angles with them, as in diagram A. If you use four nets, then just tie all four to the center pole as in diagram B.

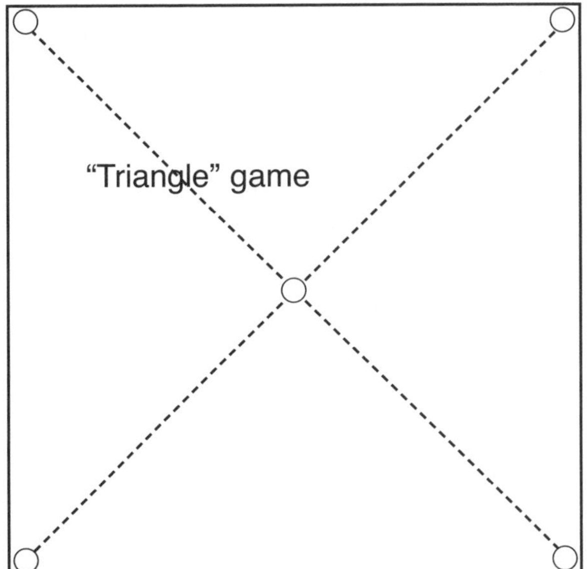

Each team takes one of the court quadrants. The game is played like regular volleyball, except that now players can hit the ball to any of the other three teams. An interesting strategy can develop since a team is never exactly sure when the ball will be coming its way.

This game can also be played with any of the other volleyball variations found in this book. Once you try this version of volleyball, your group may never want to play regular volleyball again! *Ron Fay*

GIANT VOLLEYBALL

Two teams of any number can play this funny volleyball game, which uses a giant weather balloon for a ball. Six to eight feet in diameter, the balloon is inflated with a vacuum cleaner. The entire team gets under the ball and pushes it over the net. The opposing team returns it. Giant weather balloons are available from Army surplus stores and other specialty shops. Other types of giant balloons can also be used. It's best to play this game indoors, as a slight wind can carry the balloon a long way. *Bill Tracy*

HEADBANGERS VOLLEYBALL

This is played like regular volleyball, except that players can use only their heads to hit the ball.

The rules are as follows:

- A guy must hit the ball at least once every time the ball comes over the net, or that team loses the point.
- Each team can hit the ball five times to get it over.
- The ball can bounce once each time it comes over.

You may want to add these two rules:

- Guys can use only their heads to hit the ball.
- Girls can hit the ball according to standard volleyball rules.

Otherwise, the game is played by the normal volleyball rules. This game is as much fun to watch as to play. *Jack Hawkins*

HUMAN-NET VOLLEYBALL

Use a light, large ball—like a beach ball—and divide into three teams (the third team composes the net). Mark or tape a two-foot-wide strip the net players must remain in; the other two teams may not enter the net's zone.

A regular volleyball game is then played, except that the net team plays too, earning points for each ball it can catch as the other two teams play. If the net merely knocks the ball out of play without catching it, no one scores. After each game teams rotate. *Terry Fisher*

LOTTERY VOLLEYBALL

This off-beat brand of volleyball adds the thrill of the unexpected. Divide into teams and position players conventionally. The referee should stand a few feet out of bounds near mid-court with a container of lottery tickets numbered 1 through 9 (have several of each number, and mix them up so that they can be drawn at random).

As the server serves, the referee draws out a ticket and calls out the number. The team receiving the ball must hit the ball that number of times (no more, no less) before returning it over the net. If the B team is successful, the serving team must do the same. Play continues requiring the same number of hits per play until a team fails. On the serve for the next round, a second ticket is drawn out and read, and play continues as before according to the number of hits required by the new ticket. Excitement will build on each play as team members count out hits, and you'll especially enjoy the groans when the referee calls out the dreaded number 1.

All other conventional volleyball rules prevail, but you might want to liven things up by using water balloons instead of a ball, or by playing flamingo style (on one leg). *Mark A. Hahlen*

MEGA VOLLEYBALL

Here's how to play volleyball with an extra-large group (24 players or more at a time). You need three volleyball nets, four standards, lime or tape to mark the boundaries, two volleyballs, and a ref.

Place one pole in the center and the other three

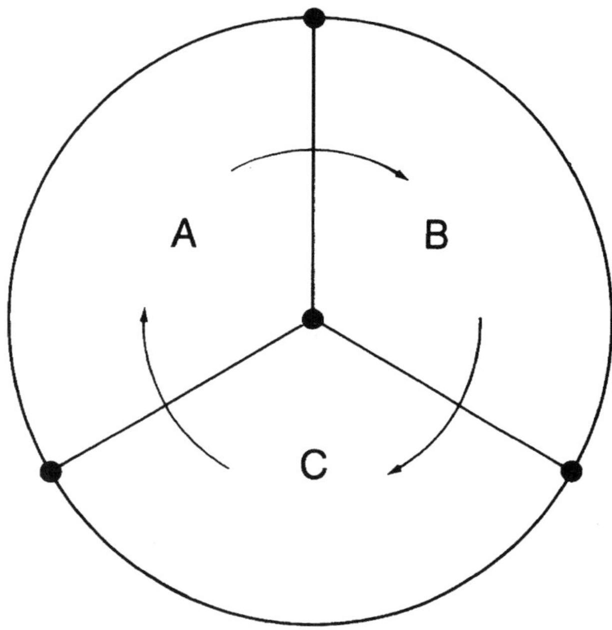

around it, so that the nets are stretched out from the center like spokes in a wheel (see the diagram). Make the boundary a circle so that each segment of the court is shaped like a pie slice (the three sections should be equal).

Play is similar to regular volleyball, except that the ball is not returned across the net to the serving team. Instead, it advances to the third team, who sends it on to the first team, thus moving either clockwise or counterclockwise around the circle. In the diagram shown, A serves to B, who volleys to C, who must get the ball back to A, and so on. To keep the game fun, don't allow spikes. For added excitement, get two balls going at once.

As in the regular game, errors include misses, out-of-bound volleys, more than three contacts with the ball by the same team before it crosses the net, and more than one contact with the ball in immediate succession by the same player. Scoring, however, is different from regular play in that 25 points are given for every error. Thus the team with the lowest score wins. *Ed Weaver*

MEGA-BAR VOLLEYBALL

This is a good variation on conventional volleyball to prevent an I'm-too-cool-to-play attitude. Purchase about six large candy bars or some other favorite munchie. Display these where teams can see them as they play.

Form two teams and play as usual, but with two exceptions. First, when you rotate, move the server out of the game and move a new player in next to him or her. Second, award a mega-bar to any server who fulfills one of the following requirements:

- Serves five points in a row.
- Serves two aces in a row (an ace is when no one else touches the ball).
- Serves the final point.

Play 11-point games so that excitement about the last point builds more quickly. Kids usually can't wait to get a chance to serve. *Todd Capen*

MIDNIGHT VOLLEYBALL

Instead of beginning a meeting with recreation, play this game after the sun goes down. Start the volleyball game shortly before dark, playing the customary rules until the genuine shout is heard, "Where is it?" Then the game changes to Midnight Volleyball.

- The game is to five points, and you win by one point.
- A person (or a team) can hit the ball as many times as needed on his side of the net—provided it doesn't touch the ground.

Play the best two out of three games—if you can stand it that long, and if parents let kids stay out that late. It's a blend of frustration and challenge swirled where blind luck determines the winners. *Vernon A. Edington*

Modified Volleyball

This game is played on a regulation volleyball court, with the same rules for scoring and boundaries. The rules for play and the strategy, however, are quite different from the traditional game of volleyball. The following modifications make the game playable for those less skilled in the techniques of volleyball and provide a new challenge for the volleyball jock.

- Each team may have four to 12 players.
- On each volley, a team is allowed five hits and two bounces (on the ground) of the ball on its side of the court.
- The game is played without a net. A mark on the poles that would hold a net, or on a wall, will indicate the height that the ball must reach on each volley. This should be about the height of the tallest player.
- Teams cannot cross over the center court line.
- There is no spiking.
- An individual player may hit the ball no more than twice in succession. If a player hits the ball, then allows it to bounce once or twice, that player can hit the ball only once more before another player must hit it. In other words, bounces don't interrupt the succession of hits by a player.
- Any person in the back line may serve the ball.
- Rotation is encouraged, but not necessary.

You may want to require each team to use five hits and two bounces on each volley so that more players will be involved in the game and additional strategy will develop. *Ed Merrill*

New Volleyball

New Volleyball is played like traditional volleyball but the scoring is nontraditional.

The object of the game is to volley the ball as many times as possible each time the ball comes over the net, return it back over the net, and hope that the other team blows it. A team volleys the ball as many times as possible without missing or fouling (up to 50 times) before hitting it back over the net. If the other team misses, the first team receives as many points as they volleyed before sending it over the net. All volleys are counted audibly by the entire team or by scorers on the sidelines, which aids in the scoring process and also helps build tension.

Other rules:

- No person may hit the ball two consecutive times.
- No two people may hit the ball back and forth to each other. Player A may hit it to player B, but player B must hit it to a third player.
- Five points are awarded to the serving team if the opposing team fails to return a serve.
- Five points are awarded to the receiving team if a serve is missed (out-of-bounds, in the net, etc.).
- Players rotate on each serve, even if the serving team scores on successive serves.
- A game is 15 minutes.
- The highest score wins.

Norma Bailey

Square Volleyball

Here is a great idea for volleyball if you have a large group with a few superstars who make regular volleyball difficult. It may not only humble those few, but demonstrate how cooperation is mandatory for Christians.

Create your playing area by setting up four portable nets in a square. Have the superstars be one team, inside the square. Divide the rest of the group into four teams, one on each side of the square. Each

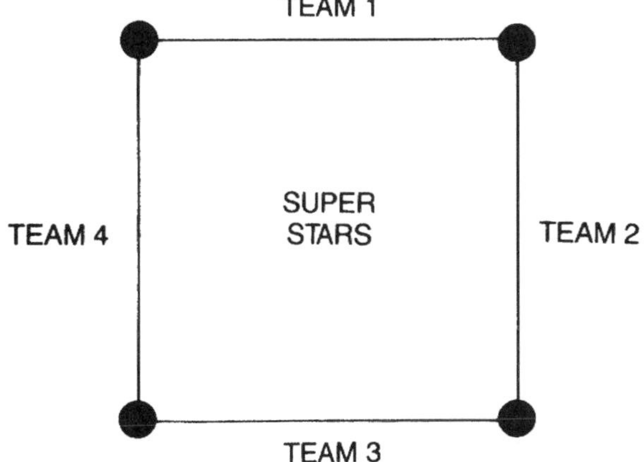

of these outside teams is given a ball with a distinctive marking of some kind.

The outside teams always serve, and the superstars must return the correct ball to the correct team. Outside teams serve all at once or two at a time. When a point is scored or a ball is dead, the team playing with that ball must wait for another team so that the two balls can be served at once.

Each team will need a referee and scorer who can watch closely for correct returns and keep track of points. Play continues until a time limit, when all scores are compared and the winning team is declared. *Ron Tipton*

Prisoner Volleyball

For this volleyball game, no particular volleyball skill is needed—just catching. Two equal teams take their positions across the net. One team starts by calling a name of a player on the opposing team, then tossing or hitting the ball over. If the other team drops the ball, that player becomes a prisoner and steps out of the game. The team can get him back by calling "Prisoner" and hitting the ball over so that the other team drops it. The object is to get the enemy team all out as prisoners. A variation would be for prisoners to become members of the opposing team. *David Coppedge*

Roofball

For this game you need a volleyball and a roof. Experimentation will tell which roofs are the best. The unique thing about roofball is that each roof produces a new challenge and a different twist to the game.

Decide what is out-of-bounds, then form a single-file line perpendicular to the line of the roof. The first person in line serves the ball from the roof. Second in line must play the ball by volleying the ball back onto the roof before it hits the ground. He moves to the back of the line and the third player plays the ball. This continues until a miss or until a played ball lands out-of-bounds. The player who is responsible for the ball going out is charged with the miss. Last one in is the winner.

Missed balls are those that don't make it to the roof, hit under the roofline, go over the roof, are completely missed, or land out-of-bounds.

To play with teams, form two lines, one for each team. The first player on team one hits the ball up onto the roof, and the first player on team two hits it up again, then back to the second person on team one, and so on. Every time somebody misses, the other team gets a point. *Larry Jansen*

Strobe Ball

Try playing the old familiar volleyball or four-square in a room lit only by a strobe light (available at electronics shops). It's surprising how difficult it becomes to keep a semblance of coordination. Kids will be swinging at balls and usually missing. *Bill Aldridge*

Superman Volleyball

Here's yet another way to add a new twist to the old game of volleyball. Simply play by the normal rules, but inflate the ball with helium. It won't float away, but watch how high it goes. Everyone will feel like Superman. You may need to increase the size of your volleyball court in order to accommodate the higher flight of the ball. *Doug Newhouse*

Table Volleyball

This is for when you have to be indoors and you don't have room to play a real game of volleyball. Divide your group into two teams. Use a regular volleyball or other soft ball. Set tables on top of one another across the room to form a net. All normal rules of volleyball stand except that all participants must stay on their knees at all times and the ball is permitted to hit the ceiling. Depending on the number of players on each team, you might permit one free bounce of the ball on each side before the ball must be returned over the net. *Jim Walton*

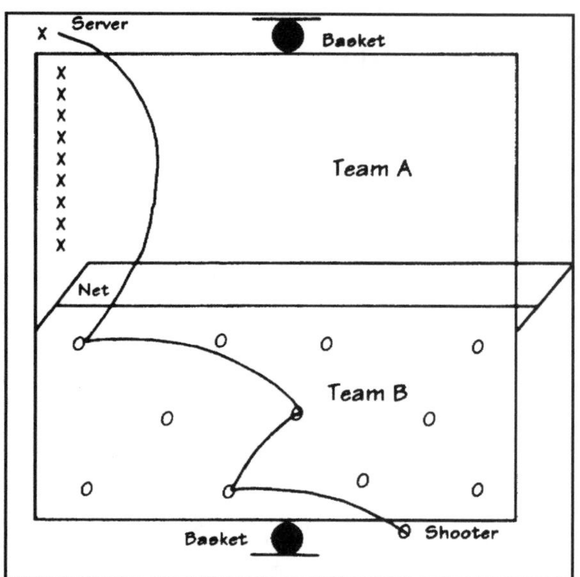

TEAM VOLLEYBASKET

Divide the group into two teams on opposite sides of a volleyball net that is set in a basketball court. The serving team lines up along the sideline facing the server (see diagram), who does a normal volleyball serve from the normal serving position. After serving the ball, the server runs to the first person in line and gives that player a high five. That player in turn gives a low five to the next person, who gives a high five to the next, and so on to the end of the line. That last person then runs to the first person in the line and starts the process all over. Each time they complete the line (the slap-happy wave) they get one point.

Meanwhile, on the other side of the net, the volleyball is volleyed among the team members until it gets to the stationary shooter. It doesn't matter if the ball hits the ground during the volley. Players just pick it up and continue to volley to the shooter, who grabs the volleyball and shoots it, basketball-like, through the hoop. The shooter keeps at it until a basket is made, which also stops the action on the serving side of the net.

At that point the volleying team lines up facing the former shooter, who is now the server. The server makes a legal volleyball serve and starts the slap-happy wave while the receiving team volleys the ball back to its shooter. The serve alternates each time after the basket is made.

There are no points given for the basket—only for completing a slap-happy wave. The first team to 21 points wins. *Brad Edgbert*

VOLLEYBOWL

This fast-paced game is exciting for all ages, but especially for younger kids. You need two volleyballs, two bowling pins, and a large playing area (indoors or out).

Divide into two teams of equal size and have each one choose a "pin keeper." Then have each team line up, all facing the same direction, in two parallel lines about 15 feet apart. Set up a pin about 10 feet in front of the first person in each line, and have a pin keeper for each team stand behind his or her team's pin. Then give a volleyball to the first person in each line.

When a signal is given, the first person in each line attempts to knock down his or her team's pin, either by rolling or throwing the ball at it. If the pin is knocked down, the team gets a point. The pin keeper sets up the pin and returns the ball to the next person in line for play. If the pin is missed, no point is earned, and the pin keeper must return the ball to the next player in line. After each attempt, the player goes to the end of the line. Team members keep rotating in this way as fast as possible until the predetermined period of play (usually five minutes) is up! The team with the most points wins.

The excitement of the game is heightened if team members shout out their score after every successful attempt and when the two-minute and one-minute warnings are given. To add a wrinkle, use half-inflated balls or two balls for each team (a headache for the pin keepers); or have players throw the ball between their legs by bending forward. *Mark A. Hahlen*

Team A	X	X	X	X	X	X	X
Team B	O	O	O	O	O	O	O

TURNOVER

Form two teams of four or more players each. Using a volleyball and regulation net and court, play volleyball, but with this difference: The player whose mistake gives the other team the serve or a point will be turned over to play on the opposing team's side.

It gets heroic as one team dwindles to two or even one player who must stand 10 or 11 opponents. *Greg Miller*

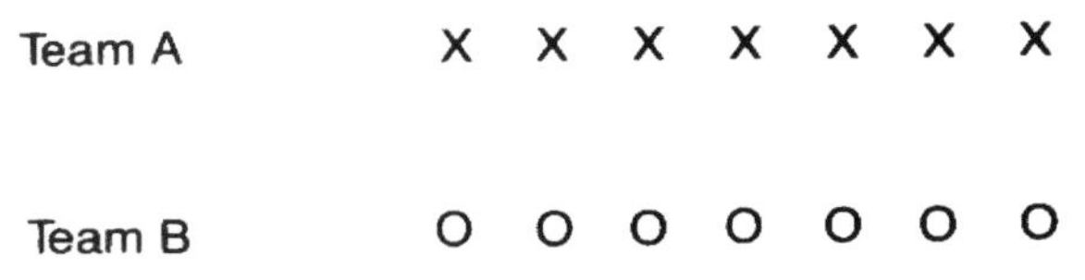

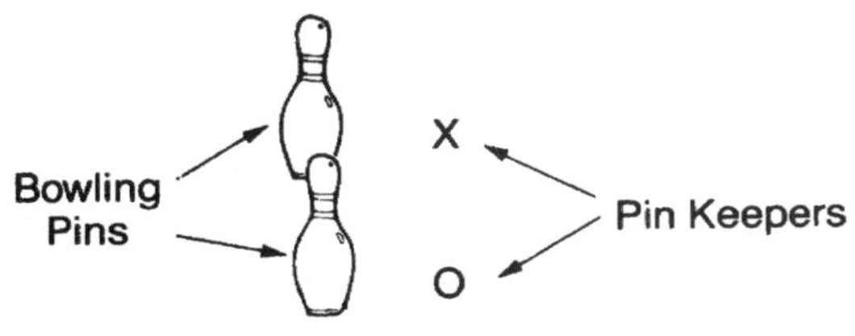

VOLLEYPIT

First make the pit: set tables with fold-up legs on their sides, like this:

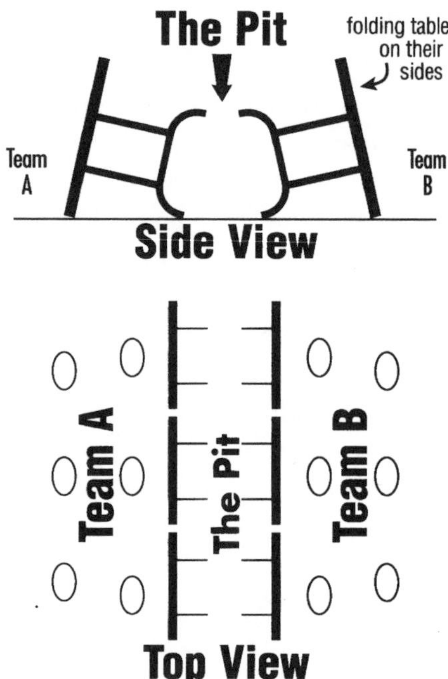

Now divide players into two teams (six to 10 on a team, depending on room size) and play volleyball the normal way, though with a volleyball-sized, very light foam ball (even hard-surfaced Nerf balls may be too heavy). The pit is the net—but woe to the players who hit the ball into the pit instead of over it! For they go into the pit themselves—and stay there, without obstructing play, until a player from the opposing team pits the ball.

If more than one player from a team winds up in the pit, they return to their team in the order they went in. Win by scoring the traditional 15 points or if all the other team's players end up in the pit.

Variation: Play Paddlepit, using a smaller, softball-sized Nerf ball and Smashball-type paddles. *Greg Hughes*

VOLLEY FEETBALL

This volleyball variation will keep your group lightfooted. You play it according to most of the traditional volleyball rules, except for one big difference—the net is lowered to within a foot or two of the floor, and players use only their feet to kick the ball under the net. Regular rules about out-of-bounds, team rotation, three-kick-per-team maximum, etc., apply.

Serving is like this: the players on both teams stand aside to let the serve reach the opposite team's back row—by traveling under the net.

After a back-row player has kicked it, players on both teams may move back into position and resume regular play. If a player in the front rows of the serving team touches a served ball before it goes under the net, it's side-out; if a player in the front lines of the receiving team touches the ball before it reaches his back row, the serving team scores a point. If the back row of the receiving team lets a served ball go out-of-bounds untouched, the serving team scores a point. When a player kicks the ball over the net, it's side-out or a point for the opposing team. Games are played to 7, 15, or 21, depending how much time you have.

Your kids will find the game a little tricky at first—they'll need to use the sides of their feet to kick with, soccer style. And you can always retreat to a smaller room with a Nerf ball and masking-tape boundaries. *Michael W. Capps*

VOLLEY TENNIS

Volley Tennis is played on a tennis court with a volleyball. It is a great game for as many as want to play, and it requires no great athletic ability. The serve is just like regular volleyball, from behind the back line. But the receiving team must allow the ball to hit the court before touching the ball. They have up to three volleys to get the ball back across the net, but the ball must touch the court between each volley. The game is played to 15 points, and only the serving team can score. Line hits are in play. This is most fun when at least a dozen people are on each team. *Ralph Bryant*

VOLLEYSLAM

Volleyslam is a baseball-like game on a volleyball court, for two teams and any number of players. Home plate is under one of the baskets, and six bases are placed in the court's corners (see diagram). The defensive team scatters itself throughout the gym. The batter stands at home plate and bats the

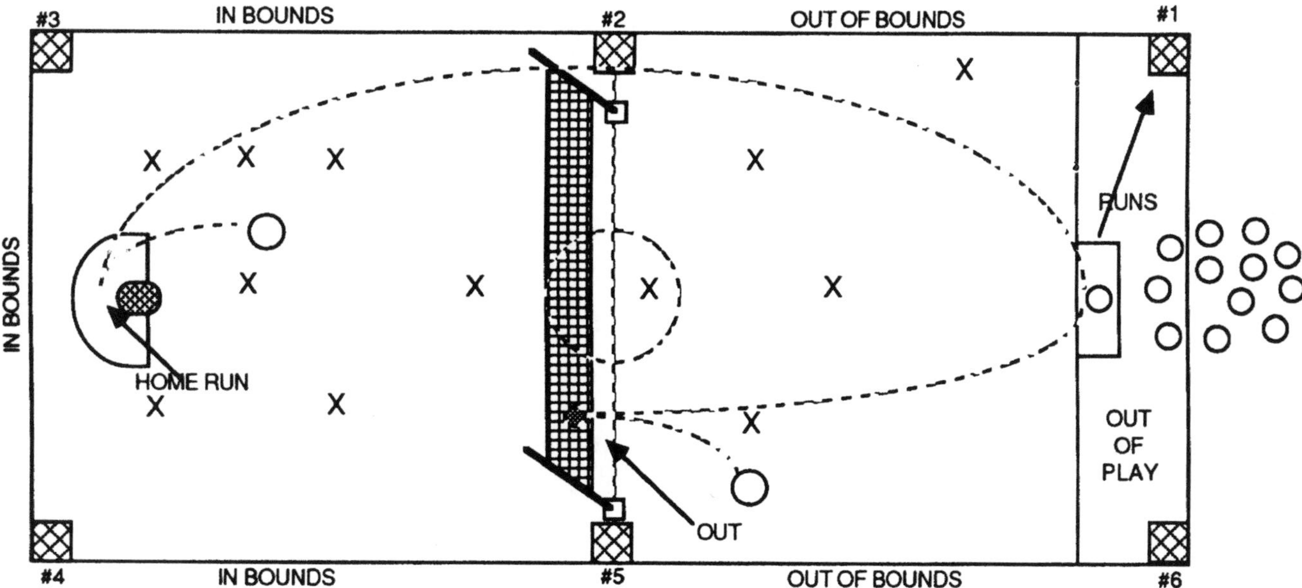

volleyball with a normal under- or overhand volleyball serve toward the far end of the court.

Outs are made only by hitting runners with the ball when they're between bases, or when a batted ball hits the net—not by catching flies. A base may hold any number of runners, and runners may pass each other. A home run is scored if a batted ball hits the backboard, rim, or net at the opposite end of the court. (Invent your own award if the ball goes into the basket—the feat certainly deserves one!)

Since there's no catcher, a thrown ball that crosses the home-base line is out of play—so runners must remain at the bases closest to them. Also notice that beyond the net, the area beyond the sidelines is still in-bounds.

All team members bat once and only once in each inning—outs retire base runners instead of determining inning length. *Phil Blackwell*

VOLLOONY BALL

On a basketball or volleyball court and across a volleyball net from each other, two opposing teams play a volleyball game—but with a weather balloon. Since getting control of the balloon is a ticklish matter, a team gets up to 10 hits before the balloon must be returned over the net. Similar to regular volleyball, a team earns points when its opponents (1) hit the balloon more than 10 times, (2) allow the balloon to touch the floor, (3) cause the balloon to hit the ceiling or lights, or (4) hit the balloon out-of-bounds.

You can make a weather balloon substitute by wrapping three lengths of masking tape around a balloon. *Phil Blackwell and Kevin J. Bueltmann*

WOLLEYBALL

This game is great for younger kids as well as challenging to athletes. Lower the volleyball net until the bottom edge touches the floor—or play on a tennis court. Use a bouncy playground ball. The game is like traditional volleyball in most ways—six-person rotating teams, scoring, no more than three hits per team per volley, no two consecutive hits by any one player.

Here are the differences: servers serve as in two-square—they bounce the ball once, then hit it over the net. Teammates can help a lagging serve over the net. The ball may bounce once (but doesn't have to) before a team returns it, as well as between the two or three hits a team makes before returning the ball over the net. *Julie D. Anderson*

Resources from Youth Specialties

Youth Ministry Programming

Camps, Retreats, Missions, & Service Ideas (Ideas Library)
Compassionate Kids: Practical Ways to Involve Your Students in Mission and Service
Creative Bible Lessons from the Old Testament
Creative Bible Lessons in 1 & 2 Corinthians
Creative Bible Lessons in John: Encounters with Jesus
Creative Bible Lessons in Romans: Faith on Fire!
Creative Bible Lessons on the Life of Christ
Creative Bible Lessons in Psalms
Creative Junior High Programs from A to Z, Vol. 1 (A-M)
Creative Junior High Programs from A to Z, Vol. 2 (N-Z)
Creative Meetings, Bible Lessons, & Worship Ideas (Ideas Library)
Crowd Breakers & Mixers (Ideas Library)
Downloading the Bible Leader's Guide
Drama, Skits, & Sketches (Ideas Library)
Drama, Skits, & Sketches 2 (Ideas Library)
Dramatic Pauses
Everyday Object Lessons
Games (Ideas Library)
Games 2 (Ideas Library)
Great Fundraising Ideas for Youth Groups
More Great Fundraising Ideas for Youth Groups
Great Retreats for Youth Groups
Holiday Ideas (Ideas Library)
Hot Illustrations for Youth Talks
More Hot Illustrations for Youth Talks
Still More Hot Illustrations for Youth Talks
Ideas Library on CD-ROM
Incredible Questionnaires for Youth Ministry
Junior High Game Nights
More Junior High Game Nights
Kickstarters: 101 Ingenious Intros to Just about Any Bible Lesson
Live the Life! Student Evangelism Training Kit
Memory Makers
The Next Level Leader's Guide
Play It! Over 150 Great Games for Youth Groups
Roaring Lambs
Special Events (Ideas Library)
Spontaneous Melodramas
Student Leadership Training Manual
Student Underground: An Event Curriculum on the Persecuted Church
Super Sketches for Youth Ministry
Talking the Walk
Teaching the Bible Creatively
Videos That Teach
What Would Jesus Do? Youth Leader's Kit
Wild Truth Bible Lessons
Wild Truth Bible Lessons 2
Wild Truth Bible Lessons—Pictures of God
Worship Services for Youth Groups

Professional Resources

Administration, Publicity, & Fundraising (Ideas Library)
Equipped to Serve: Volunteer Youth Worker Training Course
Help! I'm a Junior High Youth Worker!
Help! I'm a Small-Group Leader!
Help! I'm a Sunday School Teacher!
Help! I'm a Volunteer Youth Worker!
How to Expand Your Youth Ministry
How to Speak to Youth...and Keep Them Awake at the Same Time
Junior High Ministry (Updated & Expanded)
The Ministry of Nurture: A Youth Worker's Guide to Discipling Teenagers
Purpose-Driven Youth Ministry
Purpose-Driven Youth Ministry Training Kit
So That's Why I Keep Doing This! 52 Devotional Stories for Youth Workers
A Youth Ministry Crash Course
The Youth Worker's Handbook to Family Ministry

Discussion Starters

Discussion & Lesson Starters (Ideas Library)
Discussion & Lesson Starters 2 (Ideas Library)
EdgeTV
Get 'Em Talking
Keep 'Em Talking!
High School TalkSheets
More High School TalkSheets
High School TalkSheets: Psalms and Proverbs
Junior High TalkSheets
More Junior High TalkSheets
Junior High TalkSheets: Psalms and Proverbs
Real Kids: Short Cuts
Real Kids: The Real Deal—on Friendship, Loneliness, Racism, & Suicide
Real Kids: The Real Deal—on Sexual Choices, Family Matters, & Loss
Real Kids: The Real Deal—on Stressing Out, Addictive Behavior, Great Comebacks, & Violence
Real Kids: Word on the Street
Have You Ever...? 450 Intriguing Questions Guaranteed to Get Teenagers Talking
Unfinished Sentences: 450 Tantalizing Statement-Starters to Get Teenagers Talking & Thinking
What If...? 450 Thought-Provoking Questions to Get Teenagers Talking, Laughing, and Thinking
Would You Rather...? 465 Provocative Questions to Get Teenagers Talking

Art Source Clip Art

Stark Raving Clip Art (print)
Youth Group Activities (print)
Clip Art Library Version 2.0 (CD-ROM)

Digital Resources

Clip Art Library Version 2.0 (CD-ROM)
Ideas Library on CD-ROM

Videos & Video Curricula

EdgeTV
Equipped to Serve: Volunteer Youth Worker Training Course
The Heart of Youth Ministry: A Morning with Mike Yaconelli
Live the Life! Student Evangelism Training Kit
Purpose-Driven Youth Ministry Training Kit
Real Kids: Short Cuts
Real Kids: The Real Deal—on Friendship, Loneliness, Racism, & Suicide
Real Kids: The Real Deal—on Sexual Choices, Family Matters, & Loss
Real Kids: The Real Deal—on Stressing Out, Addictive Behavior, Great Comebacks, & Violence
Real Kids: Word on the Street
Student Underground: An Event Curriculum on the Persecuted Church
Understanding Your Teenager Video Curriculum

Student Resources

Downloading the Bible: A Rough Guide to the New Testament
Downloading the Bible: A Rough Guide to the Old Testament
Grow For It Journal
Grow For It Journal through the Scriptures
Spiritual Challenge Journal: The Next Level
Teen Devotional Bible
What Would Jesus Do? Spiritual Challenge Journal
Wild Truth Journal for Junior Highers
Wild Truth Journal—Pictures of God